The Scythians:

The White Race in Antiquity and the Philosophy and Doctrine of War

Dennis James Watson

Strategic Book Publishing and Rights Co., LLC
USA I Singapore
www.sbpra.com

For information about special discounts for bulk purchases, please contact Strategic Book Publishing and Rights Co. Special Sales, at bookorder@sbpra.net.

Book Design: Suzanne Kelly

ISBN: 978-1-63135-537-0

Dedication

The ancestral spirits whence all inspiration comes.
My late grandfather, James Oliver Watson.
My sister, Janice, for encouragement,
and my three children Keisha, Sesan, And Temu

TABLE OF CONTENTS

INTRODUCTION

NOT SOME, BUT MOST OF THE HISTORY OF THE WORLD HAS BEEN falsified, hidden, kept secret, interpolated, or as in most cases, has simply not been investigated deeply. The basis for this is the chauvinism of nations. Each nation, in order to glorify its history, adopts stories that serve to promote the national interest.

Observation has taught me that most people are ignorant not only of the real history of their own countries, but also of their own racial origins. This is very clear because one of the most obvious things observable on this planet is that most of the people are racially mixed. Men have not come to grips with what this really means, including all the Whites in America.

The contemporary view of history, both public and private, is that civilization has passed from White to Black; that is, the Whites, or the Scythians as they were called in ancient times, are the inventors and bringers of civilization. Commencing with the Greeks, European civilization has forever been on the march. Practically every White historian, known and unknown, has preached the gospel of Black enslavement to Whites!

Fortunately, Black people are seriously into oral history, and as a youngster growing up I would frequently hear people expound on the glories of the Black race and the many kingdoms we were said to have established. Research has revealed the truth of these assertions, as well as the role of the Scythians (the White race), in ancient times.

For instance, Ethiopia, in our epoch, is easily the most ancient nation on Earth—this is why Whites have even gone so far as to claim the Ethiopians as being White!

I mention this only to point out the lengths to which the Whites have gone to conceal the history of the Black race.

Incidentally, Ethiopian is the ancestral name of the Black race, not African. These words obviously have two different meanings!

The theory of relativity makes it understood that things are such in accordance with one's perspective, that energy and matter are essentially the same, changing places under a given set of circumstances: $E=MC^2$. The ancient Eastern symbol of the interchanging forces (✳) represents the same relativity. This is why the wise have said that Western mathematics is proof of the Eastern religious systems. The Nazis certainly proved this, as detailed in Ravencroft's *The Spear of Destiny*, a neat work on the occultism of the Nazi party.

In 2002, seers prognosticated a change on Earth that would alter the basic world structure as we now know it. To me, this means the Scythian race will no longer hold hegemony in its bloodied glove.

Despite all of the hoopla modern man has made over progress, the rule of the Scythians has been, and is, ruthless, barbaric, and devoid of any civilized behaviors save making war, which needs to be made plain so that we may see what is really going on.

History repeats itself not because men do not learn from it, but because the historical process is cyclic, as are all manifestations on Earth, symbolized by the comings and goings of the seasons. You do see the doctrine of reincarnation in this, don't you?

The argument that reality is what one sees with the eyes is a false doctrine, for the sun appears to rise but it is the earth that spins. In fact, as fast as the earth spins, no sensation is felt as a result. The moon sheds light, but this is an illusion. In this regard, the Whites are, according to the Dogon sage Ogotemelli, a moon race[1] that is *luna*tic, and of consequence shedding a false light, like the moon.

Interestingly, Marcia Moore says that the Whites are ruled by Virgo,[2] and all serious astrologers know that the moon is the esoteric ruler of Virgo. The moon is also the symbol of the principle of *imitation*.

In this vein, it shouldn't be difficult to comprehend that the Blacks are a "sun" race, or that the most ancient nations worshipped the Sun-Si. These sun-worshipping nations could not have been white—Whites shall never be able to harness the power of the sun to any degree for the benefit of man, but we shall!

Some of you may have read the Clavell novel *Shogun* in which he states how highly the Japanese have valued white skin from time immemorial. This is strange because the symbol of the Japanese people is the sun. In this regard, "Do not believe in something because you have read it in a book. Do not believe in something because another man has said it is true. Do not believe in words because they are hallowed by tradition. Find out the truth for yourself. Reason it out. That is realization."

October 13, 1979
New York City

---

[1] Marcel Griaule, *Conversations with Ogotemmeli.*
[2] Marcia Moore, *Astrology: The Divine Science.*

PART ONE

CHAPTER I

ORIGIN OF THE WHITE RACE

Where Do White People Come From?

EUROPE? MOST PEOPLE ASSUME THAT THE WHITES ARE FROM EUROPE. The Blacks say that they are from the caves of Europe. Let's look at this:

> The theory that the oldest human beings were what in America would be called Blacks is supported by the fact that the oldest known entire human skeletons so far discovered are negroid, as the Grimaldis of Europe, whose skeletons may be seen in the Paris Museum of Anthropology and the Museum of Monaco, and whose relics may be found from Italy to Russia and as far north as Britain and Scandinavia.[1]

Sergi of the University of Rome denied that there was a European race. "European man," he said, "was African man, changed by the effects of European environment."[2]

Now, if the oldest human skeletons found in Europe are of Black people, we must of necessity look elsewhere for the origins of the White race. There is really no need to dwell on whether the Whites come from Europe; for example, the British do not claim to have built Stonehenge as we claim to have built the pyramids. A people prior to the British built Stonehenge. No, the Whites are not from Europe.

D'Olivet, the famed Frenchman, whose bold work *The Hebraic Tongue Restored*, a classic on another level (as is his insightful *The Golden Verses of Pythagoras*), certainly ranks him as one of the more learned of the Whites. He has this to say concerning the origin of the Whites:

> . . . I shall fix across the obscurity of centuries the moment when the White Race, of which we are part, came to appear upon the scene of the world. At this epoch of which I shall seek later to determine a date, the White Race was still weak, savage,

3

without laws, without arts, without cultivation of any sort, destitute of memories, and too devoid of understanding even to conceive a hope. It inhabited the environs of the Boreal Pole where it had its origin. The Black Race, more ancient than the White, was dominant upon the earth and held the sceptre of science and of power, it possessed all of Africa and the greater part of Asia, where it had enslaved and restrained the Yellow Race and as I have just said, the White Race which was only springing up wandered about the environs of the Boreal.[3]

In developing his theme and speaking of the wanderings of the White Race, D'Olivet says:

 . . . and marching ever onward from north to the south of Europe they arrived on the shore of that sea which has since been aptly called the Black Sea, although this name belonged formerly to all the extent of waters in general which bathed the south of Europe, on account of the Black people who possessed it; as by a contrary reason, that part of the ocean which surrounds Europe and Asia on the side of the Boreal Pole is called the White Sea.[4]

I have always wondered about how these two bodies of water came by their names. Further west of the Black Sea is Bulgaria. As for the Bulgars, that word itself means "The Black People." A visitor to this part of Eastern Europe cannot help but be struck by the negroid facial features of many of the inhabitants.[5]

These Whites from the North, having learned through their interpreters that the Sudeens (Blacks) gave themselves the title of Atlanteans, that is to say, Masters of the Universe, chose that of Celts[*] (heroes), and knowing besides that on account of the white color of their skins they had been given the offensive name of Scythians, they designated their enemies by the expressive name Pelasgians, that is to say, "tanned skins." [6] You should also notice that the name Pelops, from which Peloponnesus is derived, signifies "Blackland." It was the name of Greece while occupied by the Pelasges or Black people.[7]

Our enemies, the Scythians of modern times, would like to imagine this idle speculation, but the section of the text on Greece will put an end to all dreaming.

A quick glance at a map reveals that the White Sea is territorially part of Russia. Now the Whites of Western Asia, called Europe, have always had designs of conquering or destroying Russia. This, I think, exemplifies the destructive or death principle that Whites symbolize on the earth plane—just as Blacks symbolize the creative or life principle and want to embrace Africa, the motherland, with love. The Whites, too, want to return home to Mother Russia, but their message is death. Make no mistake about it—these Scythians are a dread race, having gone so far as to poison the very air itself (the Breath of God). The earth, which holds all creatures great and small without complaint, is also being poisoned. The waters of the earth are also under attack. Consequently, it is naive for Blacks to believe that Whites plot only for our destruction, because they are waging a war against creation itself. This territorial imperative that Whites have for Russia, or Asia proper, has also been noticed by other writers:

> But consequently the fact that we have long been accustomed to regard central Asia as the homeland of the Mongolian or mongotorial peoples, it is interesting to observe that the skeletal material found at Anau shows that the people of this area definitely belonged to the Caucasoid or white group of races. [8]

Again, we find that:

> "According to Greek tradition the earliest known inhabitants of Southern Russia were a people known as the Cimmerians, then little is known. It is quite possible that the Cimmerians were distantly related to the Scythians and were originally immigrants from Central Asia. The Cimmerians were succeeded in history by the Scythians proper. It is clear from the Greek chronicles that these Scythians originally dwelt in Northern Turkistan and set upon their migration only because of pressure extended by some of their neighbors. Their entrance

upon the threshold of recorded history takes place when they moved out of Turkistan and in turn drove out the Cimmerians, making themselves the Masters of the steppes—lands of Southern Russia. [9]

To get an idea of the land area that these Scythians occupied we find that:

The immense plain which the tribes of the Scythian and all kindred nomads occupied during most of the first millennium stretches from Podolia on the western fringe of European Russia to the borders of China. It forms a single geographical unit of natural grassland, but in Asia it is broken up by the Pamirs, the Tien Shan, and the Altai ranges, whilst the Urals practically sever the Asian sector from the European. Yet communications over the whole vast tract have never been halted by purely geographical obstacles, for two passes, those of Dzungaria and Ferghana, form corridors which connect the Asiatic and European portions of the plain. [10]

This geographic position gave these Whites, just as it does the Russians of today, the strategic position to attack both Europe and Asia, and history records that they have done exactly that! The incursions that these savage hordes made on the civilized world can be readily observed in the histories of Babylon, Media, Macedonia, India, and, of course, Rome. Certain writers claim that these Whites also vied for power in Egypt under the "oppressive" reign of the "Shephard Kings," or Hykos as they were called, but this seems doubtful. [11]

Everyone knows, of course, that Egypt was at one time conquered by the Persians, but were these ancient Persians White? More will be said on this in the section on Egypt.

Getting back to Russia as the home of the White Race, Brinton says, "The most completely White communities are found among the Slavonic populations of Southern and Central Russia. Their hair is colorless and their complexion so near dead white that one anthropologist has selected the vast Roketno swamps as the original home of the White race which he thinks arose by endemic albinism." [12]

Evidently, Schopenhauer didn't even think there was a White race.[13] Be this as it may, we know on the earth plane everything seems to have its polar opposite, i.e., man-woman, earth-heaven, hot-cold, dead-alive, cat-mouse, and black-white, and though it can be said that the "Ancients" (Ancients is a euphemism for the Blacks of antiquity) held that opposites are complementary, their reasoning being that "undifferentiated energy" tends to divide itself into polar opposites, i.e., love and hate, coming from the same source—passion (*comprende?*)— so that they, that is, love and hate, are not polar opposites but a differentiation of one. This is the philosophy which underlies what these modern dogs refer to as paganism or polytheism. However, in truth, most religions appear very disturbing on the surface, and unless one knows something of what men call esoteric philosophy, religion will always appear artificial. For instance, the word "testament" is now *testa* (body) and *ment* (mind). You also see how this word *testa* is like *testes*, *si*? This gives the idea of the connection between the seed in man and his mind. Another correspondence is obviously cerebrum or cerebellum—*cere* does mean seed, does it not?

Again, a certain Pinkerton[14], researching the history of Scotland, thought the home of the White Race to be Scandinavia. This author urged his countrymen to take pride in the White barbarians. Pinkerton also made the Romans, Greeks, and Ethiopians White! I wonder why he was unable to find any facts about the Blacks of ancient Scotland.[15] At least he was able to trace the Scythians to Scandinavia, which is really next door to Russia. *The Oxford Bible Atlas* also shows Scythia as being in Russia.[16]

"Mother Russia," isn't that what they call her? Evidently the "Mother" is more progressive ideologically than her scattered children who seem intent on destroying her! Astrologers say that Russia is governed through the sign Aquarius and that this is the reason for the progressive outlook, Aquarius being a sign that can see ahead. Russian interests in space and parapsychology also bear this out.

Before I end this discussion on Russia as the ancient home of the White race, let me say that in a more remote period Blacks also occupied this particular country.[17]

Customs and Mores

We can begin our inquiry by referring to D'Olivet to see how Whites came to be called Scythians: "The name Scythians, which their enemies gave to them, signified, on the contrary, the impure ones, the reprobates. It came from the word Cuth or Scuth, applied to all things which one sets aside or which repels one or which one repels. It designated, properly, spittle. It was by this offensive word that the Black Race characterized the White, on account of the color of spittle."[18]

Herodotus, among the ancients, had much to say about both Blacks and Whites, though most of his book is about Black people. Herodotus is fun reading, and if you know that Whites are the Scythians, history begins to assume an astounding clarity:

> According to the account which the Scythians themselves give, they are the youngest of all nations. Their tradition is as follows: A certain Targitaus was the first man to live in their country, which before his time was a desert without inhabitants. He was a child—I do not believe this tale, but it is told nevertheless—of Jove and a daughter of the Borysthenes. Targitaus, thus descended, begot three sons, Leipoxais, Arpoxais, and Colaxais, who was the youngest born of the three. While they still ruled the land, there fell from the sky four implements, all of gold—a plough, a yoke, a battle axe, and a drinking cup. The eldest brother perceived them first, and approached to pick them up; when lo! as he came near, the gold took fire and blazed. He therefore went his way, and the second coming forward made his attempt, but the same thing happened again. The gold rejected both the elder and the second brother. Last of all the youngest brother approached, and immediately the flames were extinguished; so he picked up the gold and carried it to his home. Then the two elder brothers agreed together, and made the whole kingdom over to the youngest born.

From Leipoxais sprang the Scythians of the race called Auchatae from Arpoxais; the middle brother, those known as the Catiari and Traspians; from Colaxais, the youngest, the Royal Scythians or Paralatae. All together they are named Scoloti, after one of their kings. The Greeks, however, call them Scythians.

Such is the account which the Scythians give of their origin.[19]

On climate:

The whole district whereof we have discovered has winters of exceeding rigor. During eight months the frost is so intense that water poured upon the ground does not cause mud, but if a fire be lighted on it mud is produced. The sea freezes, and Cimmerian Bosphorus is frozen over. At that season the Scythians who dwell inside the trench make warlike expeditions upon the ice, and even drive their wagons across to the country of the Sundians. Such is the intensity of the cold during eight months out of the twelve; and even in the remaining four the climate is still cool. The character of the winter likewise is unlike that of the same season in any other country; for at that time, when the rains ought to fall in Scythia, there is scarcely any rain worth mentioning while in summer it never gives over raining; and thunder, which elsewhere is frequent then, in Scythia is unknown in that part of the year, coming only in summer, when it is very heavy. Thunder in wintertime is there accounted a prodigy; as also are earthquakes, whether they happen in winter or summer. Horses bear the winter well cold as it is but mules and asses are found to endure the cold, while horses, if they stand-still, are frost-bitten.[20]

On war:

In what concerns war, their customs are the following: The Scythian soldier drinks the blood of the first man he overthrows in battle. Whatever number he slays, he cuts off their heads and carries them to the King; since he is thus entitled to a share of the booty whereto he forfeits all claims if he does not produce a head. In order to strip the skull of its covering, he makes a cut round the head above the ears, and laying hold of the scalp shakes the skull out; then with the rib of an ox scrapes the scalp clean of flesh, and softening it by rubbing between the hands, uses it thenceforth as a napkin. The Scyth is proud of these scalps, and hangs them from his bridle-rein; the greater the number of such napkins that a man can show, the more highly is he esteemed among them. Many make themselves cloaks, like the capotes of our peasants, by sewing a quantity of these scalps together. Others flay the right arm of their dead enemies and make of the skin, which is stripped off with the nails hanging to it, a covering for their quivers . . . Some even flay the entire body of their enemy, and stretching it upon a frame carry it about with them wherever they ride. Such are the Scythian customs with respect to scalps and skins.[21]

From this we can easily recognize how Whites brought their ancient habits to the American Indian Wars and propagandized the Indians as being the scalpers in their history books and movies!

On worship:

They worship only the following gods, namely Vesta, whom they reverence beyond all the rest, Jupiter, and Tellus, who they consider to be the wife of Jupiter; after these Apollo, Celestial Venus, Hercules, and Mars. These gods are worshipped by the whole nation.[22]

On *la mota Buena,* or marijuana, use:

The Scythians, as I said, take some of this hemp-seed, and, creeping under the felt coverings, throw it upon the red-hot stones; immediately it smokes, and gives out such a vapor as no Grecian vapor bath can exceed; the Scyths, delighted, shout for joy, and this vapor serves them instead of a water-bath; for they never by any chance wash their bodies with water.[23]

On nationalism:

Herodotus relates two stories of Scythian kings who were put to death for adopting foreign customs, that is, the habits of civilization.[24] Hoffer has said, "The Americans are poor haters in international affairs because of their innate feeling of superiority over all foreigners."[25] This can also be seen in the hostility that the UN receives in the American press; writing the Blacks, Chinese, and others out of American history, the internment of the Japanese in prison camps during World War II, and so on.

On arts and monuments: The country has no marvels except its rivers.[26]

On guerilla warfare:

The Scythians indeed have in one respect, and that the very most important of all those that fall under man's control, shown themselves wiser than any nation on the face of the earth. Their customs otherwise are not much that I admire. The one thing of which I speak is a contrivance whereby they make it impossible for the enemy who invades them to escape destruction, while they themselves are entirely out of reach, unless it pleases them to engage with him. Having neither cities or forts, and carrying their dwellings with them wherever they go; accustomed, moreover, one and all of them to shoot from horseback; and living not by husbandry but on their cattle, their wagons the only houses that they possess, how can they fail of being unconquerable, and unassailable?"[27]

On different tribes:
Herodotus lists several tribes: the Tauri, the Agathyrsi, the Neuri, the Androphagi, the Melanchlaeni, the Budini, and the Sauromatae.

The Tauri lived by plunder and war and sacrificed all shipwrecked sailors; the Agathyrsi were fond of gold and held their wives in common with their brothers; the Neurians had a reputation of being conquerors, and each tribal member was thought to turn into a wolf at least once a year by the Greeks and Scythians; the Androphagi observed no law or justice and were cannibals; the Melanchlaeni were a tribe who dressed completely in black; the Budini had blue eyes and red hair and were considered a powerful nation. (This was to become the German nation described by Tacitus. How many Germans today can be found possessing red hair and blue eyes?) The Sauromatae was the tribe that reputedly mixed with the white Amazons of antiquity.[28] Diodorus informs us that the Amazons of Africa are older than these Whites.[29]

On outrages:

> The Scythians having thus invaded Media, were opposed by the Medes, who gave them battle, but being defeated, lost their empire. The Scythians became masters of Asia.

> After this they marched forward with the design of invading Egypt. When they reached Palestine, however, Psammetichus, the Egyptian King, met them with gifts and prayers and prevailed on them to advance no further. On their return passing through Ascalon, a city of Syria, the greater part of them went their way without doing any damage; but some few who lagged behind pillaged the temple of Celestial Venus . . . The Scythians who plundered the temple were punished by the goddess with the female sickness which still attaches to their posterity. They themselves confess that they are afflicted with the disease for this reason, and travelers who visit Scythia can see what sort of disease it is. Those who suffer from it are called Enarees.[30]

> So this is why there are more faggots among them than any other people! Also, *if my guess is right*, the Medes no doubt were a Black people, being called after Medea, the daughter of the King of Colchis.

> The conquest of Asia by Whites lasted twenty-eight years before they were overthrown. Nevertheless, this contact with more civilized people did not impress them, as subsequent history proves.

About 300 years after the death of Herodotus, another Greek writer-historian, Diodorus by name, made some very interesting commentary on these Whites.

On physique and appearance:

> For stature they are tall, but of a sweaty and pale complexion, red-haired not only naturally, but when they endeavor they can to make it redder by art. They often wash their hair in a water boiled with lime, and turn it backward from the forehead to the crown of the head, and thence to their very necks, that their faces may be more fully seen, so that they look like satyrs and hobgoblins . . . At mealtime they all sit, not upon seats, but upon the ground, and instead of carpets, spread wolves or dog skins under them.[31]

On religious belief:

> For the Opinion of Pythagoras prevails amongst them, that mens' souls are immortal, and that there is a transmigration of them into other bodies, after a certain time they live again . . .[32]

Evidently, as barbarians, the Whites knew more of religion than they do now. Incidentally, there was a Black priesthood who ministered to the spiritual and religious needs of the Whites of ancient Europe. These men were called Druids, and their influence over the Whites was destroyed by the Romans. Much has been said of the Druids, but never that they were Black. This is elucidated in a scholarly work by an Englishman named Godfrey Higgins. His text is titled *The Celtic Druids*.

On name changes according to the Romans:

> Those who inhabit the inland parts beyond Massilia (Marseilles), and about the Alps, and on this side of the Pyrenean mountains are called Celts; but those that inhabit below this part called Celtica, southward to the Ocean and the

mountain Hyrcinus, and all as far as Scythia are called Gauls.
But the Romans call all these people generally by one and the
same name, Gauls . . . Those toward the north, and bordering
upon Scythia, are so exceedingly fierce and cruel, that (as report
goes), they eat men, like the Britains that inhabit Iris.

They are so noted as a fierce and warlike people, that some have
thought them to be those who anciently overran all Asia, and were
called Cimerians, and who are now (through length of time) with a little
alteration called Cimbrians.

Anciently they gave themselves to rapine and spoil, wasting and
destroying other countries, and slighted and despised all other people.
These are they that took Rome, and robbed the temple at Delphos.
These brought a great part of Europe and Asia under tribute, and
possessed themselves of some of the countries of those they subdued.
Because of their mixture with the Grecians, they were at last called
Gallo-Grecians. They often routed and destroyed many great armies of
the Romans.[33]

On sacrifices:

According to their natural cruelty, they are as impious in the
worship of their gods; for malefactors, after they have been kept
close prisoners five years together, they impale upon stakes, in
honour to the gods, and then, with many other victims, upon a
vast pile of wood, they offer up burnt sacrifice to their deities.
In like manner they use their captives also, as sacrifices to the
gods.[34]

On sexual practices:

. . . though they have very beautiful women among them,
yet they little value their private society, but are transported
with raging lust to the filthy act of sodomy; and, lying upon the
ground on beast's skin spread under them, they tumble together
. . . and that which is most abominable is, that without any sense
of shame, or regard to their reputation, they will readily

prostitute their bodies to others upon every occasion. And they are so far from looking upon it as a fault, that they judge it a mean and dishonorable thing for any thus caressed to refuse the favor offered them.[35]

On health practices:

. . . for though they are very nice and curious in their diet, yet they have the horrid and filthy practice, to wash their bodies over with urine, and rub their very teeth with it, which is counted a certain means of health to their bodies.[36*]

Ideas of Creation According to the Ancients

The people who comprise humankind are a result of cosmic miscegenation between the Black and White races and the various combinations that have arisen. The Black man's attraction for the White woman and the White woman's attraction for the Black man have resulted in unions that are the root of what is presently called the Yellow race of Asia, esoterically symbolized by the yin-yang triagram—three—that is, the circle *O* and its division into two halves—one Black, the other White—and the trinity. Know you well that in the mystery of the trinity is contained the secret—that is, the process of creation. The Christians express this through the Father, the Son, and the Holy Ghost. Hindus express this through Brahma, Vishnu, and Shiva. The Chinese express this through the Yin Yang symbol, which also has concealed their racial origin, for the offspring of Blacks and Whites have forever been yellow or the dark-red mulatto. These unions usually took place after Blacks were hunting Whites to kill and enslave them. Before I forget the trinity, in modern words this can best be conceptualized via power, light, energy or idea, and will and form—called by the ancient Blacks *Kether*, *Chomak*, and *Binah*. This Kether is how we come by our ancestral name (k)ethiopian, that which is undifferentiated. Again, in modern times the Arabs, to whom we are accustomed, result from the unions of White men and Black women and Black men and White women—this is true, not of some, but of all the people in the Middle East. In ancient times this entire area was

Black. In the Americas, the mulatto is predominantly the result of the unions of White men and Black women.

Now, the chief reason why the White race is considered the youngest of the nations is because they were the last people to become what we call civilized; this is why the Chinese can claim to be a more ancient people than the Whites. That is, they attained civilization and culture first, meaning they were able to assimilate the great culture of the Black race, which truly is the only culture, everything else being an imitation in one way or another (note the symbolism on the American dollar)—no White people have ever created any symbols expressing divinity.

Many people, especially Blacks, feel that we have never done anything to the White race to deserve the treatment we are subjected to. This is not true! We may have forgotten, but they have not! We barred the White race from all the civilized world for untold millennia. The different people scattered throughout the world represent ancient wars and clashes that always, it seems, led to the creation of many nations. Generally, we were slaving and lusting for barbarian women. Conversely, the ancient historians all have the White race (Scythians) raiding the civilized world, which was Black only, and still is, for civilization means culture—culture, that is, to cultivate what is moral and virtuous. Morality in America is wealth and technology, which means we still have been burdened with the task of civilizing the Scythians.

The archeology, the history, and the statuary, in regards to Buddha in particular, identify Asia as one of the homes of the ancient Black race. Now, the oldest religion in China is "ancestor worship," although it really isn't ancestor worship so-called, but man's spiritual connection with the Divine.

Next to China is Russia, where the White race is and was, savages undoubtedly, hating and distrusting of civilization. The Black and White races, so far as I can tell, have never been very far from one another, the difference being that then the White race assumed the role of the marauding barbarians, a role they have played longer than any people on Earth.

The main theme that underlies all religion is that existence, or creation, came about because of the incomprehensible power of a God whose name no man knows—save the self-realized. Everything that exists depicts some animation of this God. This is what the anthropologists have misnamed polytheism.

The sacred religious doctrines say that the One becomes three; that is, the Divine divides itself and reflects different aspects of itself. It then becomes the Creator, the Preserver, and the Destroyer aspects of creation—the trinity again. It is the Father, the Son, and the Holy Ghost. The White race reflects the destructive principle of creation; we, the creative, and the marriage of the creative and the destructive yields the preserver (the Yellow race). The Chinese have preserved many things that were forgotten by other peoples—especially in the area of medicine, though just having kept the Book of Changes (I Ching) is more than enough.

Now, if the doctrine of creation says that all things originate from one, and "things" certainly do, this principle must somehow also reflect itself in the origin of the "different" races, so-called because they too originate from one source—that is, the Black race. As original humanity was Black, the White race is an extrapolation of the Black race caused either by some plague, epidemic or an experiment by a mad scientist, as Elijah Muhammad used to say. Elijah Muhammad's story was one I treated with utter contempt. How could a mad scientist create a race that would plague Black humanity? Is this possible? Consider the fact that the pyramids and sundry temples of antiquity reveal a knowledge far greater than that possessed by modern man and his childish doctrine of evolution. The sacred texts of the different peoples also reflect this: the prose of the Bible, the Bagavagita, the I Ching, and the Koran all reveal a divine man and cannot be equaled by modern pundits who can only say God is dead.

I am aware that some scholars claim a simultaneous creation, wherein people appeared in the different regions of the earth while the climatic conditions determined the hue of their skins. The one thing that is wrong with this theory is that one need only *look* at various people to see that they are mixed racially. Secondly, if this theory was factual the Eskimos would be White, would they not? The reason the Whites appear in the northern climates is because they were driven there and in time the harsh climate became natural. On another level, though, winter and cold represent the death cycle, whereas summer and heat represent the life cycle. Don't all the sciences of Whites bring death? How could the most technologically advanced society be filled with so many physically ill people if this technology in and of itself wasn't also bringing death along with "efficiency"?

To produce life, *heat* is necessary. During the creation, would this heat produce Black or White vehicles (bodies)? The sun, the ancient symbol of the beneficent creator, certainly the generator of life on this planet, is poison to the white vehicles!

Genetically speaking, white-looking albinos can be born to a Black couple but no White couple can produce a Black child.

Also, the rank distortion of history more than proves that these Whites have much to hide. Let's face it. Most people actually believe that the ancient Greeks were White, that Alexander the Great was White, that Achilles was White, that the Babylonians were White, that the Jews, the Assyrians, the Persians, and Jesus were all White. Right? Keep reading.

The ancient Germans were described by the Romans as having red hair and blue eyes. In Hitler's time, how did the Germans look? There were probably two German people with red hair and blue eyes in Hitler's time! Personally, I have never seen a red-haired, blue-eyed White person. (Never say never: I recently saw one on the subway— stoned out of his mind.) I do recall that our forefathers did—having made this the description of Typhon, the adversary of Osiris, in Egyptian theology. This was the reason why red-headed Whites would be ritualistically sacrificed by the Egyptians, being the symbol of incarnate evil, as we are so represented in modern times by the Black devil. Who were the ancient Germans mixed with so that they no longer appeared as they did in Roman times? Were there Blacks in the Roman armies? Of course. Isn't the patron saint of Germany Black? St. Maurice? This is to say that German racial purity was from the beginning bullshit, but was believed by enough men to lay the groundwork for World War II. The White American is a mongrel of another kind and actually served as an inspiration for the Nazi movement, particularly the Klan.

The Yellow Race

The lie of the indigenous development of China.

The alert reader would have noticed that throughout the narrative the lies of history have never been referred to as fables or myths, whereas a lie is exactly that and I would never give it dignity by referring to it as a myth or a fable. No, the history of China's indigenous development is a lie, as are all the other lies I have related in this book.

It was discussed earlier that ancient Black and White races inhabited Asia; also, the yellow and the dark-reddish mulatto are the colors of the offspring of Black and White unions, but mostly yellow. Anyone who has seen the children of black and white couples knows this to be so, but J.A. Rogers's *Sex and Race* is a highly illuminating volume on racial differentiation. The first men were *ptah* (pronounced *tar*), that is, the so-called Black Pygmy from whom we have evolved and whose history is so ancient that absolutely no one remembers it! This includes the Pygmies! Now the smallest men of stature are in Asia, and this also seems proof of its greater antiquity. The argument that older fossils are found in Africa says very little, since cremation is, until this very day, practiced by numerous people in Asia.

Regarding Java: *The Wayang Figures*, one day I was in the library checking out the statuary of the Buddha. I came across figurines, some of which had white faces and black bodies, others of which had black faces and white bodies. Some were a curious mixture of the two. Subsequent research revealed them to be from Java. They are said to represent the oldest inhabitants of the land. Of course I immediately found those that were plainly black and others that were plainly white, as you can see for yourself. These figurines are not only fascinating from sheer appearance but from the fact that these are obviously a dwarf race of men!

These Javanese figurines depict the origins of the yellow race. As you can see, the Wayang representing Ardjuna (Arjuna) is Black (Fig. 1). Arjuna is the famous character of the sacred Bagavagita, i.e., the personality in search of the true self (Christna).

It may do well here to point out that even in very ancient times the Whites have interpolated their bullshit into the sacred text; for instance,

19

some translation of the "gita" have Arjuna calling himself an "Aryan." As soon as I saw that I smelled a rat, and as I began to check out different translations, no Aryan shit was found anywhere. Now dig this: the Hindu of today think that the Aryans were responsible for the formation of civilization! Here are a Black people who actually think that a roving band of savages is responsible for the ancient glory of India! Castes were efficient when everything on Earth was ordered but, as a peasant can now become emperor, obviously providence prefers merit above heredity, making it plain that there is only one heredity, that is, God, the Father-Mother.

Curiously, the Chinese have Black *and* White devils! Black and White people "love" Chinese food? The Chinese have the pudgy noses of the Blacks and the eyes! In fact, the Oriental eyes are the characteristic feature of the Asiatic people, right? Right! Now here in the United States you can see millions of Blacks with these so-called Oriental eyes, particularly our women.

My own opinion as to why the Chinese claim their civilization to be a mere 5,000 years old is because this is when they came to power in that country (China) and not because Fu Sei "invented" civilization. He didn't. This has given credence to the lie among the Chinese of indigenous development, carried to an extreme by Mao Tse Tung. He was a revolutionary extraordinaire, probably the greatest leader in the twentieth century,[*] but Mao believed that the Chinese could do it alone, ignoring the fact that Communism itself comes from the West, and in the end even he was forced to "open up," so to speak, when Richard Nixon visited China.

Besides, did you know that the metaphysical and psychological elements of Chinese philosophy are of foreign origin?[38]

Civilizations do not rise of themselves but are extensions of what has preceded them—the forms may change, but the principles remain intact. In this sense the ancient Greeks were like the Chinese, in that they claimed everything and called everybody else barbarians! Most nations do likewise because they do not study their histories thoroughly enough and make assumptions that have no basis in fact; otherwise, they just lie outright. When it comes to the falsification of history, the Whites have first place, but the Chinese are not far behind.

It is also worth noting that wars between Black and Yellow men are mentioned in the *Secret Doctrine* (Vol. III). Judging from the population of Southern Asia, their populations can be seen from the point of view of a retreating Black nation being driven back by the Han people—Chinese barbarians, no doubt like the Aryans when they invaded India, that actually came to possess an advanced culture.

Further, if you go back to the art section in a library and get a book on the ruins of Ankor Wat in Cambodia, you'll see that the statuary reveal a Black people. Check it out, then check out the Cambodian people themselves—many have Afros (the hairstyles).

One Chinese scholar has rightly noted, "The oldest religion (or class of religions) in China has no name, though it was around many centuries before Buddha, Confucius, or Lao Tzu and strongly influenced the thought of the latter two. I call it Sinism. Sinism was a religion of ancestor spirits and household gods."[37]

Ancestor spirits? Household gods? Who believes in these practices more than the Black race?[38] This is easy to say since we have founded every religion of note.[39]

Many people have gazed upon the statue of Buddha, but very few have seriously considered what this says about the history of the Black race in Asia.

Did you know that the first inhabitants of China seem also to have been Negritos? Unmixed Negroes having no connection with Africa still live in southern China.

H. Imbert, a French anthropologist who lived in the Far East, says in *Les Negritos de la Chine*, "The Negroid races peopled at some time all the south of India, Indo-China, and China. The south of Indo-China actually has pure Negritos as the Semangs, and mixed as the Malays and the Sakis."[40]

You will find that wherever the Indian Ocean touches land, people are, if not outright Black themselves, mixed Blacks—this is true from India (upper Ethiopia) to Hawaii.

---

[1] J.A. Rogers, *Sex and Race* (New York, 1967), I, 31.
[2] Giuseppe Sergi, *The Mediterranean Race* (New York, 1901), p. 259.

[3] Fabre D'Olivet, *Hermeneutic Interpretation of the Origin of the Social State of Man and the Destiny of the Adamic Race* (New York, 1915), p. 6.

[4] Ibid., p. 8.

[5] Ibid. p. 83.

[*] This can be argued and refuted.

[6] Rogers, p. 118.

[7] D'Olivet, p. 56.

[8] William Montgomery McGovern, *The Early Empires of Central Asia* (North Carolina, 1939), p. 28.

[9] Ibid., p. 36.

[10] Tamara Talbot Rice, *The Scythians* (London, 1957), II, 19.

[11] Godfrey Higgins, *Anacalypsis* (1893), I.

[12] D. Brinton, *Race and Peoples*, p. 43.

[13] Rogers, p. 29.

[14] John Pinkerton, "A Dissertation on the Origin Progress of the Scythians or Goths," in *The Ancient and Modern History of Europe* (London, 1787), p. 3.

[15] Rogers, pp. 196-200.

[16] *Oxford Bible Atlas* (New York, 1962), pp. 79, 83, 91.

[17] Rogers, p. 174.

[18] D'Olivet, pp. 46-47.

[19] Herodotus, p. 206.

[20] Ibid., p. 213.

[21] Ibid., p. 223.

[22] Ibid., pp. 221-222.

[23] Ibid., p. 227.

[24] Ibid.

[25] Eric Hoffer, *The True Believer* (New York, 1961), p. 90.

[26] Herodotus, p. 230.

[27] Ibid., p. 218.

[28] Ibid., pp. 235-237.

[29] Diodorus, p. 192.

[30] Herodotus, p. 41.

[31] Diodorus, p. 314.

[32] Ibid.

[33] Ibid., p. 317.

[34] Ibid.

[35] Ibid., pp. 317-318.

[36] Ibid., p. 318.

[*] For an interesting look at urine therapy, see *The Water of Life* by John Armstrong.

[*] If there was a greater feat than the organization of 800 million people torn apart by faction, war, starvation, and Imperialism, please tell me!

[37] Gia-Fu Feng and Jerome King, *Tai Chi...A Way of Centering and the I Ching* (New York, 1970), p. 8.

[38] Ibid., p. 25

[39] See *African Religion and Philosophy*, M'biti or Muntu-Jahn, or any book on religion in Africa.
[40] See *The African Origins of the Major Western Religions* by Ben Jocamman. See *Anacalypsis* by Higgins. See *Book of Beginnings* by Massey.

CHAPTER II

EARLY CIVILIZATIONS

Babylon

> And Cush begat Nimrod: he began to be a mighty one in the earth. He was a mighty hunter before the Lord: wherefore it is said, Even as Nimrod the mighty hunter before the Lord. And the beginning of his kingdom was Babel, and Erech, and Accad, and Calneh, in the land of Shinar.(Genesis 10:8-10)

That this passage refers to Babylon will scarcely be disputed. The words Babel and Shinar are sufficient proof. Babel is translated elsewhere as "Babylon" (2 Kings 20:12, 14; 2 Chronicles 32, 33; Psalms 87; etc.). This is the exact Hebrew equivalent of the native Babel, which appears as the capital of Babylonia in the cuneiform records from the time of Hgu-Kak-rimi (about 2000 BC) to the conquest of the country by Cyrus (538 BC). Shinar is probably the equivalent of Mesopotamia, "the country of the two rivers."[1] And the Scriptures always refer to the lower part of the Tigris and Euphrates Valley, the alluvial plain through which the great rivers flow before reaching the Persian Gulf. Four facts are recorded in the passage: (1) that it became, at a very early date, a settled government under a king; (2) that it contained, besides Babylon, at least three other great cities—Erech, Accad, and Calneh; (3) that among its earliest rulers was a great conquering monarch named Nimrod; and (4) that this monarch, and therefore probably his people, descended from Cush, i.e., was a Cushite or Ethiopian.[1]

The fourth fact—that Nimrod, and therefore probably his people, was of Cushite origin—has been strenuously denied by some, even among modern critics. But ancient classical traditions and recent linguistic research agree in establishing a close connection between the early inhabitants of the lower Mesopotamian plain and the people, which under the various names of Cushites, Ethiopians, and Abyssinians, had long been settled upon the middle Nile. Memnon,

King of Ethiopia, according to Hesiod and Pindar, led an army of combined Ethiopian and Susianian forces to the assistance of Priam, King of Troy. Belus, according to genealogists, was the son of Libya (or Africa). He married Anchinoe, daughter of Nilus, and had of that issue Aegyptus. Names with the modification of Cush have always hung about the lower Mesopotamian region, indicating the primitive connection with Cush on the Nile. The Greeks called the Susianians "Kissil" and the neighboring race "Kossail." The early Babylonians had a city called "Kissi" and a leading tribe of the country was called the "Kassu." Even now the ancient Susiania is known as "Khuzistan," the land of Khuz or of the Cushites. Standing alone these would be weak arguments, but weight is lent them by the support that they obtain from the facts of language. Sir Henry Rawlinson, the first translator of primitive Babylonian documents, declares the vocabulary to be decidedly Cushite or Ethiopianm, and states that he was able to interpret the inscriptions chiefly by the aid that was furnished to him from published works on Galla (Abyssinian) and the Mahra (south Arabian) dialects.[2]

Windsor states:

> There was an Ethiopian civilization in southern Mesopotamia (Babylon), but the people in this region did not use their tribal name, Ethiopia, to designate their nationality. They called themselves by the cities they constructed and inhabited, or they called themselves by an event that happened there; for example, God confused the language of the people at the Tower of Babel (Babel means confusion in Hebrew). This is why the Ethiopian tribes called themselves Babylonians, referring to the name of the city that they constructed . . . The people who resided in the lower part of the Tigris-Euphrates Valley were Ethiopian, black in complexion.[3]

The author of *The Two Babylons* is determined to make us the "original black adversary of mankind"; nevertheless, he gives some rightful information:

. . . Cush is generally represented as having been a ringleader in the great apostasy. But again Cush as the Son of Ham, was Hermes or Mercury; for Hermes is just an Egyptian synonym for the 'Son of Ham.' Now Hermes was the great original prophet of idolatry; for he was recognized by the pagans as the author of their religious rites, and the interpreter of the gods.[4]

The author's point of view is that Black is evil. But I recall that Roman emperor Julian was also an apostate, according to the Christians. If you check out the life of Julian and his uncle, Constantine, who established Christianity as the religion of the empire, you will quickly see the difference between the apostate and Christianity.

Modern pundits have made idolatry a dirty word, dismissing the fact that the Divine Presence is everywhere, in everything, itself being the In and the Out—the worshipper and the object of worship.

All the religious rites of the "pagans" are used in modern times under different forms and styles, which the author of *The Two Babylons* himself proves in his attack on Catholicism by comparing it with the ancient Babylonian religion and rites. But the same holds true of all the other religions. The author suffers from lack of insight into the allegory and symbolism of the ancients.

Now, what were the Whites doing during the days of Babylon?

These Whites in ancient times were considered under the two general classifications discussed earlier, Cimmerians and Scythians. Marvel Comics, acknowledging this, makes Conan the Barbarian a Cimmerian. In the cuneiform writing of the Black Babylonians, they were called Gimimaya,[5] whereas the Scythians were called Ashguzaya.[6] In the Bible, the Cimmerians are said to be Ashkenaz (Jeremiah 2:27).

The Cimmerians and Scythians, as they appear in history, are always depicted as savages and barbarians and threatening to civilization.[7]

The only reason this information can be easily investigated is that the Whites consider themselves to be all the ancient people of antiquity, and they write history as such. When White historians write about the Scythians or Cimmerians, there is no mention made that these are

White people. Although somebody must know something, since books like those of Herodotus and Diodorus are not used in the classroom for students who study ancient history because of what is said about the Black race and what is said about White people.

Concerning the Mesopotamian drama, Sumer is considered to have preceded Babylon in history proper. These people, by the racist archeologists and anthropologists, are called Semetic, but it appears to me to be a civilization that was governed by Pygmies or some kind of Black dwarfs. The Egyptians had a Pygmy as one of their deities; Blacks have always (since Egypt) regarded the Pygmies as the fathers of the Black race, the taller Black being evolutionary Pygmies, or Ptah, as the sacred Black dwarf race was called by the ancients. Maspero speaks of Black and White dwarf kings of Asia.[8] These White dwarfs are also mentioned in *Oasphe and the Secret Doctrine*.

Now, I don't know whether it was the mixture of these little Blacks and Whites or the taller ones that produced the yellow race (probably a combination of both). The modern Asian is short-statured, is he not?

Incidentally, history also shows Blacks and Whites fighting together, most notably in the destruction of Nineveh, which ended the Assyrian Empire, which also was Black. Nineveh was destroyed by a combination of Medes (called after Medea, Black daughter of the king of Colchis), Babylonians, and Scythians. I recall that Livingston, in *The Zambesi and its Tributaries*, mentioned that the Black face as he saw it reminded him more of that on the monuments of ancient Assyria than that of popular White fancy.[9]

There are countless books written on the history of Babylon, Assyria, and Sumer, but never is mention made that the people were Black—never.[*] Civilization as we know it comes from the Black race, all of it.

The symbol of royalty is the lion, the animal that inhabits the environment of the Black peoples. The lion is regarded by many nations as the symbol of power, specifically the power of the will. Who amongst you thinks that this symbol was instituted by a snow-dwelling race? The lion is also the animal with a place of prominence in the ancient Chinese temples and palaces, recollecting, in my opinion, a people familiar with this animal.

"Finally, the Blackness of the Mesopotamians is also revealed in 'The Epic of Gilgamesh,' the renowned King of Uruk in Mesopotamia, it comes from an age which had wholly been forgotten, until the last century archaeologists began uncovering the buried cities of the Middle East. Till then the entire history of the long period which separated Abraham from Noah was contained in the two most forbiddingly genealogical chapters in the Book of Genesis. From these chapters only two names survived in common parlance, those of the hunter Nimrod and the Tower of Babel; but in the cycle of poems which are collected round the character of Gilgamesh we are carried back into the middle of that age."[10]

Gilgamesh, the hero of the poem, goes through a series of adventures similar to Odysseus in that his triumphs usually bring trouble. The major point of interest to me is the fact that the patron god of Gilgamesh, and his protector, is none other than Shamash, the Sun God! The Blacks are the sun race and worshippers! No White race has ever worshipped the sun, except in Florida and environs.

Uruk, the city of which Gilgamesh is king, is the Biblical Erech and is inhabited by Blacks as mentioned in Genesis 10:8-10.

Be forewarned that when reading about the history of the nations in this area, i.e., Sumer, Babylon, Assyria, Persia, etc., you will very frequently see the words "semetic," "Indo-European," and "Indo-Aryan"—disregard these interpolations, "for it is inconceivable to me, now that I have studied the ruins, how the theory of 'Semetic' . . . could have ever been formulated. Every detail . . . appears to be typically Bantu."[11]

Now this scarabacus beetle is black like darkness which lies at the beginning of all things. —Her-Bak

Ethiopia

There is no nation on Earth that can claim a greater antiquity than Ethiopia—none. The glory that was Egypt was no more than the

28

daughter practicing the arts of the elder sister, for the Egyptians did say that they came from Ethiopia.[12]

Ethiopia proper antedates what men call history. This is made strikingly clear once you comprehend that Ethiopia was also in Asia and that the African Ethiopia comes from the former!

> If my reader will examine . . . the . . . passages of the Old Testament . . . where the words Ethiopia and Ethiopian are used, he will see that many of them can by no possibility relate to the African Ethiopia. Eusebius states the Ethiopians to have come and settled in Egypt, in the time of Amenophis. According to this account, as well as to the account given by Philostratus, there was no such country as Ethiopia beyond Egypt until this invasion. According to Eusebius these people came from the river Indus, and planted themselves to the south of Egypt, in the country called from them Ethiopia . . . But there are several passages in ancient writers which prove that Eusebius is right in saying that they came from the East, but from a very distant or very eastern part. Herodotus says, that there were two Ethiopian nations, one in India, the other in Egypt . . . Dr. Shuckford gives an opinion that Homer and Herodotus are both right, and that there were two Ethiopias, and that the Africans came from India. The Bishop of Avranches thinks he has found three provinces of the name of Chus; Ethiopia, Arabia, and Susiana. There were three Ethiopias, that is, countries of Blacks, not three chusses; and this is perfectly consistent with what M. Bochart has maintained, that Ethiopia (of Africa) is not named Chus in any place of Scripture; and this is also consistent with what is said by both Homer and Herodotus.[13]

Africa was once covered with ice. We could not have been there then, nor at the time of the so-called great flood of antiquity, when it is said we went to the Himalayan Mountains to escape the deluge. The practice of magic in these mountains adds fuel to this argument, as well as the Doctrine of the Buddha, supreme in Asia, and not without influence in so-called Western religions. "The Black race is so old it has forgotten that it has ruled all Asia"!* It was the opinion of Sir

William Jones that a great nation of Blacks formerly possessed the dominion of Asia and held the seat of Empire at Sidon. These must have been the people that Mr. Maurice called Cushites, or Cuthites, described in Genesis; and the opinion that they were Blacks is corroborated by the translators of the Pentateuch, called seventy, constantly rendering the word *Cush* by Ethiopia.

> The religion of Buddha, of India, is well known to have been very ancient. In the most ancient temples scattered throughout Asia, where his worship is yet continued, he is found black as jet, with the flat face, thick lips, and curly hair of the Black . . . To what time are we to allot this black? He will be proved to have been prior to the god called Cristna.[14]

In Asia, has there been a greater influence on civilization and culture than the Buddhist religion?

We know that "Buddha is generally represented in China as a Black."[15] Further, "It is not necessary to show that the first colonizers of India were Blacks, but it is certain that the Black Buddha of India was imagined in the Ethiopian type. In the Black god, whether called Buddha or Sut-Nahsi, we have a datum. They carry in their color the proof of their origin. The people who first fashioned and worshipped the divine image in the Ethiopian mold of humanity must according to all knowledge of human nature, have been Blacks themselves. For the blackness is not merely mystical, the features and hair of Buddha belong to the Black race, and Nahsi is the Blacks' name."[16]

Continuing, F. Wilford says in *Asiatic Researches* Vol. III:

> It is certain that very ancient statutes of Gods in India have crisp hair and features of Blacks. Some have cap or tiaras with curls depending over their foreheads according to the precise meaning of the epithet, *cutibalaca*. Others, indeed, seem to have their locks curled by art and braided above in a thick knot; but I have seen many idols on which the woolly appearance of the hair was so well presented as to preclude all doubt; and we naturally suppose that they were made by the Cutila-Cesas when they prevailed in this country. The Brahmans ascribe

these idols to the Buddhas, and nothing hurts them more than to say that any of their own gods had the feature of Habashis or Blacks; and even the hair of the Buddha himself for whom they have no small degree of respect, they consider as twisted braids, like that of some modern Sannyasis. But this will not account for the thick lips and flat noses of those ancient images; nor can it be reasonably doubted that a race of blacks formerly had power and preeminence in India. In several parts of India the mountaineers still have resemblance to Blacks in their countenance and hair which is curled with a tendency to wool.[17]

Anyone can check this out for himself in any library that has pictures of the Buddha. The ancient cave sculpture of that country, long renowned for its spiritual wisdom, is the cultural heritage of the Black race, not the Aryan, as the modern Hindu is wont to surmise.

The word *India* means Black, as does the word *Egypt*—they are obviously named after their peoples. Modern scholars are fond of saying that Egypt was named after the color of the fertile soil.

The very fact that no one even considered the Black race to have had dominion in Asia seems proof enough of the superior antiquity of the Ethiopia of Asia. The people who now inhabit Asia, China included, have what would be called today an African culture (Ethiopian), as do the rest of the people who inhabit this earth, commonly called mankind. As the Black race is the epitome of all social graces and religious rites, it is right to assume that Blacks will have the more prominent place amongst men once we recognize who we really are! I mean that the religious and social amenities, through which men regulate their interpersonal behaviors, as well as their behaviors with the deity, have been handed down by the Black race.

George Wells Parker, even in 1918, never bought the shit the Whites were trying to pass off as history and wrote a beautiful little book about the Black race titled *Children of the Sun*. He begins by boldly stating:

In the morning of the world, when the fingers of love swept aside the curtain of time, our dusky mother, Ethiopia, held the stage. It was she who wooed civilization and gave birth to

31

nations. Egypt was her first born and to Ur of the Chaldees she sent her sons and daughters, who scattered empires in Asia as the wanton wind of autumn scatters the seeds of flowers. Besides the beautiful Mediterranean she built Phoenicia, and in ships with purple sails she sent her children to the blue Aegean, there to found Greece, the marvel or men and the queen of history. Troy was hers, and from that burning city fled swarthy Aneas, who set the ferment for Rome, the eternal city. Her spirit called to Arabia and out of the mystic deserts surged the Black soldiers of Islam, who welded the world into a new empire and sang their songs of love and victory in the Vales of Andalusia. On the isles of all the oceans, and from the Southern Cross bends low to kiss the restless waves to where the Arctic holds in leash its frozen world, her hand has touched. Religion, art, literature, science and civilization are hers and eternity but lives in the warmth of her radiant glow. I have chosen to call the unnumbered million of her descendants the Children of the Sun.[18]

In Gayley's *Classic Myths* it is said, "On the south side of the earth, close to the steam of the ocean, dwelt the Ethiopians who the gods held in such favor that they left at the time the Olympian abode to partake of the Aethiopian sacrifices and banquet."[19]

The Ethiopians say they were the first men than ever were in the world and to prove this they have clear demonstration. For they say they are natives of the country and not strangers that came to settle there . . . it is most probable that those who inhabit the south were the first living men to spring out of the earth. For being that the heat of the sun at first exhaled moisture of the earth and in the first production of things, influenced it with a quickening virtue, they say it is rational to conclude that those places nearest the sun should have been the first parents of all living creatures.[20]

Is it necessary to say that tropical man is never White? How about the fact that a small lie is "white" and a big lie "black"! White history is the foremost lie and propagandist tool that has been utilized to buttress the theory of White race superiority over the last four centuries. This is the race that equates gadgetry with civilization.

Getting back to the Ethiopians, we find in Volyney's text:

> The Ethiopians say Lucian, were the first who invented the science of the stars, and gave names to the planets, not at random and without meaning, but descriptive of the qualities which they conceived them to possess; and it was from them that this art passed, still in an imperfect state, to the Egyptians . . . It would be easy to multiply citations upon this subject; from all which follows, that we have the strongest reason to believe that the country neighboring to the tropics, was the cradle of the sciences, and of consequence that the first learned nation was a nation of Blacks; for it is incontrovertible, that by the term Ethiopian, the ancients mean to represent a people of black complexion, thick lips, and woolly hair . . . I have suggested the same idea in my travels into Syria, founded upon the black complexion of the Sphinx.[21]

We find:

> In the Hebrew writing Aethiopia, Kush and Zaba are controvertible terms for the same country, the Egypt beyond Egypt . . . In the time of the middle empire (of Egypt) a hieroglyphic U passed into an E. Thus we have Eti-Opia, Uti-Opia, Khefti-Opia, and Opia from Api is the first, ancestral land. Cassiopoera, the lady of the seat is the Queen of Ethiopia or Kush . . . The Aethiopians are called from the reduplicated Pih'd people of great might or (double power) (Isiah 18:27). Kefa means force, puissance, potency.[22]

J. Delouise, a famous White spiritualist, has this to say: "Blacks are more psychic than any other race of people . . . It seems like a natural power, though part of it may be called soul. If you stay more in touch with other parts of yourself, it's a lot easier to get the vibration." Delouise continues, "Scientific research backs up the fact that Blacks are more psychic. The National Opinion Research center recently did a study on the typical mystic or psychic personality, and found that more often he was Black than White . . . Black children are especially psychic."[23]

The power and majesty of the race in ancient times was our knowledge of divine forces and all that this implies—"The Double Power," i.e., the power of the magician! For further study, consult A.E. Powell's *The Etheric Double* and C.W. Leadbarter's *The Charkas*.

There are a few Greek sources in which we hear of the Ethiopia of Asia. The most famous is, of course, Homer. Homer, on the very first page of *The Odyssey*, says, "Poseidon, however, was now gone on a visit to the distant Ethiopians, the farthest outpost of mankind, half of whom live where the sun goes down, and half where he rises."[24] Now we know that the sun rises in the east and sets in the west.

Another interesting source is the famous Ethiopics of Heliodorus, evidently a Black Greek. Heliodorus wrote a romantic adventure about an Ethiopian queen, Persina, who has a daughter who is born "white." The child is given away and, upon growing up and learning her true identity, seeks to return to Ethiopia with her lover. The novel is a gem because of the view it presents of the ancient world. In this book, Heliodorus calls Hydhapes king of eastern and western Ethiopia.[25] Interestingly, the translator of this text makes the lover of the heroine, Chariclea, White through a sleight of hand. He was counting on the accepted notion that Theagenes, the hero, was a Thessalian and, therefore, a White Greek, but of course this is nonsense since the ancient Greeks were Blacks.

The Ethiopia of Africa is world-renowned, and no comment need be made here other than to say that the very name *Ethiopia* laughs at the concept of so-called White civilization, because in reality there is no such thing. Culture and civilization do not generate themselves but are simply passed from one nation to the next.

Phrygia

The Histories of Herodotus is a book that, for the most part, consists of histories of the various Black mulatto nations of antiquity. The book is full of information that identifies certain nations as Black, although Herodotus does not directly say this. He does say, though, that the Black skin and woolly hair of the "Colchian" and Egyptians means very little since there are several nations like this.[26]

The first such example begins in his opening chapter on Egypt, in which he describes an experiment by King Psammetichus of Egypt: "Now the Egyptians, before the reign of Psammetichus, believed themselves to be the most ancient of mankind . . . Psammetichus, however, made an attempt to discover who were actually the primitive race."[27]

The experiment that Psammetichus undertook was to confine two infants in closed quarters and to have a caretaker watch over them who was never to speak. After two years the children spoke the word "Becos," which, as the story goes, turned out to be the word for bread in the Phrygian language, and "of this circumstance the Egyptians yielded their claims, and admitted the greater antiquity of the Phrygians."[28]

Now remember, since the Egyptians are Black, you would really have to stretch the imagination to think that the ancient Phrygians were not Black, for the Egyptians believed the Blacks to be the first men created, as they themselves were Ethiopian.[29]

Encyclopedia Britannica offers this as its entry on Phrygia: "The name of a large district of Asia Minor in ancient times, derived from the people who the 'Greeks' called Φ PIYES; i.e., freemen. Taken at its widest extent, Phrygia comprised the whole northwest and center of Asia Minor, as far as the river Halys and the southern mountain edge of the peninsula, and had sea fronts on the Black Sea and the Aegean."[30]

Don't forget that the Black Sea was named after the Blacks who inhabited that area.[31]

Further, the ancient and sacred god of Phrygians was Cybelle, "The Great Mother," who, of course, was a Black Goddess.[32]

The principal sanctuary of Cybelle stood at Pessinus . . . Not only did the cult of Cybelle maintain itself against the religion of Phrygian . . . newcomers, but it partially absorbed them. Nay more, it more than held its own against the religions of Greece and Rome . . . The worship of Cybelle spread to Greece in the fifth century BC; in 204 BC it was officially established at Rome; in the days of the Roman Empire it has carried on the tide of Oriental immigration into every part of Italy and penetrated the western provinces as far as the Rhineland and Britain. Thus the religion of Phrygia was the most distinctive contribution to ancient Mediterranean civilization.[33]

Curiously, we find that in the "classic" *The Golden Ass* by Apuleius, the African, some confirmation of the experiment of Psammetichus exists. The Great Mother is made to say:

"*For the Phrygians that are the first of all men* call me the mother of the gods of Pessinus; the Athenians, which are sprung from their own soil, Cecropian Minerva; the Cyprians, Paphian Venus; the Cretans which bear arrows, Dictynnian Diana; the Sicilians, which speak three tongues, infernal Prosepine; the Eleusians their ancient goddess Ceres; some Juno, other Bellona; other Hecate, other Rhamnusia, and principally both sort of Ethiopians, which dwell in the Orient and are enlightened by the morning rays of the sun, and the Egyptians, which are excellent in all kinds of ancient Doctrine, and by their proper ceremonies accustom to worship me, do call me by my true name, Queen Isis."[34]

From this you can see how the Black woman, The Great Mother, was a principal goddess of the ancient world (and some European countries still worship a Black goddess).

Some of you may think that this has no connection with White Mary, mother of blue-eyed Jesus, but don't bet any money on it, as capitalist ideology proclaims. Modern theologians think that Christianity in particular is somehow distinct from so-called paganism, but this is true only in form, for in principle they are the same. This cannot be refuted, inasmuch as the Black man is the creator of all known religions, and no one knows this better than we.

On the northeastern border of Phrygia, separated by the River Holys, were the Whites (Gimarrai).[35] Here again we see civilized Blacks and, across the river, barbarians very close to one another. I see also that Apuleius called Paris (of Trojan War fame) a Phrygian shepherd.[36] Fabled Troy was on the western coast of Phrygia,[37] which also helps us identify the Trojans as a Black people. We shall discuss this further in the Grecian chapter concerning *The Iliad.*

The reader, if interested in the works of the ancients, should be warned that once blond hair is mentioned an attempt is being made to whiten a particular story, narrative, etc., particularly when reading about the Greeks.

Egypt

In the study of the history of the earth and the many nations whose very names time has destroyed, Egypt, "the land of light," stands as a beacon of the unrivaled mastery and power of the Black race on the earth plane. Evidently, the Blacks of Egypt retained a good deal of the spiritual knowledge of sunken Atlantis and the legendary Mu (Lemuria). That the Black race is associated with these two lands is borne out by the practice of magic among Blacks, which is an integral component of the cultural life of the people as seen in all our religions, including Christianity. Atlantis and Lemuria were certainly famed for their magical practices.

The Egyptians deliberately kept life in Egypt as simple as possible so as not to make the mistake of materialistic Atlantis, but generally the three nations represent a particularized consciousness in man. For instance, although the Lemurians may have been able to see directly into the nature of a thing, their relationship with the physical plane would had to have been less than ours. Nevertheless, Providence, it seems, wants us to take a good look at this creation—wonderful!

Regarding this, the secret doctrine is clear—an incomprehensible power (God, to the vulgar) has willed itself into an infinite variety of forms becoming both the slayer and the slain, the man and the woman, the right and the wrong, in what is obviously the greatest stage drama extant, each form playing his role but unable to penetrate the veil of Isis (the secret of Nature).

The Pyramids and the Sphinx of Egypt are the physical manifestations of the spiritual power and loftiness of the Black race. Both these symbols deal with man and his relationship with the Divine.

The word *pyramid* is itself revealing—*pyra*, we know, means fire, like pyromaniac. *Mid* is obviously the middle. Thus, the pyramid is the middle fire. The middle fire is the Kundalini of the Yogis, the "Ki" of the Japanese, and "chi" of the Chinese, and it is the root energy matter in man lying dormant like a coiled serpent. Alchemy, yoga, magic, Tai Chi, Akido, and tarot all aim in one way or another to release this energy, which confers divine consciousness. There are countless books on yoga explaining this process, and yoga is thousands of years old. The fact that books refer to this energy as the middle fire is most revealing.

The symbol Δ points upward—this is also the way the middle fire moves (up the spinal column). The direction is also indicative of the home of man. Man comes from, and is part of, God; he does not come from Africa or Asia or Atlantis or Lemuria (Mu). Man does not come from Earth—his body does! At death the body returns to the earth, man to God (Providence).

This drama did not fool the Egyptians. In Egypt we studied the invisible to master the visible. Nor were we dreamers, for the mastery of the arts and sciences were a prerequisite before anyone could benefit from the "inner teaching."

In Egypt we mapped the heavens and the gods who ruled there, the weight of the earth and that of the soul. Here in Egypt we laid the foundation for everything so-called Western man regards as civilization, for we are Western and Eastern man. I swear by Homer.

During the Nubia exhibition at the Brooklyn Museum, I was commenting on how Egyptian many of the artifacts were. A man named John said to me, "You are always talking about Egypt just because Herodotus said they were Black, and you show very little interest in the culture of West Africa, which is where we come from!"

This fellow did not know that the so-called West Africans seem to be the remnants of the ancient Egyptians. Their religions prove this conclusively. Secondly, no other Black nation can boast of the Sphinx and the Great Pyramid of Giza, structures that we cannot construct today, in spite of great technological advances. We look to Egypt for our greatest inspiration because our accomplishments there remain unsurpassed. Now we must try to outdo ourselves.

Who has not heard of the mysteries of the ancients? The very word *initiation* has more to do with Ethiopian universal culture than any other people.

History as Propaganda: Ancient Egypt, Greeks, Jews, Ancient Gods

"What is history," once asked the great Napoleon, "but a fiction agreed upon?" How truly has this agreement been kept by all European historians whenever the Black races are concerned! With great pains they have stated that certain people of antiquity were not Negroes and that Negroes appear upon the monuments of the ancients as slaves only.[38] There is no doubt that the historians will continue this trend until we begin writing our own books to counter the propaganda and falsification of our history.

All or most historical inquiries on Blacks should begin in Egypt:

> In many respects Egypt has long appeared to the scholar, the antiquary, and the philosopher, the most interesting country on the face of the earth. Relatively, to the various tribes who at successive eras, have founded states westward of the Black Sea and the Syrian Desert, it has with justice been regarded as the cradle of science, as well as the first seat of regular government. Even the polished nations of Modern Europe are accustomed to ascribe the rudiments of their literature and art to the ingenious people who at a period beyond the records of civil history, occupied the banks of the Nile.[39]

Who were these Nile dwellers? Herodotus, "the Father of History," traveling in Egypt in 447 BC, reported that the Egyptians were Black and the Colchians, too, were a colony of the Egyptians. He stated, "I made inquiries on the subject both in Colchis [Colchis is in South Russia!] and in Egypt . . . my own conjectures were founded, first, on the fact that they are black-skinned and have woolly hair." Another circumstance corroborative of the general accuracy of the old annalists is the establishment of an Egyptian colony in the province of Colchis. The descendants of this military association presented the dark complexion and woolly hair of Africa.[40]

Concerning the hieroglyphics:

> It has been noted that on comparing the hieroglyphics names, certain characters or bearing will be found always associated with individuals of Ethiopic descent, whilst others indicate a family from upper or lower Egypt . . . The conclusion thus obtained are altogether confirmed on turning to the ancient portraits of kings. There we find the receding forehead and high ears, peculiar to the Ethiopic or Negro race.[41]

Petrie says that the Egyptians were considered Ethiopian by the ancient writers.[42] It should be remembered that the first kings of Egypt lived not after the way and manner of other monarchs, "for among their attendants, they had neither the slaves for servants, nor such as were born in their houses, but the sons of the chief priests (after they attained to the age of twenty years)."[43] What this means is that the attendants you may see on the monuments are not slaves but the sons of priests. Egypt did have slavery: "It was a custom of the Egyptians to subject prisoners of war to this life of forced labor. A tomb in the time of Thotmos III has furnished pictures which represent Asiatic captives making bricks, and working at building under the rod of taskmasters."[44] Rawlinson says, "The use of forced labor by the Egyptian monarchs of the time, especially by Seti I and Rameses II, is abundantly witnessed to by the monuments. The kings speak of it as a matter of course."[45] Bear in mind that there were several Black nations—all of us were not in Egypt. Diodorus[46] and Herodotus[47] confirm this. Consequently, if one was a prisoner of war, one's plight was definitely slavery, regardless of color.

The importance of Egyptian studies increases when we learn that the study of history of the Blacks must begin in Egypt because more of their indestructible monuments are there; and further, because many of the artifacts archeologists have been uncovering during the past seventy-five years as Egyptian are, in fact, African.[48]

Any talk of Africa must necessarily say something on religion. Now, the first religion of Egypt was the Mystery System, a secret order whose modern versions are seen in the Rosicrucians, Masons, Illuminati, Golden Dawn, Kabbalists, and other similar organizations. In addition to the Mystery System there existed many religious cults, Osiris and Isis being the chief gods of the people. Each town had its own god. A vulture, named Nekhe, was the tribal deity of the trading city of Eileithiaspolis; a ferocious crocodile, Sebek, was the god of a second city of the name Ombos; an ibis, Thoth, was that of Hermopolis; a cat, Bast, that of Bubastis; and so on . . . It is[49] stated in *Stolen Legacy*, "The Egyptian priests possessed supernatural powers, for they had been trained in the esoteric philosophy of the Greater Mysteries, and were expert in magic. They had the power of controlling the minds of men (hypnosis), the power of predicting the future and the power over nature (i.e., the power of the gods) by giving commands in the name of the Divinity and accomplishing great deeds . . . Here it might be mentioned the Egyptian priests were the first genuine priests of history, who exercised control over the laws of nature. Here it might also be mentioned that the Egyptian Book of the Dead is a book of magical formulae and instructions, intended to direct the fate of the departed soul. It was the prayer book of the Mystery System of Egypt and the Egyptian priests received training in post mortem conditions and the method of their verification."[50]

For particulars, we see the Egyptian concept of the Ka. This Ka is an electromagnetic body, an etheric double, or an aura to the uninitiated. Modern science can now photograph this body (through Krilian photography) which hovers over the human form, so this is not religious nonsense but scientific fact. More than a few African tribes believe this concept. It is remarkable that the Twis, Gas, and even the Ewes use the same word: Kra, Kla, Klama—there is a great temptation to link this with the Egyptian concept of the Ka.[51] In religious matters, the Egyptians at all periods, except the educated at the end of the eighteenth dynasty and probably under the Saites, were in the mental condition of the Negroes of the Gold Coast and Niger Delta. Marvelous mysteries, occultly harboring deep truths, are assigned to them by the classical and modern imaginations. They had mysteries like the Ashantis or Ibo.[52] The Black race still practices magic. The most

41

popular, Voodoo, encompasses an exceedingly complex religion and magic with complicated rituals and symbols that have developed for thousands of years.[53]

If Voodoo be hush-hush, ponder this:

> The Africans and their descendants (Black people) everywhere need not defend their traditional religious philosophies . . . because within the three most accepted religions in Europe and the Americas—Judaism, Christianity and Islam—often called Western religion; Africans have been the founders of said religions and their teaching along with Asians hundreds of years, and in some cases thousands of years before they were known in Europe.[54]

This is not so unusual when you consider:

> . . . that these people (Egyptians) stand prior to all other nations in reference to the present time; and a s far as we can discern, they were the inventors of sculpture, painting, architecture, iconography.[55]

What about the Sphinx? Massey has told the world:

> The type of the great Sphinx, the age of which is unknown, is African, not Aryan or Caucasian. The Egyptians themselves never got rid of the thick nose, the full lip, the flat feet, and week calf of the Nigritian type, and these were not additions to any form of the Caucasian race . . . The single Horus lock, the Rut, worn as a divine sign by the child Horus in Egypt is a distinguishing characteristic of the African people . . . The African custom of the children going undressed until they attained the age of puberty was also continued by the Egyptians.[56]

Herodotus and Diodorus on the Wonders of Egypt

HERODOTUS:

"The Egyptians they went on to affirm, first brought into use the name of the twelve Gods, which the Greeks adopted from them, and first erected altars, images and temples to the gods . . ."[57]
"The women attend the market and trade, while the men sit at home at the loom.[*] [Ha. The men are trying to control spiritual transcendence.] . . . sons need not support their parents unless they choose, but daughters must, whether they choose or not."
". . . they are the only people in the world—they at least and such as have learnt the practice from them—who use circumcision."
". . . they are religious to excess far beyond other men."[58]
". . . by calling the dove black the Dodonians indicated that the woman was an Egyptian. And certainly the character of the Oracles of Thebes and Dodona is very similar. Besides this form of divination, the Greeks learnt also divination by means of victims from the Egyptians."[59]
". . . with respect with the Egyptians themselves, it is to be remarked that those who live in the corn country, devoting themselves, as they do, far more than any other people in the world, to the preservation of the memory of past actions, are the best skilled in history of any men that I have ever met."[60]
"The Egyptians have also discovered more prognostics than all the rest of mankind . . . Medicine is practiced among them on a plan of separation; each physician treats a single disorder, and no more; thus the country swarms with medical practitioners, some undertaking to cure diseases of the eye, others the head, others again of the teeth, others of the intestines . . ."[61]
". . . that Perseus belonged to their cities by descent. Danaus and Lynceus[*] were Chemmites before they set sail for Greece, and from them Perseus was descended."[62]
"It is said that the reign of Amasis was the most prosperous time that Egypt ever saw, the river was more liberal to the land, and the land brought forth more abundantly for the service of man than have ever been known before; while the number of inhabited cities was not less

than twenty thousand. It was King Amasis who established the law that every Egyptian should appear once a year before the governor of his canton, and show his means of living; or failing to do so, and to prove that he got an honest livelihood, should be put to death. Solon the Athenian borrowed this law from the Egyptians and imposed it on his countrymen, who have observed it ever since. It is indeed an excellent custom."[63]

". . . In social meetings among the rich, when the banquet is ended a servant carries round to the several guests a coffin, in which there is a wooden image of a corpse, carved and painted to resemble nature as nearly as possible, about the size of a cubit or two cubits in length. As he shows it to each guest in turn, the servant says, 'Gaze here, and drink and be merry; for when you die, such will you be.'"[64]

DIODORUS:

"And therefore the Egyptians affirm that letters, astronomy, geometry, and many other arts were first found out by them; and the best laws were made and instituted by them. To confirm which they allege this as an undeniable argument, that the native Kings of Egypt have reigned there for the space of above four thousand and seven hundred years, and that their country, for all that time has been the most prosperous and flourishing kingdom in the world, which could never have been so, if the inhabitants had not been civilized, and brought up under good laws, and liberal education in all sorts of Arts and Sciences."[65]

"For it was judged, that by the harangues of lawyers, a cloud was cast upon the truth and justice of the cause; inasmuch as the arts of rhetorically juggling tricks of dissemblers, and the fears of them that are like to be overthrown in their cause, have wrought upon many to wave the strictness of the law, and to turn aside from the rule of justice and truth: and indeed it is often found by experience, that offenders brought to the bar of justice, by the help of a cunning orator, or their own rhetorical flourishes (either through a fallacy put upon the court, or taking insinuations, or melting compassions wrought by the speaker on the judge), have escaped: therefore the Egyptians concluded, that if all the accusations were put into writing and consideration of what was there set down, the sentence would be more exact and just. And so by that means crafty and ingenious fellows would be no more favored than those that were more dull, nor the experienced artist more than those that were ignorant and unskillful, nor the audacious liar more than those that are modest and sincere; but all would have equal justice. . ."[66]

Persia (Iran)

Many stories are told concerning Persia under Camyses and its conquest of Egypt. What is not said is that these ancient Persians were Black.

When reading Herodotus I was struck by the fact that he disputed the Egyptian claim of relation to the Persian royal family. Even if this were true, I thought, the Egyptians themselves could never have made the claim unless the Persians were a Black people. So I checked it out:

> If you have ever studied the history of Persia you will remember that historians classify it as the first great White civilization in the history of the world. So wonderful was the Persian Empire and so magnificent was its civilization, that one cannot well blame historians for trying to claim it for the White race to the exclusion of all others. But the claim has fallen before the modern study of the Persian people. The primitive civilization of Persia has been called Elamite, and the Elamites let it be said, was a branch of the great federation of African races. J. de Morgan in his work on Persia tells us: 'Besides the Sumerian civilization in Babylonia we have in the Valley of the Farum, in Persia, evidence of an early civilization which we call Elamite, which is only being explored. Whether the Elamites and Sumerians were akin, and how early Elamites civilization was, we do not yet fully know, but certainly the cuneiform script was in use there at a very early period.'[67]

I quote this to impress upon you the fact that the cuneiform script, so often spoken of by students and writers of ancient civilizations, was that form of writing primitively and exclusively used by that great federation of African people who inhabited Asia.

We discover in Grecian mythology that Perses was the founder of the Persian race. Now Perses was the son of Perseus, the famous hero who sprang from the Argive race, and African people who settled in Greece, and Andromeda was a princess of Ethiopia, whom Perseus rescued from death imposed upon her because her mother boasted that her daughter's beauty surpassed that of the Neriads. Couple this with the significant fact that in *The Shah Nameh*, the Persian epic, we find that the first ruler of Persia, Kaimers, was an Ethiopian, and that he clad himself and his people in tiger skins because it was the symbol of royalty among the Ethiopians, and you will begin to understand how important myths and traditions are in establishing the relationships between races and nations. In this same epic we read that Zohak, one of the great Persian heroes, was none other than Nimrod, the mighty African hunter and builder mentioned in the Bible. We read also of many princes of Persia who married Ethiopian and Yemenite women, and it would not be out of place to mention that later in her history, when Persia was besieged by her enemies, her king sent an embassy to Ethiopia, carrying her precious epic and the Persian crown jewels, asking the Ethiopians if they would keep them safe until Persia was free from her enemies. Ethiopia kept them for eighty years and returned them all when Persia asked for them again. When the Persian king received them from the Ethiopians he said in his speech of thanks that Persia never feared for their safety because of the kinship that existed between the peoples of the two countries. The statement that the Persians were a White race is purely an invention on the part of historians.[68]

I found out that the surname of Darius was Orchus.[**] Herodotus said that Darius was the tallest and handsomest man in Asia. At the library I was able to verify my results (see figures #).

Greece

It has been assumed, and falsely so, that the ancient Greeks were a White people. Many generations have died thinking this, and all who live today believe this. The general confusion by both Blacks and Whites concerning this and other ancient peoples is that Blacks are only associated with Africa and the Whites with Europe, and as I have shown previously, this is false. As I write this, it is even clearer we have struggled with this White race on all continents—Asia, Europe, Africa, the Americas—and it still continues.

The most famous of all Greeks is Homer, obviously a Black man because Heliodorus in his novel says he was an Egyptian.[69] And, as the Egyptians were a Black people, as were the early Greeks, who according to tradition, sacred and mundane, were themselves colonists from Egypt who left that land after a civil war.

> After the civil war broke out Egypt between Armesis and Rameses, surnamed Dorith and Gopth, or Danaus and Egyptu , and whose result had been the expatriation of Danaus and the Passage into Greece of great numbers of Egyptian colonies . . .[70]

I mentioned earlier that the name Pelops, from which the name Peloponnesus is derived, signifies Black land. It was the name of Greece while occupied by the Pelasges or Black people.[71]

Beeton states:

> Aegyptus – son of Belus and brother of Danaus to whose fifty daughters he gave his fifty sons to marriage. Danaus had fled to Argos being afraid of his brothers fifty sons, they followed him from Egypt into Greece.[72]

This is Grecian allegory to explain the exodus into Greece. The reader, if he has not fallen asleep and read *The Iliad*, must recall that Horner called the Greeks by the name "Danaans" several times, that is, after Danaus, in this most famous book.

The same story is contained in Gayley's *Classic Myths*,[73] along with the genealogy of Danaus and other dynamite. (The reason many White writers give up information unknowingly is that when discussing ancient history they never see themselves as the Scythians but change places with the Blacks in the history books.)

Now Argos, the most ancient dwelling place of the Greeks, was said to have been founded by Phoroneus, the son of Inachus.[74] This name is Ina-Chus—and you do recall that *chus* and Ethiopian are interchangeable. Don't forget, "names with the modification of *cush* have always hung about the lower Mesopotamian region, indicating the primitive connection with Cush on the Nile."[75]

In latter times these Black men, called Greeks, became a mixed people, and after much race mixing with the barbarians have an appearance of White people in contemporary times. The mythology of the Greeks is in accord with this. According to this mythology, the Greek people (of latter times I might add) themselves seem to have come into being as a result of miscegenation. Zeus, the "Father of the Gods," who is of Ethiopian ancestry, mates with the fair Greek maiden, Io, and has a mulatto son, Epaphus, who is born in Egypt. Eschylus, a great tragic poet of ancient Greece, says of this union:

> . . . and thou shall bring forth Black Epaphus, thus named from the manner of Zeus ingendering . . . fifth in descent from him fifty maidens shall return to Argos (Greece), not of their choice but fleeing marriage with their cousin kin.

Eschylus adds:

> . . . call this the work of Zeus, and this his race sprang from Epaphus, and thou shall hit the truth. This was the symbolic way of saying that the Argives or Greeks were of mixed blood. One of the titles of Zeus was Ethiops.[76]

Nevertheless, it is still clear that originally these Greeks were Blacks. Herodotus in his text refers to these unions and people as Greco-Scythians, as distinguished from "pure Greeks."[77] The term "Gallo-Grecian" is used in Diodorus to indicate these mixtures.[78] Today we call the offspring of these unions mulattoes.

Further, Grecian art, which you can check out right now, contains precisely and sequentially the race mixing that took place. By examination of these Greek vases one can see they contain the figures of Black warriors and White women. Looking closer, you will find that White male figurines are not shown until latter times. Of special interest is that most of the male figures on Grecian vases have Afros. When these Greeks were letting their hair grow into dreadlocks they were called by Homer the "long haired Archaens" in *The Iliad*!

Doubtless, the Black Grecians had a large White slave population. The Black attic figures on Grecian vases pictured with White women can only mean that the White men are subdued and were more than likely slaves or dead. For women are the spoils of war. Once the men are beaten the soldier can then screw their women. This is a universal practice among men at arms and needs no further commentary.

In Plutarch, but really Plutarchus, a Greek of note, we find a curious story:

> On another occasion Agesilaus gave orders that before his prisoners were put up to be auctioned by the dealers in the spoils of war, they should first be stripped of their clothes. The clothes found plenty of buyers, but the spectators burst out laughing at the sight of the men and their naked bodies, for these were white and tender as they had never been exposed to sun or wind, and were regarded as useless and worthless.[79]

When the two Greek city-states Phocis and Thessaly were at war, an interesting episode is recorded: ". . . that is the slaughter of the Thessalay infantry by a night sortie of picked Phocians who had been colored white according to the stratagem of the Elean seer Tellius . . ." [80]

Aristotle did say: "The nations inhabiting the cold places and those of Europe are full of spirit but somewhat deficient in intelligence and skill, so that they continue comparatively free, but lacking in political organization and capacity to rule their neighbors."[81]

Aristotle would be amazed to see the progress of a people he considered deficient in intelligence. The Phocians colored themselves White, no doubt to fool and frighten the Thessalians into thinking they were being attacked by barbarians! There was the laughter of the crowd on seeing the naked bodies of White men. There is the tradition sacred and mundane of the passage into Greece great numbers of Blacks after a civil war in Egypt between Amasis and Ramases. This story has been allegorized by the Greeks with the story of Danaus and his fifty daughters. The "Greek Vases" themselves tell the entire story. Just look at the hair of the men on the vases, and disregard all commentary when checking out art books in libraries. A picture is worth a thousand words.

Western civilization is credited with having it genesis in Greece, *si?* And since the Greeks were Blacks, what is really being said here? Actually, these Black Greeks are given credit for what really is Egyptian; that is, the White men who have written history lay the foundation of "their" civilization in Greece because it's in Europe. This way civilization can be given to the Whites. Certainly this text will destroy this lie. The veracity of what has already been stated can be checked out by any conscientious or hater of truth for truth is.

Originally, I became interested in the Greeks from reading the great J.A. Rogers (*Sex and Race I, II,* and *III*) and following up on books that he was using as footnotes. One such book was *The Children of the Sun* by George Wells Parker, which was twenty-nine pages of delight! Parker made me do the research and is proof that you cannot fool the people all the time! Parker stated:

In the year 1884, Alexander Winchell, the famous American geologist, upset Americans with an article appearing in the *North American Review.* From it I quote the following: 'The Pelasgic Empire was at its meridian as early as 2500 B.C. These people came from the islands of the Aegean and more remotely from Asia Minor. They were originally a branch of the sunburnt Hamitic stock that laid the basis of civilization in Canaan and Mesopotamia, destined latter to be semitized. Danaos and his daughters, that is, the fugitive "shepherds from Egypt," sought refuge among their Hamitic kindred in the Peloponnesus about 1700 B.C. . . . In time they occupied the whole of Greece and Thessaly. Before 200 B.C. they established themselves in Italy. Thus do we get a conception of a vast Hamitic empire existing in prehistoric times, whose several nationalities were centered in Mesopotamia, Canaan, Egypt, Northwest Africa, Iberia, Greece, Italy, Sicily, Sardinia, and Central Europe an intellectual ethnic family, the first of the Adamites to emerge into historic light . . .'[82]

In Black English, the above means that civilization as we know it comes from the Black race and, contrary to popular opinion, it is the Black who has tried to civilize the White.

The slave trade (in fifteen to seventeen countries) allowed "whiteness" to be propagated, or better said, the *gun* and the power derived thereof, concocted a history in which the Black people, who were and are everything, to be "history-less." The Whites then changed places and claimed to be all the people in classical antiquity who were Black, and this includes the archetype, Jesus Christ, on whom more will be said later.

Getting back to the Greeks, I have said that the Whites prefer to have Greece as the beginning of European civilization while at the same time concealing and hiding the fact that in classical antiquity Greece was Black. Along with this is the "whiteout" on Egypt from whence all Grecian learning came.

First of all, "the term Greek philosophy to begin with is a misnomer, for there is no such philosophy in existence. The ancient Egyptians had developed a complex religious system called the Mysteries, which was the first system of salvation. As such it regarded the human body as a prison house of the soul, which could be liberated from bodily impediments through the discipline of the arts and sciences and advance from the level of a mortal to that of a good. This was the notion of the *Summum bonum* or greatest good, to which all men must aspire, and it became the basic of all ethical concepts. The Egyptian mystery system was also a secret order, and membership was gained by initiation and a pledge of secrecy. The Egyptians developed a secret system of writing and teaching and forbade their initiates from writing what they learnt. After nearly 5,000 years of prohibition against the Greeks, they were permitted to enter Egypt for the purpose of their education."[83]

We learn that Thales, the celebrated Greek astronomer, was taught by the Egyptians six centuries before the birth of Christ to calculate eclipses and determine the equinoctial points.[84]

In reference to the humane treatment of the insane, Clark says:

Plato may have urged it upon the Greeks, but he as well as Ascelepeades, who has ever been regarded as the first to practice this mode of cure Egyptian by education and some say the latter was Egyptian by birth.[85] Nor shall we forget . . . that Lycurgus, Solon, and Plato borrowed from Egypt many of those laws which they established in their several commonwealths and that Pythagoras learnt his mysterious and sacred expressions, the art of geometry, arithmetic and transmigration of souls in Egypt.[86]

Further, that all the Grecians swear by the name Isis and that in all their manners and customs, they are all together like the Egyptians."[87]

The Greek gods were also borrowed. "Almost all of the names of the gods came into Greece from Egypt."[88]

We think it not too bold to maintain that most of the scientific and literacy acquirements which distinguished the Greeks, while the rest of Europe was in a state of barbarism, were derived from there intercourse with the scholars of Thebes and Memphis. In fact, at one time no Greek was accounted truly learned until he sojourned a certain period on the banks of the Nile; conversed with philosophers on the mysteries of their science; studied the law, government and the institutions of the most remarkable people who ever existed; examined and explored their everlasting monuments and in some measure initiated into the wisdom of the Egyptians.[89]

Now that we have changed the Greek from White back to Black and showed where they were taught, the veracity of their fame as philosophers should be investigated also, for on close inspection we find that Plato, an oil peddler[90] in Egypt and first in fame among the Grecians, probably didn't write those doctrines attributed to him. Concerning the writings, they are disputed not only by such modern scholars as Grote and Schaarsmidt, but by ancient historians Diogenes, Laertius, Aristoxenus, and Favorinius (80–150 AD), who declared that the subject matter of the Republic was found in the controversies written by Prothagas (481–411 BC), at the time of whose death Plato was a boy. Furthermore, the authorship of Plato rests only upon the opinion of Aristotle and Theophrastus, both of whose aims were the compilation of a Greek philosophy with Egyptian materials, which they could do very easily since Egypt at that time was long under a foreign yoke.[91]

If the reader wishes to pursue this further they need only get a copy of *Stolen Legacy*.

The Greeks (Blacks and mulattoes) were the vainest motherfuckers who ever lived. This is immediately apparent in their reference to the Persians, who they call barbarians. Now the Persians (Blacks of Asia) certainly weren't barbarians, and neither was Socrates guilty. The Greeks put to death one of the wisest men of antiquity; this crime will forever add infamy to their name. Being Black didn't make these motherfuckers saints. To study the Greeks is the study of progress and history of the West—that is, incessant warfare, unbridled rivalry amongst the states, and an inability to join together for common aims except for short durations.

To get an idea of the sheer vanity of these Greeks, one should check out Thucydides's *On the Athenian Democracy* or Plutarch's *Lives*.

(As the Greeks copied most things from the Egyptians, the one thing that they left out was the matriarchal family system, which in the end spelled ruin for them because the foundation of the state was on shaky ground. The Greeks were patriarchal or farther right, which really means that the women aren't shit. In Egypt, descent was passed through the female line, so the brother married his sister to keep his inheritance.)

The patriarchal system of the Greeks led to homosexual practices, which always foreshadow the doom of any state, historically speaking that is. The Egyptians were "anti-faggot"[92] and from all accounts their civilization lasted longer than any other. Fuck you, Mayor Koch.

A word on slavery:

> All the social and economic conditions of antiquity are based on the institution of slavery, and without it would have been impossible; in fact, slavery is so closely interwoven with the whole life of antiquity that even the political development of the ancient nations and their achievements in the domain of art and industry would be inexplicable without the existence of a large slave population. So great was the importance of slavery

in antiquity that any account of Greek life incomplete, which did not give some slight sketch of these peculiar conditions.

The institution of slavery in Greece is very ancient; it is impossible to trace its origin, and we find it even in the earliest times regarded as a necessity of nature, a point of view which in even the following ages the most enlightened philosophers adopted. In later times, voices were heard from time to time protesting against the necessity of the institution, showing some slight conception of human rights, but these were isolated opinions. From the very earliest times, the custom was that captives taken in war, if not killed or ransomed, became the slaves of the conquerors, or were sold into slavery by them. This custom was universal in the Homeric age, and it continued to exist in the historic periodalso, so that not only was it adopted in the contest between Hellenes and barbarians, but even in the numerous feuds between Hellenes and Hellenes. They often condemned their own countrymen to the hard lot of slavery. In the historic period, the slaves of Greece were, for the most part, barbarians, chiefly from the district north of the Balkan Peninsula and Asia Minor. The Greeks held towns on the Black Sea and on the Asiatic coast of the archipelago . . .[93]

The above passage is saying that most of the slaves of Greece were White because it is they who inhabited the "district north of the Balkan Peninsula." There were Black slaves in Greece (Aesop), but evidently the majority were White.

Check this out: one of the greatest poems in Western literature is "Prometheus Bound" by Aeshylus. Prometheus is the Titan who stole fire from Zeus to aid mankind. For this audacious act he is sentenced to be nailed to a rock in Scythia! Force, a henchman of Zeus, is made to say in the first two lines: "Far have we come to the far spot of earth this narrow Scythian land, a desert all untrodden."[94] The worst punishment Zeus could think of was to send Prometheus to Scythia, the land of White men. Zeus, you will recall, is a Black god.

At one time in Sparta during the reign of King Archidamus a great earthquake occurred, which, as in the blackout in NYC, sparked a slave revolt. "In this situation, the Spartans sent Pericleidas to Athens to ask for help. This is the man whom Aristophanes makes fun of in

Lysistrata, where he shows him sitting by the altar with a white face and a red cloak begging for an army."[95]

The Athenians

The most famous of the city-states in Greece was Athens. The Athenians themselves always claimed to be kindred of the Egyptians.

> That the Athenians likewise are a colony of the Saits which came out of Egypt, and are their kindred, they endeavor to prove by these arguments; (that is to say) that they only of all the Greeks call the city Astu, from Astu a city among those people of the Saits: and that for the better government of the commonwealth, they divide their people into the same ranks and degrees as they in Egypt do, to wit into three orders; the first of which are called Eupatride; employed for the most part in studying liberal arts and sciences, and are advanced to the highest offices and placed of preferment in the state, as the priests of Egypt are. The second order of men are the rustic and country people, who are to be soldiers, and take up arms on all occasions for the defense of the country, like to those who are called husbandmen in Egypt, who furnish out soldiers there. In the third rank are sectioned tradesmen and artificers, who commonly bore all necessary and public offices, which agrees exactly with the order and usage among the Egyptians.

They say likewise, that there were some of the Athenians' generals who came out of Egypt. For they affirm, that Peteos, the father of Menestheus, who was a captain in the Trojan War, was an Egyptian and afterwards was King of Athens . . . Erechtheus likewise, one of the kings of Athens, they say was an Egyptian, which they prove by these arguments, viz. That whereas there was a great drought (as all confess) almost over the whole world, except Egypt only (because of the peculiar property of the place) which destroyed both men and fruits of the earth together, Erechtheus transported a great quantity of corn to Athens out of Egypt, because they and the Egyptians were of the same kindred; with which kindness the citizens were so effected, that they advanced him to the kingdom. After which, he instituted the festivals, and taught the Egyptians rites and mysteries of Ceres in Eleusina.[96]

"There is another custom in which the Egyptians resemble a particular Greek people, namely the Lacedaemonians (Spartans). Their young men, when they meet their elders in the street, give way to them and step aside; and if an elder come in where young men are present, these latter rise from their seats."[97] This is common all over West Africa right now!

Religion

Dionysius stated: "It was the first and highest praise of Athens that in every matter, and at every season, she followed the gods and accomplished nothing without divination and oracles."[98]

There were many oracles in Greece, the two most famous being the Oracles of Delphi and Dodona, the former for Apollo, the latter for Zeus. They were consulted by many nations in the ancient world on all serious matters. Many so-called scholars have tried to explain this agency, believing it to be the machinations of a shrewd priestcraft. Temple, in his interesting book *The Sirius Mystery*, is the latest to attempt an explanation of this phenomenon. But what all these men have failed to grasp is that there were, and are, spiritual entities that work through the oracular medium for the guidance of man. If these men had simply asked themselves if any oracles still exist they would have found out that they do, particularly in Africa, where the veracity of the oracles can be checked out very easily, as you could go to Queens where there is an Akan shrine (oracle) under Denizulu. It should also be noted that when the Athenians neglected the shrine at Delphi this was the beginning of their fall from power. So:

> The religion of ancient Greece, like that of Egypt, was established by the Blacks. Not only were the Grecian gods Black, as was said, but the two most important Oracles of Greece were established by Blacks, namely those of Dodona and Delphos. The first according to Herodotus was founded by two black doves who flew across the waters from Egypt, the black doves being symbolic of black priestesses. He said also

56

that the cries uttered in the Greek temples during the Hellenic rites sounded as if they had come from Africa.[99]

The Iliad

To the Greeks, *The Iliad* was the Bible and considered their finest literary achievement. This epic poem by the blind poet Homer is required reading for all college students in the Western world. Indeed, the merit of this book is far greater than the Whites suspect. The story is about the ten-year siege of Troy by the Greeks to recover Helen, the wife of Menelaus—"The face that launched a thousand ships." The main character is Achilles, probably the most famous figure in Western literature.

The translators of this text, the great Alexander Pope leading the way, have interpolated this book with a sleight of hand, particularly in Book One, where the goddess Athena appears to check the wrath of Achilles, who is enraged at Agamemnon; as Athena appears, she is said to grab Achilles by his "yellow hair."[100] My favorite translation of this work (Chase and Perry, now out of print) also has this ridiculous "yellow hair" passage.[101] Lattimore, though, translates this as "fair hair."[102] Rieu has used "golden locks" in his translation.[103]

This yellow hair bullshit means White, and the sole intent is to set the tone of the epic and seduce the reader into the acceptance of a white Achilles, which up to now was passé. Chase and Perry made an error which made me investigate this classic a bit more closely. The error was the use of the word *blameless*.

The ancients had an epithet that they used to describe the character of Blacks. This epithet was "blameless."[104] Homer uses this term in *The Iliad* and *The Odyessey*. Thus we come by the term the "Blameless Ethiopians," who antiquity considered were the favorites of the gods. Homer has the gods actually leaving the Olympian abode to partake in the festival of the Ethiopians.[105] We were called blameless to signify our reverence and piety for things celestial and divine. This is not difficult to understand, if you compare the religious nature of White and Black people. It's obvious that there is no comparison at all. Blacks are still, and distinctly so, the most religious people on Earth. My father believes this to be our chief weakness, and so did I before I got hip! Weakness properly considered can be your greatest strength (King,

Malcolm, and Gandhi prove this point; religion, properly considered, has and is the foundation of great strength. Malcolm particularly was no "turn the other cheek" philosopher).

Anyway, speaking on the "Blameless Ethiopians," the term made famous by Homer, in the Chase-Perry translation the appellation *blameless* is use to describe all the major characters of this epic, identifying the characters as Ethiopians. The Blacks are considered the noblest race. Chase-Perry also stated: ". . . so long as Achilles was angry, for the latter was much the best, and so too were the horses which bore the blameless son of Peleus"; and if this is not so, how could Achilles ask his mother, the goddess Thetis, to punish Agamemnon for the injustice done him? She replied in these words, according to Pope:

The sire of gods and all th'etherial train,

On the limits of the furthest main. Now mix with mortals, nor disdain to grace

The feats of Ethiopia's blameless race.

Now follow the story line: Achilles wants his mother to beseech the gods to punish Agamemnon for fucking over him. His mother is telling him to be cool because the gods are always conscious of the feats of Ethiopia's blameless race. In other words, Achilles is definitely Ethiopian, otherwise the passage makes no sense. His mother is merely answering his question and trying to soothe him.

You want more? How about the fact that Achilles is the fastest runner of all the Greeks? If I say the word "swift," what comes to mind, Black or White? (Ever see a white horse at a race track?)

Achilles is also depicted as being the most handsome man of all the Greeks, and this is significant when you consider that Herodotus, the so-called Father of History, said that "The Ethiopians . . . are said to be the tallest and handsomest men in the whole world."[106]

Grecian vase painting likewise depicts Achilles as a Black, particularly the more ancient vases.

I must admit that I was thoroughly pleased with myself when I made this particular discovery about the "blameless son of Peleus" (Achilles). I knew that I was the first to unlock this secret, but I also knew I had to check one more book to be absolutely certain. This book, *Anacalypsis* by the learned Godfrey Higgins, had this to say concerning Achilles when speaking about Meminon: "This is the Memmon who was said to have been sent to the siege of Troy, and to have been slain by Achilles; and who was also said, by the ancient authors to be an Ethiopian or a Black."[107] (There goes my glory!)

In the Lattimore translation, the blameless son of Peleus has his name spelled Achilleus.[108]

Those of you who are familiar with *The Iliad* know that the story ends with the death and funeral of Hector. The death and funeral of Achilles was dealt with in another book that is no longer extant but is categorized by the ancients nevertheless; this would be insignificant if it were not for the interesting title of this last book, namely, *The Aithiopis*. I repeat, *The Aithiopis*. This settles the question for me; the reader may think whatever the fuck he wants to.

Oh yes, before I forget—in *The Iliad*, just being Black was a sign of utmost distinction (and rightly so!), which is why we find passages (in the Chase-Perry translation) in the text that read:

> The Grecian horsemen, Nester, said to him, you are right in all you say, my friend. I have blameless sons . . . [Book X]." Further in this text the characters connected with the "blameless," implicit and explicit, are as follows: Achilles (Book II), Glaucus (Book II), Asclepius (Book IV), the Trojan priest of Hephaestus, Dares (Book V), Aeneas (Book V), Anchises (Book V), Hector's wife, Andromache (Book VI), Teucer (Book VIII), Neleios (Book V), and Polydamas (Book XII). Hector is not called blameless (but his wife is), but we can say that no doubt he was dark because we do find this passage: "and glorious Hector sprang within, his face like swift night. (Book XII).[109]

Lattimore has this: "Then glorious Hector burst within with dark face like sudden night."[110]

Other characters called blameless, directly or through inference, in Chase-Perry are Zeus, Minos, Deucalion, Idomeneus (Book XIII), Menelaus, Paris (Book XIII), Satnius (Book XIV), Ajax (Book XVI),

Patroclus (Book XVII), Erichthonius, Tros (the Trojan king), Ilus, Assaracus, Ganymede, Tithonus, Priam, Lanpus, Clytus, and Hector (Book XX).

I also said earlier that Apuleius in *The Golden Ass* calls Paris a Phrygian shepherd. Troy was a city in the country of Phrygia that we deduced was a country of Blacks in Asia, based on the first page of Herodotus in his chapter on Egypt, in which he relates the experiment of the Egyptian king to determine which is the older nation, Phrygia or Egypt.

The Odyssey

I hope the reader is willing to spare me the task of writing about the Blackness of Odysseus. Suffice to say that the name of his son is Telemachus, you dig?

For divergence sake, the following is an interpretation of one of the adventures of Odysseus.

ODYSSEUS AND THE CYCLOPS – HOMER

The view from Bedford Stuyvesant:

This particular adventure of Odysseus has always been a favorite of mine. The heroes are trapped in a cave by a giant Cyclops with one eye in the center of his forehead. They escape the monster by putting a stake through the monster's eye while he is in a drunken sleep. As the cave is full of sheep, Odysseus has his men hang to the bottom of the sheep as the Cyclops lets his sheep out to pasture. Now blinded, he has to try to make sure that the other men within the cave who blinded him do not escape; but Odysseus's plan thwarts him! This is more or less the gist of the story.

Interpretation:

Initially, the Cyclops asks Odysseus what is his name. Odysseus, of many councils, answers "No-man"; that is, he is not a thing, he is not what he appears to be, and he is actually saying that he is God, because that which dwells within is No-man!

The men are trapped in a cave by a Cyclops, that is, man is trapped in a Cycle and will be devoured (die) and be reborn unless he is able to penetrate the "middle eye" (pineal gland of Divine Consciousness).

This can be facilitated by resolute inventiveness (the craftiness of Odysseus). "The Third Eye" is not awake (the drunken sleep of the Cyclops), and as soon as one becomes passive or submissive (the sheep, which is the means of escape) coupled with the stake (one pointed concentration), they can then escape the Cyclops or Cycle.

Oh yes, another point concerning the stake—it is "heated" and phallic, once again affirming the ancient doctrine of the transmutation of the spermal energy through heat (that is, rhythmic breathing that creates heat in order to raise the sexual force to increase the ability to concentrate as well as stimulate and awaken the pineal gland, the so-called third eye; the ancients also called this the philosophers' stone, that is, the pineal gland[*]).

Alexander the Great

Was Alexander a Scythian (White)? Hell no! Just like Ptolemy, I must remind the reader that the Scythians, in Ptolemy's words:

> . . . are White in complexion, straight-haired, tall and well nourished, and somewhat cold by nature, these too are savage in their habits because their dwelling places are continually cold the wintry character of their climate, the size of their plants, and the wildness of their animals are in accord with these qualities we call these men too, by a general name, Scythians.[111]

Alexander was a Macedonian, not a Scythian. Macedonia, the country that borders the Black Sea, is named after Macedo, who was said to be the son of Osiris, the great Black god of Egypt.[112]

The passage of Arrian in his *The Campaigns of Alexander* makes this strikingly clear:

> A few days after the events previously recorded Alexander was visited by a deputation from a tribe known as the Abian Scythians [Homer, by the way, mentions these people with approval, calling them 'the most righteous of mankind'.[*]] They are Asiatic and have kept their independence, thanks, as much as anything, to their poverty and fair dealing. Another deputation came from the European Scythians, the most

numerous of all the European people. Alexander instructed certain officers of the companions to return with delegates ostensibly to conclude formally a pact of friendship with their country, though his actual purpose was rather to gather up information about Scythia – its geographical peculiarities, the customs of its people, their numbers, and military equipment.[113]

The above passage has just killed the White Alexander the Great! The passage also shows that the Scythians are the most numerous of the European peoples—meaning that other people also inhabited Europe.

The reader should also be aware that there is indeed a tradition that identifies Alexander as an Ethiopian, the story being that his real father was Nectanebo, the King of Egypt, and as this story is also included in the Ethiopic text translated by Budge, I see no reason to deny it.[114]

One of the stories of Alexander concerns his killing his friend "Black" Cleitus, and after this incident Alexander immediately tried to kill himself.[115] (You still think Alexander was a Whitey?)

Undoubtedly among the Macedonians, Cleitus was exceptionally Black in color, so they called him Black Cleitus. Among the Whites, when a person is exceptionally White they call him Whitey—we still do this and so do they.

Plutarch, Arrian, and other authors also record a few clashes that Alexander had with the Scythians.

I have seen the coin on the cover of the Penguin Classic that purports to be the coin of Alexander (Plutarch's *The Age of Alexander*), but this, like a mosaic that I've seen recently, hardly favors the "blameless" and are therefore false, just as are the White gods and goddesses of Greece.

Alexander, as most Blacks, was needful and respectful of the gods, and at least one author has also mentioned Alexander's recourse to magic in the building of Alexandria. This it would seem also indicates the "blameless."

Frankly, the Whites only gained control of Europe in the fifteenth century with the expulsion of the Moors from Spain, and later from France, by Charles Martel, although this contact with the Africans was enough to bring Europe out of the dark ages that had lasted a thousand years—you forgot? So the Whites, our slaves, for what looks to be millions of years, have finally come into their own—savages with shirts and ties.

Of course I could say more things about Alexander, but I would be here all day relating various stories that identify that hero as one of the blameless.

The story of Alexander would not have been included in the Ethiopic text if he were not one of the blameless, would it?

Rome

History has shown that the ancient Trojans and Greeks were Black people, as have archeology, anthropology, and other related disciplines. What about the Romans? Well, you have to keep in mind that the people of southern Europe at that time were dark people, Blacks and mulattos. If this were not so, Sallust would never have said, "In mapping out the earth's surface most authorities recognize Africa as a third continent, though a few admit only Asia and Europe as continents, including Africa in Europe."[116] Including Africa in Europe?! You would certainly have to stretch your imagination to think that White people would consider Africa part of Europe.

You wouldn't have to do much research to find out that the earliest inhabitants of Italy were Black people.[117] The nation that dominated Italy before the Romans was the Etruscans. Any serious investigation of these people will easily reveal them as you know who![118] Now tradition states that these Blacks "were the third of the constituent elements which went to farm the city of Rome."[119] It should also be noted that "the busts of the Roman Caesars are often Black."[120]

The following passage by Plutarch puts an end to all idle speculation about the so-called White Romans. It also illustrates that the ancient Gauls and Celts were Black people. Rome, in the time of Gaius Marius, was threatened with a massive invasion from northwest of Teutons and Cimbri:

> At first what was reported about the number and strength of the invading armies seemed incredible; later it appeared that the rumor fell short of truth. Three hundred thousand armed warriors were on the march and hordes of women and children

in much greater numbers were said to be marching with them, all seeking land to support these vast hosts and cities in which to settle and live, just as, before their time, as they had discovered, the Gauls had seized the best part of Italy from the Etruscans and were still occupying it. Who these people were and from what part of the world they had set out to fall on Gaul and Italy like a thunder cloud no one knew; *for they had no contact with the southern races and had traveled a very great way*. The likeliest guess seemed to be that they were some German tribes whose territory extends up to the northern Ocean. This conjecture was based on their great size, the light blue color of their eyes, and the fact that the German word for plunderers is 'Cimbri.'

There are some, however, who say that the country of the Celts is so wide and extensive that it stretches from the outer sea and the subarctic as far as Lake Maeotis and the part of Scythia bordering on Pontus, in which region there is a *mixture of the two races*, Celts and Scythians.

Others say that the Cimmerians, our first knowledge of whom comes from the Greeks, did not constitute an important part of the entire race; they were merely a body of exiles, or a minority, which was driven out by the Scythians and crossed from Lake Maeotis into Asia under the leadership of Lygdamis. Meanwhile, the greater and most warlike part of the race lived at the end of the world by the outer ocean in a land of shade and forest so thick that the sun was never visible because of the size and thickness of the trees. (All this Homer found useful in his account of the visit of Odysseus to the land of the dead.) According to this theory, the native tribes set out against Italy from this part of the world, being originally called "Cimmerians and then, by a not unnatural change, Cimbri."[121]

The aforementioned passage by Plutarch indicates that the Romans were not White—and neither were the Celtics and Gauls. Eventually all three changed color due to the constant race mixing with the Whites. And, as Whites have written most of the history (his-story) they have made themselves the Egyptians, the Ethiopians, the Greeks, the

Romans, the Celtics, and the Gauls, but in fact were none of these people. Remember, whenever reading ancient history:

> Those who live under the more northern parallels, those I mean, who have the Bears over their heads, since they are far removed from the zodiac and the heat of the sun, are therefore cooled; but because they have a richer share of moisture, which is most nourishing and is not there exhausted by heat, they are White in complexion, straight haired, tall and well nourished, and somewhat cold by nature, these too are savage in their habit because their dwelling places are continually cold. The wintry character of their climate, the size of their plants and the wildness of their animals are in accord with these qualities. We call these men too, by a general name, Scythians.[122]

Don't forget this name, and use it in your history courses in discussions of the ancient world. Challenge every and any textbook, course, and instructor who does not acknowledge the Black race as the founder of civilization, and then prove it through what are known as primary sources. The irony of much of this is that Whites, in their delusion to see themselves as all the great people of antiquity, have written excellent histories concerning Black people who they just assumed were White!

Plutarch says that the Celtics and the Scythians were different races, but he's not the only one, for in the famed *Anacalypsis* we find:

> A great nation called Celtae, of whom the Druids were the priests, spread themselves over the whole earth and are to be traced from the rude gigantic monuments from India to the extremity of Britain. Who these can have been but the early individuals of the Black nation of whom we have been treating I know not, and this opinion I am not singular. The learned Maurice says 'Cuthites,' i.e. Celts, built the great temples in India and Britain and excavated the former. And the learned mathematician, Reuben Burrow, has no hesitation in pronouncing Stonehenge to be a temple of the Black curly haired Buddha.[123]

In studying the Romans or any ancient people, all words and names should particularly be considered because "in those early times, when language was analogical and nearly perfect, all appellations were significant, and represented some quality, or some religious symbol."[124] In this regard, consider the name Pubins Terrentius Afer, famous for having said, "I am man and nothing human is alien to me." Afer means the Black.[125] Robert Graves of *I, Claudius* fame wrote a book on Terence, endeavoring to make him White on the opening page! Since Terence was born in Carthage, Graves says that he was a White Berber. Plutarch also informs us in *The Life of Coriolanus* that names are given that stem from bodily peculiarities. Among the examples he gives is Nigers,[126] which signifies the Black.[127]

We then discover that some of the most illustrious Romans bore the surname Niger, or the Black, as Percennius Niger, one of the greatest emperors. Septimus Severus, another emperor, was born in Africa. Macrinus and Firmus, other emperors, were Moors. Macrinus came from most humble parentage and was probably an ex-slave, as his ears were bored in slave fashion. Hannibal and his African troops must have brought a great deal of Black strain into the Roman population.* For thirteen years they dominated the peninsula from the Alps to Naples. Hannibal himself was a full-blooded Black with woolly hair, as his coins show.[128]

The Punic Wars were race wars between the Blacks of North Africa and the so-called White Romans for hegemony and empire. I thought the same prior to my in-depth research of ancient Italy.

We must not forget "Gracchus, in ancient Rome, the name of a plebeian family of the *sempronian gens.* Its most distinguished representatives were the famous Tribunes of the people, Tiberius and Gaius Sempronius Gracchus . . . usually called the Gracchi."[129] History records that members of this family also served as consul (today's equivalent is president) during the Republic.

As the empire expanded it became more and more mulatto. If anything, these mulattos were contemptuous of the Whites, as is seen in the readings of Tacitus when he calls the Britons slaves in this fashion: "And so the population was gradually led into the demoralizing temptations of Arcades, baths, and sumptuous banquets. The unsuspecting Britons spoke of such novelties as 'civilization,' when in fact they were only a feature of their enslavement."[130]

This same author, without question the greatest of all Roman historians, gives the well-known description of the Germans—blue-eyed and red-haired[131]—the same description, as we have stated earlier, of the murderer of Osiris.[132] This has an interesting parallel in modern times with the Germans and their attack on Christ, who as Osiris has forever represented divine consciousness.

Further, "it is a well known fact that the people of Germany never live in cities and will not even have their houses adjoin one another . . . they do not even make use of stone or wall tiles; for all purposes they employ rough-hewn timber, ugly and unattractive looking . . ."[133]

Again we find Publius Scipio, the elder, conqueror of Hannibal, stating:

> Had two sons . . . two daughters, one of whom became the mother of the Gracchi. A man of wide sympathies, cultured and magnanimous, Scipio easily won the friendship of Phillip of Macedon and the native princes of Spain and Africa. Though essentially a man of action, he was also something of a mystic in whom contemporary legend saw the favored of Jupiter Capitloinus as well as the spiritual descendant of Alexander the Great. One of the greatest soldiers of the ancient world, by his tactical reforms and strategic insight he created an army which even defeated Hannibal and asserted Rome's supremacy in Spain, Africa, and the Hellenic East.

Don't forget that Alexander was Black, as Jupiter was. For in Latin we find: "*Ham, sub Jovis nomine, in Africa Cultus.*"[134] Of the generals most admired by Hannibal, Scipio was second best.[135] Pyrhus, a Greek, was first, and himself third, meaning Hannibal was not commenting upon Scythians, but on other Blacks skilled in the art of war, an art that we must resurrect and utilize for our own constructive ends.

The Romans considered the Trojans to be the founders of their state. Virgil's classic poem *The Aeneid* makes this clear, as does Livy, who says, "Romans and Albans were both of Trojan stock; Lavinium had be settled by men of Troy, Alba by men of Lavinium . . . the two people ended by amalgamating."[136] The Trojans were a Black people, Troy being a city in Phygia.

There is a story, very romanticized, about a German named Schliemann. This Schliemann became famous. As he set out to prove that Troy did exist and was not just a fable, he found Troy! This is what he said: "It looks to me that this civilization belonged to an African people."[137]

There is one other people who amalgamated with the Romans. These people were called the Sabines, and more than likely were also Black, because they believed themselves to be a Spartan colony, according to Plutarch in his *Life of Numa*.[138]

Oye, the population of Rome was originally like that of Haiti, then like that of Santo Domingo, then like that of Puerto Rico.

Professor Sergi of the University of Rome remarked:

> Until recent years the Greeks and Romans were regarded as Aryan, and then as Aryanised people; the great discoveries in the Mediterranean have overturned all these views. Today, although a few belated supporters of Aryanism still remain, it is becoming clear that the most ancient civilization of the Mediterranean is not of Aryan origin. The Aryans were savages when they invaded Europe; they destroyed in part the superior civilization of the Neolithic populations, and could not have created the Greco-Latin civilization. The primitive population of Europe originated in Africa and the basin of the Mediterranean was the chief center of movement when the African migrations reached the center and north of Europe.[139]

It has been noted that the people of Rome "always measure the greatness of a man's spirit by his capacity to make much of himself in words . . ."[140]

Are we lacking in this regard? Just the example of Muhammad Ali is enough! Dr. King had no match as an orator, except, perhaps, Malcolm X, great in his own right. I have yet to hear a White man gifted in oratory enough to impress me, save those tapes I heard of Adolph Hitler, which sounded very inspirational, even though I don't speak German. The Nazi movement was satanic, so his inspiration certainly was![141]

This information on the Romans contradicts all previous dialogue concerning this subject and is obviously far more factual, notwithstanding Gore Vidal's wretched book *Julian*, the recent movie *Caligula*, and all other pseudo attempts to portray the civilizations of the ancients as White.

Julian was one of the more learned and interesting of the Roman emperors. He was initiated into the older religious systems and was opposed to Christianity. He was a philosopher and a warrior, a combination that is seldom found in the West. His virtues far outweigh the polemics of his attackers. Vidal's book is a travesty.

After the fall of the Roman Empire, civilization was once again centered in Africa with the rise of Islam. Europe then plunged into the Dark Ages for a thousand years.

The Romans had a curious practice, which is peculiar to Blacks, in the settlement of disputes and arguments. During street play, regardless of the game, but specifically (usually) basketball, when there is a questionable call the fellows "choose," that is, the two disputants thrust out fingers and the one who correctly chooses whether the fingers will total odd or even sums is the winner. The Romans called this *morra*.[142]

As the empire progressed, two Black men and one White man were engaged in a struggle as to who would be the next Caesar. They were Pescennius Niger, Septimus Severus, and Clodius Albinus, that is, Clodius the White. Gibbons, the English historian, says that "Clodius Albinus, governor of Britain, surpassed both his competitors in the nobility of his extraction, which he derived from some of the most illustrious names of the old Republic."[143] Gibbons footnotes this assertion, but it's obvious that he's errant on this matter, on how to back this statement up about the nobility of extraction. The truth is that Whites really don't believe "White is beautiful." If they really did they would never spend billions of dollars on suntan oil and run to wherever they can find the sun so as to get darker, right?

Anyway, contrary to Gibbons's assertion, we find in *The Lives of the Later Caesars*:

In the end, while the republic was in the greatest upheaval, when it was announced that there were three emperors, S. verus Septimus, Pescennius Niger and Clodius Albinus, the son of the Delphic Apollo was consulted as to which one it would profit the republic to have as emperor. He is said to have produced a Greek verse somewhat as follows: Best is the dark one, good is the African, worst is the white one.[144]

In the end it was Severus, the African, who won the crown.

We find in *The Jewish War*, Aggripa II pleading with the Jews not to challenge the might of Rome, and in so doing Josephus has him speak these words:

Almost every nation under the sun bows down before the might of Rome; and will you alone go to war, not even considering the fate of the Carthagenians, who boasted of great Hannibal and their glorious Phoenician ancestors, but fell beneath Scipio's hand? The Cyrenians (Spartan by descent), the Marmardae (a race that extends to the waterless desert), Syrtes, whose very mention terrifies, Nasamonians, Moors, Numidians with their vast numbers—none of them could resist Roman skill at arms. This third of the whole world, whose nations can hardly be counted, bounded by the Atlantic and the Pillar of Hercules* and supporting the millions of Ethiopians as far as the Indian Ocean, is subdued in its entirety.[145]

The above is sufficient to prove that Blacks were indeed everyone who Whites have been portraying as themselves. This naturally includes the Black Jews, whose numbers were greatly diminished in the war with Rome, a war, judging from the above, they should never have fought!

Besides, who does not know that "on every side Roman masters have German slaves . . ."?[146]

Finally, Pliny the elder, in his classic *Natural History*, yields another comparison between the White and Black races, as follows: ". . . or it is beyond question that the Ethiopians are burnt by the heavenly body near them, and are born with a scorched appearance, with curly beard and hair, and that in the opposite region of the world the races have white frosty skin, with yellow hair that hangs straight; while the latter are fierce owing to the rigidity of their climate but the former wise because of the nobility of theirs."[147]

The only way man can rise to higher level of consciousness is by mastering his body and conquering his physical desires. The ancient Sages said that the less man needs the more he becomes like gods, who use nothing and are immortal.

—Hotema

[1] George Rawlinson, *Egypt and Babylon From Sacred & Mundane Sources* (New York, 1885), pp. 1-2.

[2] Ibid., pp, 5-6.

[3] Rudolph R. Windsor, *From Babylon to Timbuktu* (New York, 1969), p. 15.

[4] Rev. Alexander Hislop, *The Two Babylons or The Papal Worship Proved to be The Worship of Nimrod and His Wife*, pp. 25-26.

[5] H.W.F. Saggs, *The Greatness That Was Babylon* (New York), p. 125.

[6] Ibid., p. 133.

[7] Ibid., pp. 133, 134, 137, 143.

[8] J.A. Rogers, *Sex and Race* (New York), I, 61.

[9] Ibid., p. 42.

[*] H.W.F. Saggs, a learned "scholar" on Babylon, never mentions Genesis 10:8—"Cush begat Nimrod." This is deliberate, for this man is a Biblical "scholar" also!

[10] N.K. Sanders, *The Epic of Gilgamesh* (New York, 1972), p. 7.

[11] Rogers, p. 264.

[12] Godfrey Higgins, *Anacalypsis* (1833), I, p. 54.

[13] Ibid., pp. 54-55.

[*] Higgins, *Anaclypsis*, Vol. I, p. 58.

[14] Ibid., pp. 27-59.

[15] Ibid., p, 52.

[16] The Rev. Alexander Hislop, *The Two Babylons* (1959), p. 57.

[17] Gerald Massey, *A Book of the Beginnings* (New Jersey, 1974), I, p. 18.

[18] J.A. Rogers, *Sex and Race* (1967), I, p. 268.

[19] George Wells Parker, *The Children of the Sun* (1918), p. 5.

[20] Charles Mills Gayley, The Classic Myths (Toronto), p. 43.

[21] Diodorus, p. 151.

[22] See Count Volney, *Meditation on the Ruins of Empire*.

[23] Gerald Massey, p. 35.

[24] J. Delouise, "Blacks are More Psychic than Whites," *H.E.P. Magazine* (May 1976), pp. 40-41.

[25] Homer, *The Odyssey* (Penguin Classics, 1974), p. 25.

[26] Herodotus, p. 115.

[27] Ibid., p. 81.

[28] Ibid.

[29] W.M. Flinders Petrie, *A History of Egypt* (New York, 1897), I, 12.

[30] *Encyclopaedia Britannica* (1958), XVII, 851.

[31] Fabre D'Olivet, *Interpretations*, p. 83.

[32] Higgins, I, pp. 138-139.

[33] *Encyclopaedia Britannica* (1958), XVII, 853.

[34] Lucius Apoleius, *The Golden Ass* (London, 1962, translated by William Adlington), p. 264.

[35] *Oxford Bible Atlas* (Toronto, 1965), p. 70

[36] Lucius Apoleius, p. 258.

[37] *Oxford Bible*, p. 82.

[38] George Wells Parker, *The Children of the Sun* (Omaha, 1918), p. 33.

[39] M. Russell, *View of Ancient and Modern Egypt* (London, 1883), p. 17.

[40] *The History of Herodotus*, translated by George Rawlinson (New York, 1928), p. 115.

[41] Russell, p. 56.

[42] George H. Wathen, *Art, Antiquities, and Chronology of Ancient Egypt* (London)

[43] W.M. Flinders Petrie, *A History of Egypt* (New York, 1897), I, 12.

[44] *The Historical Library of Diodorus the Sicilian*, in fifteen books, translated by G. Booth, Esq. (London, 1817), I, 73.

[45] *Manuel d'Histoire Ancienne* (Paris, 1883), II, 269.

[46] George Rawlinson, *Egypt and Babylon* (New York), p, 144.

[47] Diodorus, I, 155.

[48] Herodotus, p. 115.

[49] Chancellor Williams, *The Destruction of Black Civilization* (Dubuque, 1971), p. 1.

[50] Arthur Weigall, *Akhnaton* (New York/London, 1970), p, 14.

[51] George G.M. James, *Stolen Legacy* (Private Printing, 1954), p. 54.

[52] H. Debrunner, *Witchcraft in Ghana* (Landon, 1959), p, 15.

[53] *Encyclopaedia Brittanica* (1958), VIII, 53.

[54] *Gallery of Antiquities* (London: British Museum), preface.

[55] Mile Riguad, *Secret of Voodoo* (New York), p. 1.

[56] Yosef ben-Jochannan, *African Origins of the Major Western Religions* (New York, 1973), p. 19.

[57] Herodotus, p. 82.

[*] Metaphor for occult study, the Creator being the Divine Weaver (architect) of the universe.

[58] Ibid., p. 93.

[59] Ibid., p. 101.

[60] Ibid., p. 106.
[61] Ibid., p. 108
* Founders of Grecian civilization.
[62] Ibid., p. 110.
[63] Ibid., p. 144.
[64] Ibid., p. 107
[65] Diodorus, p. 72.
[66] Ibid., pp. 78-79
[67] George Wells Parker, *Children of the Sun* (Omaha, 1918).
[68] Ibid., pp. 14-15.
** Sexual Secrets
[69] *The Greek Romances of Heliodorus, Longus and Achilles Tatius* (London, George Bell and Son, 1901).
[70] Fabre D'Olivet, *Hermeneutic Interpretations*, p. 200.
[71] Ibid., p. 221.
[72] Beeton, *Classical Dictionary* (1871).
[73] Gayley, *Classic Myths*, p. 207-228.
[74] Ibid., p. 207.
[75] George Rawlinson, *Egypt and Babylon from Mundane and Sacred*, p. 5.
[76] *Sex and Race, Vol. I*, p. 79.
[77] *Herodotus*, p. 210.
[78] *Diodorus,*p. 317.
[79] Plutarch, *The Age of Alexander "Agesilans"* (Penguin Classic), p. 33.
[80] Philip A. Stadter, *Plutarch Historical Methods*, p. 34.
[81] Aristotle, *Politics, VII*, v.6-vi.1 ((Loeb Classic Library), p. 565-567.
[82] George Wells Parker, *Children of the Sun (The Hamitic League of the World)*, 1981, p. 23.
[83] James, *Stolen Legacy*, p. I.
[84] Edward Clark, *Daleth* (London: Tickner and Fields, 1864), p. 3.
[85] Ibid., p. 6.
[86] *Diodorus*, p. 97.
[87] Ibid., p. 35.
[88] *Herodotus*, p. 99.
[89] Russell, *A View of Ancient and Modern Egypt*, p. 159-160.
[90] *Everybody's Plutarch* (New York: Dodd, Mead & Co., 1931), p. 66.
[91] James, *Stolen Legacy*, p. 107.
[92] Nik Douglas and Penny Slinger, *Sexual Secrets* (New York: Destiny Books, 1979), p. 336-337.
[93] Alice Zimmenn, *Home Life of the Ancient Greeks* (New York, London: Funk and Wagnalls Co.), p. 519-520.
[94] Mack, Knox, McGalliard, Pasinetti, Hugo, Wellek, Douglas, *World Masterpieces #1* (Norton Pub.), p. 280.
[95] Plutarch, *The Rise and Fall of Athens* (Penguin Classic 1978), p. 159.
[96] *Diodorus*, p. 35.
[97] *Herodotus*, p. 127.

[98] *Thucydides Mythhistoricus*, Francis M. Conford (Univ. of Penn. Press – Phila., 1971), p. 178.

[99] Rogers, *Sex and Race*, Vol. I, p. 80.

[100] Alexander Pope, *The Iliad*, Bk. I.

[101] Hurd-Perry, *The Iliad*, Bk. I.

[102] Richard Lattimore, *The Head of Homer* (Univ. of Chicago Press, 1951), Bk. I.

[103] Rieu, E.V., *The Iliad*, Bk. I (Penguin Classic, 1950).

[104] Homer, *The Iliad*, Bk. I; b) Homer, *The Odyssey*, Bk ?; c) Snowden, *Blacks in Antiquity*, p ?; d) Gaskell, *Dictionary of Myths & Scriptures*.

[105] Homer, *The Odyssey*, Bk. ?.

[106] *Herodotus*, p. 153.

[107] Higgins, *Anacalypsis*, p. 35.

[108] *The Iliad* (Lattimore translated), Pheome Book UNW of Chicago Press.

[109] Ibid., p. 25-26.

[110] *The Iliad* (Lattimore), p. 270.

* The pineal gland which is now atrophied secretes a hormone which confers spiritual consciousness when stimulated by concentration and sexual energy, or LSD.

[111] Ptolemy, *Tetrabiblos* (Loeb Classical Library, 1971), p. 123.

[112] *Diodorus*, p. 24-26.

* Line 6, Chapter 13 (*The Iliad*):-The fact that Arrian says that Homer "approved" of these Scythians means he did not approve of the "others"?

[113] Arrian, *The Campaigns of Alexander* (Penguin Classic, 1978), p. 201.

[114] Burge, A.E.W., *Life and Exploits of Alexander the Great, Vol. II* (London, 1896), p. 3-32.

[115] Plutarch, *Age of Alexander* (Penguin Classic, 1979), p. 309.

[116] Sallust, Jugurthine, *War/Conspiracy of Cataline* (Penguin Classics, 1963), p. 1.

[117] J.A. Rogers, *Sex and Race* (New York), I, 86.

[118] Higgins, I, 166.

[119] *Encyclopaedia Britannica* (1958), VIII, 784.

[120] Higgins, p, 801.

[121] Plutarch, *Fall of the Roman-Republic Gauis Marius* (Penguin Classics, 1972), pp. 23-24.

[122] Ptolemy, *Tetrabiblios* (London, 1971), p. 123.

[123] Higgins, p. 59.

[124] Ibid., p, 352.

[125] Rogers, p. 86.

[126] Plutarch, *Plutarch's Lives* (1936), p. 104.

[127] Rogers, p. 86.

* The Punic Wars

[128] Ibid., pp. 86-87.

[129] Titus Livius (Livy), *The History of Rome* (New York), IV, 96.

[130] *Encyclopaedia Britannica* (1958), X, 588.

[131] Tacitus, *The Agricola and The Germania* (Penguin Books, 1970), p. 73.

[132] Ibid., p. 104.
[133] See Parker, *Children of the Sun.*
[134] Tacitus, p, 114.
[135] Higgins, I, 45.
[136] Plutarch (Pyrhus), *Age of Alexander* (Penguin Classics, 1979), p. 392.
[137] Livy, *The Early History of Rome* (Penguin Books, 1971), p, 57.
[138] Parker, *Children of the Sun*, p. 23.
[139] Plutarch, *Selected Works and Essays* (New York, 1951), pp, 32-33.
[140] Parker, p. 24.
[141] Plutarch, *Fall of the Roman Republic* (Penguin Books, 1972), p. 21.
[142] See Trevor Ravenscroft, *Spear of Destiny.*
[143] Suetonius, *The Twelve Caesars* (Penguin Classics, 1979), p. 60.
[144] Edward Gibbins, *The Decline and Fall of the Roman Empire*, I, p. 108.
* Gibraltar
[145] *Lives of the Later Caesars* (Penguin Classics, 1979), p. 232.
[146] Josephus, *The Jewish War* (Penguin Classics, 1969), p, 152.
[147] Pliny, *Natural History* (Loeb Classic), p. 321.

CHAPTER III

RELIGION

Digression on the Color of the Ancient Gods (Jesus Christ)

WHAT COLOR WERE THE ANCIENT GODS? THE LEARNED MR. HIGGINS says that Osiris and his bull were Black; all of the gods and goddesses of Greece were Black; at least this is so in the case of Jupiter, Bacchus, Hercules, Apollo, Ammen, and the goddesses Venus, Isis, Hecate, Diana, Juno, Metis, Ceres, and Cybil. The Multimammia is Black in the Campidoglio in Rome, and in Montfaucon's *Antiquity Explained*, the God Christ, as well as his mother, were described in their old pictures and statues to be Black. The infant God in the arms of his Black mother, his eyes and drapery white, is himself divinely Black. I make references to the cathedral at Moulins, the famous Chapel of the Virgin of Loretto, the Church of the Annunciata, the Church of St. Lozaro, and the Church of St. Stephen in Genoa, Pisa, in San Francisco, the Church of Brixen, in the Tyrol and that in Padua, the Church of St. Theodore in Munich (in these last two churches the whiteness of the eyes and teeth and the studied redness of the lips are very observable), the church and a cathedral in Augburgh, where the Virgin and Child are large as life, in Rome, at the Borghese Chapel Maria Maggiore, the Pantheon, a small chapel of St. Peter's on the right side upon entering near the door and, in fact, to almost innumerable other churches in countries professing the Roman religion. If I had wished to invent a circumstance to corroborate the assertion that the Roman Christ of Europe is the Christna of India, how could I have desired anything more striking than the fact of the Black Virgin and Child among the White Germans, Swiss, French, and Italians? The Roman Christna is Black in India, Black in Europe, and Black he must remain—like the ancient gods of Greece, as we have seen.

Godfrey Higgins states:

> The circumstance of the black god of India being called Christna, and the god of Italy, Christ, being also black, must appear worthy of deep consideration.[1]

White Jesus then, must be of recent creation.[2]
This from Parker:

"Hence the blue-eyed, golden haired, and pale skinned gods and goddesses that grace the canvasses of our art galleries and theater curtains are merely camouflage, a subtle attempt to hide the truth and perpetuate a lie."[3]

In fact:

We have undoubted proof that it was the Negro who originated not only religion but Christianity as well. The fact is significant because no matter what some may think of religion, it was the source from which came all our learning, art, science, and culture in general.[4]

Christ Esoterica

Jesus Christ is basically a metaphor for divine consciousness, or spirit, and has nothing whatsoever to do with a historical person. All men should aspire to Christ, that is, divine consciousness. Jesus is the personification of a principle within you, not a dying god on a cross, for men do not die—the resurrection!

Christ being crucified on the cross is the spirit that has impregnated matter—the body. That which is crucified is the spirit, the cross, the human form, the mortal sex body in which the "doer" operates on Earth. Jesus on the cross is the divine self in form, the infinite within the finite, the Son of God dead on the cross, that is, ignorant of spiritual force while in the body. The ancients called a man dead if he had no spiritual knowledge.

This is not a new doctrine. *Gaskell Dictionary of all Scripture and Myth* describes Jesus of the Gospel as "A Symbol of the Indwelling Higher Self or Divine Spirit in man, evolving toward complete manifestation."[5]

Alice Baily expressed the following: "The great Presiding One, within the Council Chamber of the Lord, pondered the nature of the Son of Man who is likewise a Son of God."[6]

Vivekananda says, "Each soul is essentially divine. The goal is to manifest this divinity within by controlling nature, external and internal. Do this either by work, or worship, or psychic control, or philosophy—by one or more or all of these—and be free. This is the whole of religion. Doctrines, or dogmas, or rituals, or books, or temples, or forms are but secondary details."[7]

The nature of men is that they seek or see the solutions of problems that confront them as being outside of themselves. Thus, only Jesus is divine, whereas men are mortal! Isn't this alleged to have made Christ say, "Ye shall be as I am," that the kingdom of heaven was within? It is only in the sleazy, low-life, money-loving, sex-mad milieu in which we live that men cannot accept an idea of themselves as gods—small gods, but gods nonetheless.

This is the principle that underlies the doctrine of magic, for the magician wants to know and control everything by the power of his will, including the devil, angels, spirits, demons, the sun, the moon, and the stars. The magician knows that there is only one will, and since he has use of this he must be part of the One, an extension of the divine flame encased in form, divine fire in a liquid container (man's watery body).

How can you say Christ is not also the symbol of the sun and his disciples, the twelve signs of the zodiac? Do you think the ancients were as stupid as men today? Look at the monuments we have left: the Bible, the I Ching, the Bhagavad Gita, *The Iliad.* It is easier to fly to the moon than it is to comprehend these profound texts!

> We feel we shall have to overcome a great many prejudices, and that those who agree with us that Bacchus and Hercules[8] are nothing else, but the sun,[9] will not easily agree, that the worship of Christ is nothing more than the worship of the Sun . . . Everyone takes good care, to guard against anything, which might destroy the illusion of an ancient prejudice, which education example and the habit of believing have fortified.[10]

> Plato called the Sun the Son of God . . . thus Mithra and Christ were born on the same day, and that day was the birthday of the Sun. They said of Mithra that he was the same God as the

Sun, that he was the light that lightens every man, that cometh into the world.[11]

The crime of converting the Solar God of the Universe into a certain man who walked the earth, and excluding all the rest of mankind, caused the great Roman Empire to pass out of the light of knowledge and sink into the dreadful gloom of the long Dark Ages.[12]

St. Augustine, a Black African, wrote *The City of God* in part to say that Christianity wasn't the cause of the fall of Rome.[13]

As to Christ and the solar myth, we know that from December 21-24, the sun is at a 23'260 declination in the Southern Hemisphere for four days, meaning the sun is standing still for four days, hence the winter solstice (*sol* - sun, *stice* - still).

On the twenty-fifth of December the sun begins its ascension, or is reborn, as the ancients used to say. The reason the ancients allied their religious myths with astronomical phenomena was that they viewed the position of the sun in the heavens to be related to cyclic states within the soul (sol), codified into the science they called astrology.

The sun as his namesake, Christ has forever been the symbol of the divine consciousness being the greatest symbol on the physical universe of the divine power—right? Right!

"The Son of God is indeed our Lord Jesus Christ, but he is also your own true self, your higher self . . ." – R.J. Campbell

The Aim of Evil

The evil hierarchy that is currently very influential in the world has one theme, one scheme, and that is to keep mankind from seeing the light of Providence, specifically within and generally without. The entire plan is geared to keep man on the lowest levels of consciousness and glued to a materialist conception of reality, which the theory of relativity ($E=mc^2$) has already belied. *E*, or energy, is equivalent to what is referred to as spirit.

79

The satanic influence (evil) wants to prevent the second coming of Christ (divine consciousness)—the "second" coming because man has already seen Christ once, that is, has had divine consciousness in the original creation. This makes so much sense!

"Progress" is measured in terms of how close one is able to get to the divine. Each stage toward this goal was designated initiation by the ancients. Initiation as such is practiced more by, and is an indigenous cultural feature of, the Black race. The Masonic rites, and those of the Elks, the Shriners, and all cults good and evil no more than mimic the practices of the Blameless, not just here, but everywhere. Cult means to cultivate.

Run Down on the Trinity

All things that exist in the phenomenal world that have been created by men (gods) follow a threefold process, or trinity, as the ancients were wont to call it. For a thing to exist it must first be an *idea* in somebody's head. Secondly, this idea must then be acted upon to bring it to realization, therefore *will* is necessary to produce the action (most people live in the first stage). Thirdly, the action spurred by the will yields the *form* of the original *idea*. (Whose idea is man and the cosmos?)

This the Christians have called the Father, the Son, and the Holy Ghost; but what is really meant is idea, will, and form. The same holds true for the Kabbalist who calls this Kether, Chomak, and Binah (the White Jews openly claim no trinity—this is untrue), and the Hindus who call this Brahma, Vishnu, and Shiva, but they still mean the threefold process of creation.

This threefold principle of the ancients was called the Creator, the Preserver, and the Destroyer. This principle is duly symbolized by this circular order: that is, the one that divides itself into two. The ancients of Asia, being clever, divided the circle O and made it appear thus:

As this book makes mention of war (to say the least), it is necessary that some reflection be made concerning the destroyer aspect of creation. The destroyer corresponds to the form aspect sequentially. This is given further weight by the form aspect corresponding to the planet Saturn, who in mythology devoured his own children. Saturn represents time that destroys form, which is the external aspect of itself.

Do not ignore the relationship between time and form, for time also governs when things come into manifestation. This is why men say that "there is nothing like an *idea* whose time has come."

This also explains how in time the White race would rule (destroy) and also how in time we would rule (create) again. No race has created, lived, and died in more civilizations than we, since this life is wretched with its hatred in the family, the street, the school, the UN General Assembly, the White House, the Kremlin, Peking, Calcutta, and South Africa. I too was once engulfed in the global disease of hatred, enjoying every minute of it. It is easy to draw energy from hatred. This is why hatred is popular.

The White race represents the destructive forces of creation (i.e., the defacement of the Sphinx of Egypt by French cannon). It is impossible for us to hate them more than they do us. They hate us much more. We as a race are simply incapable of this kind of hatred. Our history, as outlined by the noted author of *The Destruction of Black Civilization*, substantiates this assertion. We have dealt with White treachery from positions of power and have never done to them what they have deserved—save Dessalines. I love White people now! Love them to death! Love does kill—Cupid has a bow and arrow, right? Love hurts and kills, and as I now write this I am convinced that more people are killed by love than by hate. So hate, although a mighty power, cannot overpower love. Hate can never love love.

But love can love hate. This is what Dr. King did. He loved hate, and hate was enraged and killed him. Now love is telling people to love hate, but use weapons to help hate incarnate remanifest itself. Whenever hate gets in the way (of love) it must be removed. Are there not stories of the wars in heaven?

Submission to satanic forces will lead these dirty slaves of Satan (Saturn) to destroy humanity. Who is going to oppose them if we do not? World peace or nuclear death. It is very important that we command a world voice on the international situation, not as individual groups, but as a united people. How do we unite? That's easy — warfare, sacred and mundane — that is, magic and physical violence.

The difference that distinguishes good from evil is the purpose and intent of the action.

Unity

Basically, religion has enlightened the few and made ignorant the masses. The priest class must accept the weight for this, as they are the interpreters of the divine message: "a little knowledge is a dangerous thing." As the goal of all religions is communion with God, the priestcraft has neglected to tell men that the God they've been seeking is within themselves. This knowledge has been hidden in the mass of symbolism, allegory, and the like.

The learned priestcraft regarded the body as a replica of the universe: "As above, so below!" To give meaning to the doctrine they found (and symbolized) and give correspondences between all that was outside of man and what was inside of man — astrology shows most of this. Now the riddle of the Sphinx has been solved — man! You must comprehend the symbolism of the Sphinx to really appreciate this. Just reflect on the human head rising above the animal body.

Man is God, but unmanifest. Manifest in form he is Christ or Buddha, or Christna, or Mithra, etc.

To manifest this God within oneself all kinds of practices ensue, the most obvious being celibacy. Others are alchemy (changing lead to gold, that is, animal man to spiritual man — gold — through chemistry), yoga (which means "union" — the different yogas represent the various approaches one may take to accomplish the goal), and magic. The whole practice of magic is based on the fact that man is God, for only God can make something out of nothing! The magician takes for granted that the only thing that exists in the universe is God. Only God exists and everything that we see is one of the infinity of forms (disguises is a better word — thus the ancients portrayed the Nameless One as the fool or the joker in tarot — for the wisdom of God is foolish to the unlearned).

The so-called differences in religion, like the differences in men, are for the most part surface and petty. These religions make much of themselves by calling the supreme god by different names, but who are they kidding? "The most ordinary man of letters does not fall into this error. He knows, with Plutarch, that different places and names of do not make different Gods; that the Greeks and Barbarians, the nations of the North and easily that infinity of attributes to the unity of the essence . . ."

Men believe that Judaism, Christianity, and Islam are different religions. Each one teaches a bottom-line philosophy of the God-Man. This point must be conceded on the basis of newly acquired information, which is that all three have a hidden aspect. Judaism has Kabala (which has the trinity the Jews claim they don't have). Islam has Sufism, which is more like Kabala and Buddhism. Christianity has King Arthur (the soul), the Knights of the Round Table (the capacities of man), and the search for the Holy Grail (the pineal gland, which secretes a hormone awakening the divine consciousness).

The pineal and other glands that affect the consciousness were found to be affected by LSD, allowing millions of acid heads to perceive the higher unity amongst men and the universe. This vision was too strong for many, to whom "separateness" is everything—this group comprises those who commit suicides and those having bad trips.[14]

What most people don't comprehend about acid (LSD 25) is that a person on a "nice trip" sees through all the trappings of society.

These new doors of perception quite naturally led to spiritual investigation in the seventies. The government wisely (on its part) put the clamps on acid, probably the only drug in the history of the world the government has banned!

Acid, you see, allowed men to perceive and comprehend phenomena that were usually the fruit of years of spiritual discipline—years! Many have experienced these states of awareness, so that when Sacthidananda, Chimoy, Iyengar, and the rest are preaching the good word, they know it to be true from experience and now seek a discipline where they can experience these states naturally—yoga!

In this modern sense, Timothy Leary was playing Osiris, the "awakener," and the United States government, the administrative agent of the power of the White race in America, was playing Typhon, trying to obliterate the "light," as the rule of law and order in America is based on satanic forces.

> "Concerning deity and nature, and the relationship of man to both, the teachings of the New Testament do not differ from those of any other ancient religious cult or philosophical system. However, dissimilar these various systems may be in their external form of expression, their nomenclatures, symbologies, and formulations, they are yet at one on every fundamental proposition. This essential unity of all the old religions and philosophies is clearly apparent to everyone who studies and compares them with a mind open to receive truth from any source and a heart in sympathy with the nobler aspirations of humanity which seek expression in every age."[15]

Today, with the increasing interest in Eastern religions, "Chinese" Taoism is also being checked out. But here again we find that all the doctrines of Taoism, not some, all, arise from Buddhism. I discovered this when reading *Tibetan Yoga* by Wyeth, a classic in the genre.

All religions are simply modifications of one another to suit the particular temperament of the people to whom they are presented. For instance:

> The difference between the religion of Moses and that of the surrounding nations, consisted merely in this: the latter had become corrupted by the priest, who had set up images in allegorical representation of the heavenly bodies or zodiacal signs, which in long periods of time the people came to consider as representations of real deities. The true and secret meaning of these emblems, the priest, that is the initiated, took the greatest pain to keep it from the people . . . the sole object of the initiated was, as it yet is, to keep the people in the state of debasement, that they might be more easily ruled. Thus did the Magi in ancient, and thus do the chief priests in modern times, wallow in wealth on the labour of the rest of mankind.[16]

There was an Aquarian who, by his life, at least proved the truth and unity of three of the great religions, Hinduism, Christianity, and Islam. This man, called the God-Man of modern times, was Ramakrishna, the great teacher of the sage Vivekanada. [17]

There are many texts that deal with the unity of religion, but what is usually not mentioned is that it is the same people who are also the founders of these religions, which in truth also accounts for the implicit unity that is found in them.

---

[1] Godfrey Higgins, *Anacalypsis* (New York, 1965), I, pp. 138-139.

[2] Ibid., p. 139.

[3] Parker, *Children of the Sun*, p, 27.

[4] Rogers, *Sex and Race*, I, 282.

[5] Gaskells, p. 407.

[6] A. Baily, *The Labours of Hercules*, p. 60.

[7] Vivekanda, *A Biography*. Swami Nikhilamanda

[8] See Alice Baily, *The Labour of Hercules*.

[9] Higgins, *Anacalypsis*.

[10] Charles Francois Dupuis, *The Origin of All Religious Worship* (New Orleans, 1872), p. 215.

[11] Ibid., pp. 233-234.

[12] Hilton Hotema, *Ancient Tarety Symbolism Revealed* (Lakemont, Georgia, 1969), p. 71.

[13] Dr. Ben Jochamman, *African Origins of the Major Western Religions*.

[14] Fabre D'Olivet, *The Golden Verses of Pythagaras* (New York, 1975), p. 17.

[15] James M. Pryse, *The Magical Message According to Icannes — Commonly Called the Gospel According to (St.) John* (New York, 1967), p. 7.

[16] Godfrey Higgins, *Anacalypsis*, I, 95.

[17] *Vivekananda: A Biography* by Swami Nikhilanda Advatta (Calcutta, 1971).

CHAPTER IV

CHURCHWARD AND THE LOST CONTINENT OF MU

(Lemuria)

BLACK SCHOLARS TELL THEIR STUDENTS THAT IT IS NECESSARY TO READ the works of the most biased observers. Inevitably, they reveal things that quite disprove that which they are claiming. James Churchward and Mu is an example of such.

Mu, The Motherland

Mu was a continent in the mid-Pacific that was sunk in a great cataclysm of earthquake and fire. The people of Mu, or the Lemurians as they are sometimes called, were said to have laid the foundations of all the religions and sciences on earth. Churchward, the leading investigator on Mu, said that they were a White race with black hair. Is this true?

The truth is, with all the heavy research Churchward put into his works, his attempts to make the Whites the ruling race is comical, tragi-comedy.

Let's begin in Chapter II of *The Lost Continent of Mu*: "The record of the destruction of Mu, the Motherland of man, is a strange one indeed. From it we learn how the mystery of the white races in the South Sea Islands may be solved and how a great civilization flourished in the mid-Pacific and then was completely obliterated in a single night."

What White races of the South Seas? The only mystery in the South Seas is what all those Black people were doing in the middle of the Pacific Ocean, many of whom were indistinguishable from Africans!

> The dominant race in the land of Mu was a White race; exceedingly handsome people, with clear white or olive skins, large soft, dark eyes and straight black hair. Besides this white

race, there were other races, people with yellow, brown or black skin.

Churchward justifies this by citing a document called the Troano MS, which has pictures of Indians and Blacks, but no Whites.

In Chapter III, we find: "One of the most startling discoveries is that the natives of the Polynesian group of South Sea Islands are a White Race."

Now, even if you consider that the Whites have been mixing with these islanders for the last five centuries, you would still have to stretch the imagination considerably to consider the Polynesians a White people. Tropic man is never White.

Further, Mu was called the "Empire of the Sun," which means the Blacks; they were exceedingly religious, which again excludes the White people.

In Chapter V, we find:

> Lower Egypt was settled from the Motherland via Mayax and Atlantis, both of which lay west of Egypt, therefore to reach the place of reincarnation from lower Egypt, and to travel back over the same road by which their fathers came, the soul had to travel back to the west.

The upper Egyptians came to Egypt from the Motherland by way of Burma and India. Both of these countries lie to the east of Egypt, so that the souls of the upper Egyptians to arrive at the place of reincarnation and travel back over the same road by which their fathers came, they had to travel back to the east.

When Churchward first published this in 1959, the ancient Egyptians were a White people!

Churchward claimed that The Egyptian Book of the Dead was really a memorial to the sixty-four million who went down in the destruction of Mu, the Motherland.

He goes on to say that:

> Mackenzie asserts that Osiris was an ancient king. What people he reigned over Mackenzie does not say; but by

inference it would be the Egyptians; if so he is wrong again, because when Thoth started the first lower Egyptian colony at

Sais, he taught the Osirian religion, as various papyri show, and that was 16,000 years ago. From two different sources I find it stated that Osiris lived in Atlantis 18,000 or 20,000 years ago, and that he was a great religious teacher—a Master.

The two Egyptian cults form another convincing proof that the advent of man on earth was on Mu, and that Mu was situated in the Pacific.

Here Churchward not only identifies the Blacks with Mu, but also with Atlantis. It cannot be forgotten that Osiris is a Black god, though you wouldn't think so if you saw the picture Churchward uses in his book!

In Chapter VIII, Churchward really puts his foot in his mouth:

Hermes Trigmegistus in his writings said: Oh Egypt! Egypt! Of all thy religion, fables only will remain which thy disciples will understand as little as they do thy religion. Words cut into stone alone will remain telling of thy pious deeds The Scythians, or dwellers by the Indus, or some other barbarians will inhabit thy fair land.

It's amazing that, with all the learning Churchward had, he was unaware that the Scythians were the Whites! But then most people did not know this. They should know now!

Churchward's own research reveals that, upon the destruction of Mu, the survivors went to Atlantis, India, Burma, Egypt, Ankor Wat in Cambodia, and Mexico. It can easily be demonstrated that Blacks occupied all these places. Churchward himself says that Osiris reigned in Atlantis.

Also, if Whites of any type had escaped Mu they would have appeared somewhere as a civilized group in later times, but all the places Churchward mentions were, and are, occupied by Black people.

There are huge stone Black faces found all over Mexico. Some of these can be seen on the mountains on the road to Mazatlan from

Mexico City. There are also pyramids in Mexico and this is more akin to the Blacks than the Whites.

Now we are not denying that the Whites lived in the ancient world. We are saying that the monuments in all these places reveal the presence of a Black people and if the Whites held power in any of these places, they left nothing to reflect it.

CHAPTER V

DIGRESSION ON THE JEWS (White)

IT WAS SAID EARLIER THAT THE ANCIENT JEWS WERE BLACK. IF THIS claim is true, does this negate the White Jew's claim on the Holy Land?

Because the "White" Jew holds economic and military power, he has used this, as well as the wholesale falsification of history, to put his false claim forward for land rights.

These so-called White Jews come by their religion through miscegenation. If this were not so, we wouldn't see so many of them with natural Afros—would we?

When letting the hair grow became the style in the sixties, we rediscovered that the hair of Blacks grows straight up when groomed and appears as a natural crown on the heads of the Blameless. When ungroomed, it grows into what is called dread or war locks. This is the type of hair seen on the Greek god Dionysius. This crown-like growth of hair is seen among all White people, particularly the Jews. But by now all of us have seen Whites with Afros.

Any kind of curling hair is proof positive of miscegenation. Only the hair of the Blameless curls (the hair curls because it acts as an antenna and conductor of electrical force—divine energy. Who hasn't heard of Samson and his hair? The only unique hair on the planet is the hair of the Blameless).

The White Jew is fond of saying that the Bible is his deed to the Holy Land! Let's look at this:

According to this bit of Jewish folklore, Noah cursed Ham's son, Canaan. Now, according to this same source, the eldest son of Canaan was Sidon, the ancestor of the Phoenicians and founder of the great cities of Sidon and Tyre. The Phoenicians were the greatest explorers of antiquity. They circumnavigated Africa, colonized Britain and worked the tin mines there, and founded Carthage and a colony or two in West Africa.

Their glory certainly dims that of the ancient Jews. As for another son of Ham, Mizraim, he was the founder of Egyptian civilization, according to this same Jewish folklore. Now the Bible also says that the sons of Ham had been delivered to the sons of Shem as slaves of the Egyptians for 430 years. As for the supposed sons of Japhethio—they were another people who, according to the Bible, Ham's eldest son, Canaan, was to serve. But when the Phoenicians, the sons of Canaan, were at their height of glory, the Nordics were sunk in the depths of savagery and cannibalism, and they remained so for a full thousand years after the glory of Phoenicia faded. In short, never had a curse worked so much in reverse as this alleged one of Noah's. As for the sons of Ham being Black because of a curse, we shall see later that in all probability the sons of Shem, from whom the Jews are supposed to be descended, were Black themselves. According to the Bible, the eldest son of Shem was Elam, and the Elamites were a Black people.[1] And if we consider the Hebrew language, I shall say without any partiality that the Hebrew contained in the Sepher (Genesis) is the pure idiom of the ancient Egyptians.[2] Tacitus (80 AD) says that many Romans of his time believed that the Jews originated in Ethiopia, having left there to escape oppression from Cepheus. Moreover, it is only in the White man's land that the Jews are White, this being the result of the mixing with Whites. In the Black man's land they are Black. If some Romans believed that the Jews were of Ethiopian ancestry, there must certainly have been Black Jews in Rome. Negroes were very well known to the Romans.[3] Do not the kings of Ethiopia possess the title "the lion of Judah"?

The Bible says that the Jews are Black: "Are ye not as children of the Ethiopians unto me, O children of Israel? Saith the Lord" (Amos 9:7).

The mistake of the Jews is also exemplified by Ida Greidanus, chairwoman of the faculty of Passaic Community College. To quote this witless woman, "People who live in the north (snow) are healthier than people who live in the south (sun). That is why the Nordics have always ruled the world." No, I made no mention of syphilis, smallpox, or the bubonic plague, nor did I remind her that the darker races consider the Whites a disease-carrying race. They are the only conquerors in history whose very presence has continually brought death. I made no mention of the cyclical passing of world domination from nation to nation. I can only reflect on what this attitude has meant to the largely Hispanic (mulatto) and Black student populations!

Not forgetting the Jews, Albert Einstein agrees with me: "The Jews, however, are beyond doubt a mixed race, just as are all the other groups of our civilization. Sincere anthropologists all agreed on this point, assertions to the contrary all belong to the field of political propaganda and must be rated accordingly."[4]

How we long to become that which we hardly believe we are.

—Sufi

---

[1] J.A. Rogers, *Sex and Race* (New York, 1967), I, 60.
[2] Fabre D'Olivet, *The Hebraic Tongue Restored*, translated by Nayan Leuise Redfield (New York, 1976), p. 16.
[3] Rogers, p. 92.
[4] Albert Einstein, *Ideas and Opinions* (New York, 1954), p, 196.

CHAPTER VI

BLACKNESS

The Light comes from the Darkness in order that Darkness can reveal itself.

—The Secret Doctrine

. . . the most consistent account of the origin of the world and of the gods is given by the poet Hesiod, who tells us that Chaos, the Yawning abyss, composed of void, mass, and darkness in confusion, preceded all things else. Next came into being broad blossomed earth, and beautiful love who should rule the hearts of gods and men. But from Chaos itself issued Erebus, the mysterious darkness that is under the earth, and light, dwelling in the remote regions of sunset.[1]

Out of chaos is born Erebus (formless matter) and Night, both of whom are Black.

You say, "Yes, but chaos means confusion!" But *does* Chaos mean confusion? How could it? We find this word as the root for terms such as *Tao*, *tarot*, *Torah*, and *cosmic*. Before criticizing, check the fact that the first three mean law, just as the latter means order, but the words are certainly interchangeable. Women use cosmetics to put their faces in order, right?

The confusion definition is good, insofar as it applies to the law of opposites, confusion being the opposite of order. The word *chus* is derived from *chaos*, meaning that the children of Cush (the Ethiopians) are the guardians of the law and order (celestial).

A reading of *Indaba My Children* by Mutwa will more than convince you that traditional tribal life is characterized by a pronounced and clear order, to the point of what kind of meat can be eaten by an individual attending a festival!

The children of night and Erebus are light and day.[2]

Again, on darkness we find in Gaskell's darkness a higher aspect: it is symbolic of the inscrutable source of the one and the all, under the terms, the absolute, the potential, the unknowable, and the unmanifest.

"With the Egyptians, Darkness was the mystery of all mysteries. As Damacus on first principles says: 'Of the first principle the Egyptians said nothing; but characterized it as a darkness beyond all intellectual conceptions—a thrice unknown darkness.'"*

"In the beginning darkness existed enveloped in darkness. All this was undistinguishable water."

Rig Veda Mandala (X 129) stated that Black indicates either the unmanifest and potential of ignorance and evil. This explains the Black figures of the higher gods and goddesses and the Madonna, and the lower gods and demons.**

The aforementioned being slightly true, the reasons the gods are Black is because the people who fashioned them are Black. With the rule of the Scythians we find that the gods have been changed from Black to White.

Now according to the Jews, Binah (Saturn) is the first crystallization of form arising out of Chomak (the will). The color of Saturn (Binah) is Black. Astrologers account this the planet that is sacred to them (the Hasidics), and Saturday (saturn) is their sabbath, lending weight to the truth that Saturday is the Sabbath, and not Sunday (sun) as the Christians practice. This also seems to confirm, as has been stated, that Jesus is a sun god.

Why do priests all over the world wear black? Of all colors, why black? (The Hindu wear orange, according to the ancient solar principle.) To find our answer we need to know the nature of the color black. Well, what is the nature of black?

"Scientists and manufacturers have long sought a way to make the surface of objects pure black, because a pure black coating or paint will absorb all light, including the energy in it."[3]

The aforementioned was said in the context of solar devices and answers our question very clearly: the nature of black is that it absorbs light and explains our deeply spiritual nature and why we have created every religion on earth. This accessibility to light, which is the symbol and vehicle of truth, wisdom, and knowledge, is also why we shall come into our own again.

The wisdom and knowledge of the Divine appears to men as greater and greater light! This seems the best reason for the wearing of black by White so-called priests.

Going back to Gaskell's dictionary, we find: "Ethiopians, Noble or Blameless—Symbolic of activities upon the higher planes. Buddhic faculties of truth, wisdom and love."

We can be assured that these qualities emanate from Ethiopians coming from Ether.

"The fiery aether, which has no weight, formed the vault of heaven, flashing upward to take its place in the highest sphere."[4]

This is one reason why we called the highest sphere in Judaism Kabala, after ourselves (k), ether, the sphere of undifferentiated consciousness—God.

It's fitting that we should end this digression with a note about the Scythians from Professor Arnold Ehret, who had this to say concerning the color white:

> In my first published article I promulgated the gigantic idea that the White Race is an unnatural, a sick, a pathological one. First, the color skin pigmentis lacking, due to a lack of coloring mineral salts; second, the blood is continually over filled by white blood corpuscles, mucus waste with white color; therefore the white appearance of the entire body. The skin pores of the White man are constipated by white, dry mucus; his entire tissue system is filled up and fitted out with it. No wonder he looks white and pale and anemic. Everybody knows an extreme case of paleness is a 'bad sign.' When I appeared with my friends in a public air bath, after having lived for several months on a mucusless diet with sun baths, we looked like Indians and people believed that we belonged to another race.[5]

. . . for the war gods

> *Oh Netzach grant me victory over my enemies, send them to*
>   *Yama!*
> *Oh Netzach to die in your sleep in the midst of enemies is*
>   *the only sin!*

*Oh dread goddess play your war music help us to be MEN
      again.*
*Oh Netzach how can I go through the Halls of Osiris? What
      shall I say to Maat?*
*Oh Netzach, guide me in the coming struggle, grant me
      Divine weapons, access to the magical powers of old,
      but more than this*
*Oh star of my rising, strengthen my Will—Hateful war calls
      me, the game of tearless men.*

*To everything there is a season, and a time to every purpose
      under the heaven.*
*A time to be born, and a time to die; a time to plant, and a
      time to pluck up that which is planted;*
*A time to kill, and a time to heal; a time to break down, and
      a time to build up;*
*A time to weep, and a time to laugh; a time to mourn, and a
      time to dance;*
*A time to cast away stones, and a time to gather stones
      together; a time to embrace, and a time to refrain from
      embracing.*
*A time to get and a time to lose; a time to keep and a time to
      cast away;*
*A time to rend, and a time to sew; a time to keep silence,
      and a time to speak;*
*A time to love, and a time to hate, a time of war, and a time
      of peace.*

—Ecclesiastes

*. . . China has already found, that in this world the nation that
has trained itself to a career of unwarlike and isolated ease is
bound in the end to go down before other nations which have
not lost the manly virtue and adventurous qualities.*

—Theodore Roosevelt, *The Strenuous Life*

[1] Gayley, *Classic Myths* (Xerox College Publishing), p, 4.
[2] Ibid.
* G.R.S. Mead, *T.G. Hermes*, Vol. I, p. 91.
** Gaskell, p. 113.
[3] *The New York Times*, Science Times, Cl 1/15/80.
[4] Ovid, *Metamorphoses* (Penguin Classics), p. 29.
[5] Arnold Ehret, *Mucusless Diet Healing System* (California, 1972), p. 72.

PART TWO

THE PHILOSOPHY AND DOCTRINE OF WAR

It was an immutable and unchallenged law among beast and men alike, that all must submit to the stronger, and that power belonged to those supreme in arms.[0]

—Josephus, *The Jewish War*

A force is that which makes changes in the position of bodies, and sometimes changes in the body itself. No body or matter, however infinitesimally small or ponderously large, can make any change without the aid of force.

—James Churchward, *The Cosmic Forces of Mu*

In Principle

To move a pencil you need force. Everything in life requires some force to change its existence. Now, if we are talking about changing the social, economic, and political position of a people, we are talking about a force of warlike proportion.

Admittedly this is a difficult premise to accept. Look at Mugabe in Zimbabwe. He's acting like he doesn't want to fight anymore. Aren't the Whites doing everything they can to sabotage Zimbabwe, if not inside the country, then outside of it? Of course they are.

The border countries of South Africa have no choice except to unite, if for no other reason than to spread the military power of South Africa.

South Africa is beset both externally and internally and will eventually have to fight wars on external and internal fronts, wars that it can never win. The development of nuclear weapons in South Africa is idle dreaming, unless the Nazis there intend to use them within their own borders.

Again, as there can be no change without the aid of force, our history becomes clearer and clearer.

I read the autobiography of Frederick Douglass. I could distinguish no difference between his times and ours, meaning the power relationship has remained the same. The forms of the relationship have changed, but the substance is the same—consistent in the relationship has been the use by Whites of force and terror and our reluctance of these uses or inability to use them. This has stabilized our relationship. This is the cycle we have to break in order to become whole again.

Aren't there more Blameless fighting champions than there are among any other people? Hasn't history commented that Hannibal was the most daring and sagacious of generals? What about the awesome Scipio Black (conqueror of Hannibal), Alexander the Great, and Pyrrhus?

If we know who we are, can our enemies escape our wrath? Force is a principle in life, not the ideation of a revolutionary, the creation of the ruling class, or the vision of the Mafia.

The state owes its origin to war . . . agriculture, slavery, and territoriality are the primary factors underlying state formation, but the force which actually welded them together to produce the state was war.

—Schuman

Law of Strife and the Acme of War

The state has been referred to as a biological organism or cell, and the analogy still remains, for we have the microcosmic (cell) reflecting the macrocosmic (universal). The cell divides itself, doesn't it? We've seen this doctrine before, haven't we?

In this incarnation, I have observed that the nature of men is such that they will not even do what is good for them unless compelled by force, threat, or subterfuge.

The state must have laws that regulate the behavior of its populace (taxes, laws against crime, etc.). If laws exist, then force exists.

War then is the organizing mechanism of the state. We need look no further than the history of the United States. Let's see, we have Cuba, China, Vietnam, Mozambique, Zimbabwe, etc. Each of these states was newly born from war. Should I forget Israel?

There is a law of strife that exists in the universe, no doubt associated with the Venusian Vibration, the catchphrase of Venus being "Victory through strife."

The ancients put this knowledge to good use, as can be seen in the Bagavagita, *The Iliad* (which literally means "the strife"), and the Bible.

Now one can easily say that a major theme in all three books is conflict or strife. We can also say that these works cannot be interpreted literally for their true meanings, since, for the most part, these are the works of Black people (with White interpolation when possible).

Black people teach through allegory, symbolism, metaphor, parable, fable, and myth. We even speak cryptically: "That's mean," meaning good. This use of cryptic language comes under the heading of slang, but it is really a way of communicating that is closed to the uninitiated. So-called Black English is actually the most popular English. If it were not, people wouldn't be using so many words which originate in the Black American community.

Esoterically, these three books deal with man and his struggle to awaken his higher nature or self, covered in a panorama of earthly conflict, war being the greatest endeavor man can undertake on earth.

The Bagavagita concerns itself on the surface with the struggle of the Pandavas and the Kurus for the "kingdom" of India, the former representing the desire for self knowledge of the higher self, the latter representing desire as a whole.[1]

The central characters in the drama are Arjuna, a Pandava prince (the personality) and Christna (the higher self), the charioteer of Arjuna.

The Pandavas have been driven from the kingdom of the blind king Dhritarashtra (the body) by the Kurus (the lower desires).

As the story opens, Arjuna is reluctant to struggle because the Kurus are family relations—cousins, uncles, grandfathers, etc. No kingdom assumes value through the slaying of one's relatives. From this beginning a dialogue ensues between Christna and Arjuna, in which Christna urges Arjuna on to fight, and in so doing expounds on the immortality of the soul, the doctrine of death, reincarnation, duty, etc. What a story! It is told in war drama—simply because the conquest of one's self, that is, the lower desires of that self, is a great war and is best symbolized by such. The Buddhist expresses it this way: "If one man conquers in battle a thousand times a thousand men, and if another conquers himself, he is the greatest of conquerors."

Similarly, in *The Iliad* we have Achilles (the personality) driven to and fro by his affections—anger, lust (bisexuality, as in the Pope translation Patrocleus is called his "best beloved"), excessive pride, love of glory, etc. Achilles is seeking himself in the world and is slain, whereas Arjuna, though a warrior as Achilles, seeks truth and glory within himself and is victorious by slaying the Kurus (lower desires).

In Gaskell's *Dictionary of All Scriptures and Myths* (a must text for all those who have an inclination to study religion or occult science) we find this on Agamemnon:

Agamemnon (Astreides), son of Atreus: a symbol of the desire
mind . . . which is the offspring of illusion (Atreus). 'Nor do
thou (Achilles) son of Peleus, feel inclined to contend against a
king (Agamemnon); since never yet has any sceptre-bearing
king to whom Jove have given glory, been allotted an equal
share of dignity.'

—*The Iliad*, Book I

The interpretation by Gaskell reads:

Nor must the personality (Achilles) begotten of the higher
self (Peleus) seek to exterminate and crush out the desire mind
which has its own purpose in the soul's evolution . . .[2]

Evidently, the ancients felt strife to be an important doctrine. If they
did not they would never have disguised their wisdom in dramas of
struggle.

The Bible is full of wars too, isn't it? The war panorama was
applied also because it exemplified the manly virtue—courage—as did
the Roman Circus.

The strife doctrine is also apparent in Egypt with the struggle of
Osiris (Black) against Typhon (White). Further, the Egyptians taught
that "the world becomes, through incessant strife of complementary
forces."[3] For example, the strife of the Black and White races has
literally produced mankind.

It has been seen how war, always inevitable between the two
races, because the races all strive for the dominion and
usurpation of the earth, had developed much useful knowledge
in the White Race, and put it in condition to struggle
advantageously against the Black Race.

—D'Olivet

The Whites in America, to their credit and our disgrace, have been
practicing the highest form of war on us. The highest form of war is to
subdue your enemy without fighting. With a combination of terror,
welfare, a few jobs, unemployment, and the media they have subdued

104

fifty million strong! All of this is masked in a gross covering of materialistic consumerism where the American working, unemployed, on welfare, or in the Mafia is desirous of a new car, a color TV, a yacht, a plane, or any item that he feels will round out his life, as if material possessions shield him from the force of life!

This tactic is successful because the nature of men in war is that, when surrounded with no means of escape, they will fight to the death. Therefore, American society allows various avenues of escape (jobs, welfare, drugs, school, training programs, etc.) and by doing so is able to isolate and murder whomever it wishes. Man is a creature of immediate self interest.

War is the father of all things.

—Heraclitus

Observations on the Doctrine of War: The Martial Chronicles

Oh, sons of the sun (the sun was the symbol of reason to the ancients, who comprehended it to be the balance between synthetic and abstract analysis on one level and congregative and segregative thinking on another). In this day and age, the race appears desperate for an ideology that shall save it. It is necessary that something very fundamental be averred, namely that if war be politics with bloodshed, and politics be war without bloodshed, the central question involves fighting, not ideology!

Organizational unity should be based on the recognition of the following: 1) The army is the chief component of state power, 2) Force is the key issue and deciding factor in politics, 3) We are already at war; we are just not participating righteously, and 4) Only an organization designed for political violence can lead our race out of this morass and take our struggle to a higher level (*organized around the need to engage in violence to psychologically regenerate the race*—this is the lesson Fanon wanted us to learn).

Organized violence is the key factor that distinguishes us from the other ethnic groups in America.

Beloved

Beloved, we must plot the ascension (Coltrane) of the race over the next century. This can only happen if we do two things—join the American gun culture and exercise our citizenship within the empire which we can do as strong and fearless men. America will act as a springboard to our triangular organization of the Diaspora, just as it did for the slave trade. This time it will be America, Brazil, and Africa, the three great strongholds of the Black race.

At home in America, we will enforce an armed draconian-fascist hold on our communities to enforce discipline on the youth, emphasizing education, spirituality, physical strength, and love of self and kind. I recall when I was reading *The Golden Age of Black Nationalism*—an excellent page turner—the author, an arrogant asshole, calls Garvey a fascist. This made me reflect that for all his scholarly insight he knew nothing of the nature of Black people, who require discipline, not freedom. Freedom has millions of us in jail. Freedom has men thinking it's all right to father children and not take care of them. Freedom has more Black males reading Iceberg Slim and Donald Gaines than Dubois, Douglass, George Jackson, and Dr. Welsing (see book list). Freedom has Black Christians *believing* that mystical Jesus was White and not Black—doubting the esoteric symbol of the sun, even when they are told that the oldest church in Christianity is the Coptic Church of Ethiopia. Are we fucked up or what? All this nonsense calls for a fascist kick in the ass—get your guns!

How are we to reclaim that which was ours without fighting for it? When you go to the malls on the planet Earth in America, Asia, Europe, Russia, South America, etc., you see diamond and gold stores. Diamond and gold are the two most precious stones on man's earth. Where do they come from? Africa! How are all these people selling that which comes from our homeland? They took it! How did they take it? They took it by force and violence. They were willing to fight and die to take what is ours. Can we do less to get it back?

My son asked me the other day, "Where is our Mao?" We almost had him in Marcus Garvey, who gave us the ideological vision for ourselves and Africa. The Black Panther Party almost had it, but they pushed the political ahead of the military agenda. We see the same thing in present South Africa. They (the Blacks) can't nationalize the gold and diamond mines because they lack the military to do so. The main component of state power is the military. Yes, even in America!

Don't forget, our children, the various nation states, have been warring against us for 10,000 years. Untold, told millions have died. The Europeans and Arabs have devastated us during this period.

Look at the map of Africa. As you go northeast, you get what men call the Middle East. No, what you get to is northeast Africa! You forget this land was attached to Africa, divided from it by the Suez Canal. That area north and south was anciently was named Cush, biblical Ethiopia. It was taken from us by Arab invaders. We are not seceding anything to anyone on ancestral lands.

America can train us in the military arts, which is why we must be pro-patriotic. We must become strong in a strong America. We are getting into gun culture to prevent White citizens, be they the police, vigilantes, or Joe Blow, from killing us without consequences. This has to happen so we can act and speak as men and reap the benefits of true American citizenship.

Murder as State Policy: Minority Groups in the State (Empire)

Beloved, our issue is one of manliness. There is no manhood; hence, the support of gay rights is absurd when we can't even manifest as men! The state, all states, view minorities within them as a Trojan horse that will one day emerge and kill them in the night. If we look we will see the scenarios worldwide of minority groups in various states suffering from one or another form of oppression. The doctrine is to keep these minorities in check. In America, it is done with murder and political and institutional racism. Murder is the best form of oppression, because it keeps the people in both psychological and emotional fear, and it has worked for centuries.

The Trayvon Martin case in Florida illustrates the point. A White kills a Black unarmed youth and is allowed to go free. The Whites seek to form a dialogue around what is clearly premeditated murder. This drama is historic, is it not? Do we need to name all of our people this has happened to while we chase a blind goddess? Don't you think the ancients knew what they were doing when they made justice blind?

Countries or Empires

Beloved, we have to take our own justice, the way real men do, and allow the blind goddess to go on her way. The Black man has no rights Whites are bound to respect. This ruling is still in effect! These killings of our people are humiliating to witness as men and constantly lower our self-esteem. It is Willie Lynch all over again, but instead of humiliating the slave male in front of his woman, now they do it across the nation. Stop crying! I have the solution! *The great American gun culture.* This is the only part of the American cultural matrix that we are not involved in, and at the same time it is the most important for us and Africa! Guns will psychologically free us from fear and 393 years of murder and lynching. When a murder occurs, or some other outrage that requires a manly response, we can take care of the situation; which to date, to our disgrace, we have been unable to do.

A Call to Arms

Brothers and sisters, we need a weapon. Some twenty-first or twenty-second-century hardware that will give us the capacity to wage war as the gun did for the White man. Meanwhile, join the American gun culture and learn the science of weaponry. Until this is done, we will continue to be second-class citizens. An armed citizen is a true American.

The Motherland

There's a psychic connection between the homeland of a people and their relationship to the world at large. When the homeland is strong the people carry themselves with strength and pride. Lacking this, they have to become organizational killers to get respect, i.e., the Italian Mafia. Italy is not a strong country, Colombia is not a strong country, but they have organizational killers that you must respect.

When the Kazars (Jews) got Israel, they became an incredibly strong people. Who gave a fuck about the Chinese? Now they are a power on Earth, and the modern Chinese reflect this. Africa is weak, and so are we. Having no organizational killers weakens us even further.

Listen: China united because of the Japanese invasion during a civil war between the nationalists and the communists. In Africa we have ready-made enemies. To unite the people around, we have the Whites in the south and the Arabs in the north.

Nasser

Nasser, the late former president of Egypt, once remarked that "the Jews left Egypt Black and came back White." This being said, you ever wonder why the mulatto Arabs never cited this in their struggle against Jews, whom they have been fighting since 1948? The answer is simple. If they call into question the legitimacy of the White Jew on the land question, it would then open the land question that the Arab nations occupy in general, and the Palestinians in particular. Remember, this is called the Holy Land.

Sidebar: two Jehovah's Witnesses came to my house for a religious talk, one White, the other Black, both females. When I brought up the fact that the oldest church in Christianity is the Coptic Church of Ethiopia, the Black female said, "Are you trying to say that Jesus was Black?" Then the White one chimed in, "Everyone knows Jesus was born in the Middle East!" The reader should be clear that what men today call the Middle East in reality is northeast Africa. It is ancient Cush/Ethiopia separated by the European Suez Canal. The Middle East, my ass. This is northeast Africa, and when we get our military shit together we will reclaim it, as we will all of Africa.

All that has been taken from us has been by people better organized militarily against us and having better weapons of war. This is how we lost India also. There are still countless millions of Black people in India who once held sway there, and the present-day Hindus who claim the spiritual heritage of that nation are built on lies. They are not who they say they are either.

I cannot emphasize enough the major importance of getting knee deep into the American gun culture, which has always been open to us. How else are we to quell our fear and develop the necessary mindset to call forth the spirits of Sesotros, Lycugus, and the great Hannibal in our children? I was watching the American History Channel the other day, which was showing Hannibal as White! Then you have all these movies showing Greek gods as White, the godlike Achilles as White, Paris, who ran away with Helen, as White, and Helen of Troy, the face that launched a thousand ships, as White. Yes, the same Paris that is the capital of France. The Trojans and the Greeks of antiquity were Black.

Bobby

I was talking to my friend Bobby, and when I said, "You can't be an American without a gun." He couldn't see what this had to do with voting and slick laws being passed to prevent our people from voting. Voting is a right given to all citizens. Black citizens were murdered trying to exercise this right. It was so bad that Congress had to pass the Voting Rights Act to ensure that we were able to do so. At one time, when Marius was Consul in Rome and in the middle of a fight with one of Rome's enemies, soldiers fighting with the Romans refused to fight any further unless they were granted citizenship. This Marius granted immediately. Later, when asked by the Senate why he did such a thing, he replied that the din of warfare decided the issue! With us, the din of warfare has decided the issue. Acting as men, anyone who dares to interfere with our voting rights by a fallacious argument to law should be fought or slain. Our resume in war has granted us this right. Fearless manliness guarantees it.

Cuba

LA TIERRA DONDE MACEO

The Blacks of Cuba, like the Blacks of America, fought valiantly in the wars of their nation, each time thinking that this participation would lead to normalization of citizenship rights. This never happens. In fact, in most cases their rights as citizens worsen. Both the jails of Cuba and America are filled with Blacks, namely because they don't have access to those means within the society that would cause them to thrive. This is called racism or White supremacy—a make-believe doctrine of superiority of Whites as a defense mechanisms for their lack of color living in a world of color.

Blacks in Cuba should be plotting their ascension to state power, since they are the majority in that nation. Many are already in the armed forces, and all they need to do is tum those guns on any who would like to stop them from gaining state powers. Sidebar: The Black Cubans will also be crucial in the wars in Africa and the unification of the continent. The Black world already owes them an incredible debt for the role their military played in holding back the racist South African military; many of the sons of Cuba died in that conflict.

The Gun Culture of America

BLAMELESS

In order for us to manifest as men, we must put ourselves in the gun culture of America. Why? All of the psycho-social nuances that affect us as a people, from education to bullshit criminality, are rooted in *fear*. The psychology of the gun eliminates this psychosis that cripples us in degrees unimaginable.

We live in a nation with well over 100 million armed White people—men, women, and children. Psychologically, this enhances their boldness. You have a Black president speaking at a public forum and Whites show up displaying guns, asserting our Second Amendment rights in open disrespect for the office and its Black president. Reflection will reveal that what King and Malcolm had were two things that gun culture will give us: fearlessness and truth telling.

White people, whose social and economic well-being are based on lies, make believe, and fear, guard them with gun psychology. We must do the same, but add truth to this dynamic. We can never be men if we are unwilling to stand up and speak the truth, which is why our politicians are worthless. For example—when are we going to confront the following: the Tuskegee syphilis experiments, AIDS, and the incarceration of Black youth on phony drug charges? There is no war on drugs, only the war on Black youth by racist police forces. Drugs are predominantly controlled by governments, which use the profits for much of its covert ops.

We should also be aware that police murder is state policy, no matter how random it appears. The aim is to instill fear in Black people. That is why police murder Black people regardless of age or gender, in or out of their homes. Anyway, in the *Los Angeles Free Press* there was an article by Allen Ginsberg, a poet of some renown in the hip community. His article was about the drug culture and how drugs were the chief conduit for the incarceration for Black youth in America, and linked it as a government operation. During these times, Bob Dylan had a song called "Subterranean Homesick Blues" with the line "Must bust in early May/orders from the DA/Look out kid, no matter what you did." (This meant arrest as many Black youths as possible; the summer is coming when rebellion is right.)

Self Discipline

Black and Hispanic leaders need to take a serious look at the drug trade in regards to its impact on the systematic incarceration of their young males. They need to stop making believe that the federal, state, and city authorities have a sincere interest in bringing about the elimination of drugs in our society. The tremendous profit reaped through drugs makes it an integral part of the American economy. However, for our purposes, what should concern us is that drug selling is used as the primary vehicle for the incarceration of our youth. Initially, one would think that if you are selling drugs, you should go to jail. On the surface this sounds correct, but if we probe deeper we will see that the kingpin drug lords and traffickers don't even go to jail. We also have not confronted the various governments, including the US, in their duplicity concerning drug trafficking. The CIA has been linked to drug trafficking for years and in books too numerous to name, the latest being *The Crime of Patriots*. The real deal is that the White high school dropout has a better chance of getting employment than a Black college graduate under twenty-five.

History and experience teach us that America is simply not interested in justice for Blacks or Hispanics. This is the scene: the government, through its secret police, the CIA, brings in narcotics. These narcotics are then distributed to various dealers throughout the land. Black and Hispanic youths who have no jobs and no prospects of getting one can sell drugs and make lots of money. Remember, the real American ethic is that you may do whatever you wish—just don't get caught. Moral outrage over the drug trade is nothing but political show, false and hypocritical. The hidden agenda is funneling minorities to jail and maintaining a social edifice of corrupt and decadent police and callous judges, with an army of lawyers on both sides (though clearly the client with the most money will go free, with the exception of Blacks and Hispanics, who have their assets taken). Are there any cases of the authorities ever doing this to the Mafia? Inevitably, although the drug trade originally served two purposes, crazy profits and the incarceration of the brothers, it has crept into the crevices of our American society, which translated means that White America is now also afflicted with rampant drug use. There is one great difference. The police do not arrest or prosecute to any extent White male youths for drugs, the exception being the poor Whites.

We Are

This is from a book called *We Are*, which is about becoming galactic humans. This book doesn't mention us directly, but it's not hard to infer who these ancient people were. For example, the occultist Manly Hall, in his extraordinary book *The Secret Teaching of All Ages* (written at the age of twenty-eight!), mentions the past when the zodiac was in flower and there were probably no White people on Earth! Or if you never read Tacitus, Godfrey Higgins's *Anacalypsis*, or Gerald Massey's books on Egypt you wouldn't know that the ancient Jews were Blacks. If you read Josephus's *The Jewish War* you get the same thing, although every interpretation possible is used to get the reader to think that those Jews who fought the Romans were White. The ancient Greeks were Blacks, as were the first Chinese. So, when Elijah was talking about the Asiatic Black man, he spoke the absolute truth.

This is the Problem Age

Our race is millions of years old. In fact, it is the only race! It has already been established that we are the mothers and fathers of humankind. The nonsense of a White race, a Yellow, a Brown, etc., has no validity. Mystical and spiritual writing that I have read over the past few years claims that we once shared this planet with a dinosaurian and a reptilian species with whom we fought for dominion. Both of the species were older than us. In the book *Morning of the Magicians* it is said that a chemical substance that is left after a nuclear explosion is found all over the earth. Perhaps it is the remnants of very ancient wars! Or of a time when we were fighting each other in Lemuria and Atlantis, when we destroyed the firmament, when Mother Earth was in an eternal spring?

Can We Talk?

There is an absolute phenomenon in this world that only the dull-witted could deny (or a people drowning in self-delusion). First, we are living in a world where we are ruled by armed men. Our history says we have been bought across an ocean by a fierce people better armed than we. Second, respect is never earned; it is demanded. Many people do not understand this. The murder of Martin Luther King Jr. should have taught everyone that they do not respect us. Remember what happened to Jackson at the Democratic Convention. No matter what your powers, be they oratory, scientific, historic, athletic, or whatever, the Black man has no right a White man is bound to respect. Justice Taney (of the Dred Scott decision) said that social acceptance is based on whether you can entertain them; hence, the historic popularity of sports and clowns. In turn, many do not respect themselves.

There is only one conclusion that can be drawn from the first and this concerns our knowledge of arms, which is still wanting. How could this be after 300 years? You mean to tell me that men (I use the term loosely) cannot even discuss the instruments of our enslavement and our use of same? Is this not the greatest dishonor? Secondly, there can be no honor without force; there can be no psychological progress in men without that—no. This does not mean trying to overthrow the US government, you idiot. Americans organize force to get a better piece of the pie, not to overthrow the government!

The Destiny of the Black Race

Think about it: we came here by force. All other groups came of their own volition. There has to be a cosmic/divine purpose for us being placed here and the reason is to bring this country and the world into the light. As a people we have been through, lived through, fought through, developed through, and gave birth to more nations than any people on Earth (see *Anacalypsis*). It is our destiny through America to put the world in order through both material and spiritual warfare. The wickedness that abounds across the planet is sustained by lies, the chief one being that the Black race has no history, when in fact all of history is ours, East and West.

Tour de force, I recall, when reading Dr. Ben's *The African Origin of the Major Western Religion*. In his intro, he said he was raised a Jew, but when he started studying history he learned that the Black race started all the religions, so being a so-called Jew was not even necessary, since we could lay claim to all of them. Presently, you have all these White pundits claiming the mystery system from Egypt. All the secret societies, all in imitation of the former Rosicrucian, Masons, Templar, and Illuminati, teach the Man-is-God doctrine as the basis for the creation of a socialist new world order (the one-world order). Of course the planet needs a one-world government. Humanity is one family and we are its parents. DNA has already proven this. The problem is that White men, demonically led, cannot and have proven themselves incapable of leading such an enterprise. Obviously they are not unaware of Public Enemy's "Fear of a Black Planet."

In the summer of 1968, in the mountains between Mexico City and Tulica, I took what is known as the sacred mushroom. I was twenty-four years old and an avowed agnostic, sometimes atheist. I had smoked marijuana and tried LSD, but nothing prepared me for this mushroom. I was going to school in Mexico at the time, and some White friends said that they had experienced God. I found this outrageous and laughed my ass off at such an assertion. I was with a Mexican friend, Fernando Lozano. The friend brought us some mushrooms that they had brought back from the state of Oaxaca, where the mushroom grows around the town of Huatla. When I ate the mushroom I threw up, but as I did so, a white light went up my spinal column—I saw it! All is one, all is one. I was able to look through the floor into the next apartment. Fernando and I started communication telepathically. We were so frightened that we ran out of the apartment and took a bus into the city, but we had to come right back because our senses were being overwhelmed by the environment. When we got back to the apartment, we finally calmed down and went into meditation. I knew everything, all that was and all that was to be. In the center of my being there was the feeling of divine energy. In yoga, they call this *kundalini*, where men go in caves and try for thirty years to get what I experienced.

When I told this story to my friends in the summer of '72 we literally took a caravan down there. The doctrine is this: Only God Exists. There is nothing outside of this existence. Everything in creation is part of this being. This includes animate and inanimate

115

objects. This being appears to us obviously in a myriad of forms with different grades of its essence. Firstly, man was not the first created being. You forget the angels? Now the creation of man caused problems because Ethiopians were endowed with powers not given to other sentient beings. Proof of this is that man can draw a "magic" circle and call forth angels, devils, elementals, or demons, and all must obey him. I don't suggest you try this, but there are hundreds of books on how you can. The Black race in antiquity was famous and feared for its powers in these matters. Being colorless, they have created myths about themselves (White world supremacy) that have poisoned the globe. They put Obama in office to clean up the image after the Katrina fiasco, but it's difficult for a leopard to change its spots.

"Beloved"—I love when Farrakhan says that!

Listen: our history on this planet is immeasurable in time, but traceable in the ancient empires of Ethiopia, Chaldea, Babylon, Egypt, Greece, Atlantis, Assyria, Persia Cush, India, etc. More than any people, we can tell when the decadence of an empire is evident and the decline sets in. All empires have a life cycle of youth, middle age, old age, and death. But the key is always the same. The empire subtly shifts form, from an underpinning of spirituality to one of sexuality. This is foreshadowed by the rise of homosexuality within the state and the amoral acceptance of it by people thinking it no more than acceptance of so-called sexual freedom. It slowly begins to undermine the moral character of the state by uncharted sexual permissiveness, and pedophilia also increases. We got sick of it in Greece and made that the death penalty; they caught Socrates's ass and made him drink poison as a lesson to others. Our empires of the past lasted thousands of years because when homosexuality began to show its proclivity we suppressed it; when we couldn't, we fell.

In the later days of Babylon, the priests had all the virgins in the state come to the temple of Venus and sell pussy. Some women were said to be there for years! But this is an example of sexual permissiveness that we fell under. The marriage of a man and a woman is considered sacred in any culture you can find on this planet, and none have a ritual sanctifying same sex marriage. Even America, with its slave foundation, had a spiritual undertone to it, if for no other reason than the greatest spiritual race on Earth was here. All nations have a spiritual underpinning, but life itself is spiritual, not material. Why the fuck do you think communism is a failure? They recognize civilization as economic and define man in his relationship to production. However true that is, there is no spiritual underpinning, and failure is inevitable. Man is a spiritual being. How the fuck can you have a state that says there is no God? The Chinese are a spiritual people.

War Footing

When Professor Small and Dr. Jefferies said that the race had been at war for 10,000 years, it dawned on me what kind of fighting we were doing besides marching and protesting the various injustices against us. I remember Malcolm thought those methods were unbecoming for a man. He was right. Then came the Black Panther Party, the argument subculture, nationalism with shotguns in hand, with the rhetoric of revolutionary socialism and intercommunalism. Man, I loved that stuff. Hey, Newton, Bobby Seale, D. Cox, Fred Hampton, Eldridge Cleaver, George Jackson, and Angela Davis calling cops pigs! I remember Cox, who recently passed in Paris, calling Israel the beachhead of US imperialism in the Middle East in the late '60s and '70s. As I understand it, an internal struggle within the Panthers developed, like all revolutionary groups, over the need to create a revolutionary consciousness among the American people or an underground armed struggle.

As the future generation of males, you have an obligation and a sacred duty to throw off the shackles of fear and lead our people to war. Redemption cannot accomplish this task without weapons; hence, the need to study the sciences and math (what your parents never told you).

Our Will

Our will to accelerate this process in fifty-five countries is generally the result of colonialism and bullshit tribalism that disgracefully led to Rwanda. Could Rwanda have happened if Africans knew our history? Who our enemies are?

Students, we need a weapon—a ray gun, lasers, atomic, nuclear, biological, or chemical. A lack of melanin is something to combat what is being used against us by demonic White forces. This clown shit is over. Turn up your game and join this war through relentless study of the sciences, math, and occult sciences. Remember the name of Egypt was Kemet, where we get the name chemistry. The self hate must end. We have a 10,000-year-old war on our hands. I don't give a fuck about you wanting to be a rapper praising an Italian mobster bullshit or a pro sports phenom. If you rap you better come off like Immortal Technique, Nas, etc.—all those brothers trying to wake your dumb asses up. Brush your hair in the sink with water and you will see all the numbers—how the fuck can you say you don't like or understand math? Be and act like the God within you. Our shit is so deep and profound. The depths to which these crackers have gone to keep us away from the knowledge of our true self knows no bounds. We are the masters of the universe. Think of all the things we have been able to accomplish with every fucking institution in the nation against us! You don't know math, you don't know science, and you are pussy. This is what we need to fight this war, not you singing lyrics to that asshole with the tattoos. They color your body and make you darker, you fucking idiots. We already have color, beautiful color. Will you kindly wake the fuck up!

And you sisters, don't think I forgot about your dumb asses. How are you giving up some pussy to someone who never takes you to a movie, treats you to McDonald's, or takes you to meet his family, nor can you bring him home with you because his drawers are showing? Check the mentality. We want to govern the world—all people do who vie for power on Earth. These drawers-showing motherfuckers are dressing for jail and not rulership. Psychologically, showing your ass means fuck society—okay, I get that. On the other hand, it says you have no place in it—but you do, you are just too pussy to take it.

For the Pussy and Squeamish

You do realize that our kids are running around with guns and killing each other in absolute misguided frenzy, to the point that we (adults) are afraid of them? Do you really think that would remain as serious a problem as it is now if we were an armed population? Inevitably, there are going to be some glitches, some unnecessary killings, and collateral damage, but how are we going to get gun-toting youth under control in our communities if we don't have guns ourselves? Explain that shit to me. Talking to them is a waste of time. We can't even convince them to pull their pants up, which unconsciously is saying "fuck society." In a place like Chicago where Blacks seem to have better political organization than in New York, their youths are as buck wild as they are in any other urban city. I think as a people the gun will give us greater political savvy than we are currently demonstrating. The Panthers had it right. Their mistake was the rhetoric of socialist revolution, which in my youth had great appeal, but empires are not overthrown, and America is certainly not 1917 Russia. If you require more information on empires you can read the following two classics, one old, one new . . . *Meditations on the Ruins of Empire* by Count Volney and *Civilization or Barbarism* by Diop.

Rwanda

Rwanda happened because of tribalism. Tribalism will be a major obstacle to overcome toward the unification of Africa. The Africans like to say that we in America lack the culture of Africa. This is not true. What we lack is the tribalism, which gives the clans the nuances that makes them differentiate themselves, and in this day it is reactionary. We live in an epoch or empirical economic and military nationalism of the great states—Europe, Russia, America, and China. The Black race cannot compete against this, with fifty-five fragmented states created by nineteenth-century European colonialism. This situation will put us at least more than a century away if Africa follows the growing pains of continental unity. To circumvent this, we need to infiltrate the major and minor state as a fifth columnist, with the Garvey ideal of Africa as a global power . . . By "we," I mean the African Americans and our brothers from the West Indies who have gives us Marcus Stokely, Tony Martin Padmore, Eric Williams, C.L.R. James, Walter Rodney, etc.

I spoke earlier on the need to acquire military training and going into Africa. The difference between us and the Africans is that the White man has beaten the tribalism out of us with his system of savage slavery. It is now very easy to see ourselves as one people. This is not the case in Africa. The goal is to create an awakening consciousness of who we are and what we were. We are going to start this here in America when we join the American gun culture. The wealthy among us, who are "conscious," must flood Africa—Nigeria, South Africa, Ghana, and the Congo in particular—with certain books: *How Europe Underdeveloped Africa, The Destruction of Black Civilization, The African Origin of the Major Western Religion, The Cultural Unity of Black Africa, African Origin of Western Civilization,* and *Neocolonialism.* There must also be a neverending, constant barrage of propaganda against the Arabs and South African Whites, with an incessant call for a unified African army to assemble these two groups and run them the fuck out of Africa.

Unite the Planet

At one point I thought it would be possible through America to unite the planet, so as to fortify the earth as we go to war with the aliens who are having our people and children for breakfast and using our women to breed humanoid hybrids—this is going on now.

Police Policy

Do not kill police. Under no circumstances are police officers to be killed when we have joined the American gun culture. The state has 101 cop shows on the air. Those paramilitary bastards are an integral part of the state apparatus, as were the Praetorian Guard of old. We fuck them indirectly. They kill a child, then find theirs. Barring that, then find the wife or mother. Go biblical: an eye for an eye. Become merciless.

Follow me: can you fuck with the Italians? No. And you know why! How about the Russians? No, and you know why. The Albanians, the Colombians, etc. . . . . Can you fuck with the Blacks? Yes, because we don't bring the rain. Of all these groups, once we start we will be the most feared, because the night is more fearful than the day. Also, target the police chiefs and their union heads, but never the officers. You remember when that White cop Sullivan killed Eleanor Bumper, a Black grandmother, with two shotgun blasts, and then they made him the marshal of the St. Patrick's Day Parade as a reward? I was so ashamed of my fear and cowardice. I couldn't look in the mirror or fall asleep for months. Remember Emmett Till and the three girls in the church bombing? And you wonder why as men we are so fucked up.

Fear was so real to Alexander the Great that he went to the desert to sacrifice to the god FEAR.

We must join the American gun culture and create a new weapon. Find out what the Irish did to us in New York City in 1861. You saw and heard about the Cotton Club, you saw *The Godfather*; they were killing each other so they could bring heroin to whom? I just heard somebody say "forgive." I'm not forgiving shit. With the American gun culture, we have vendettas to answer. No wonder we are second-class citizens. A real American would go get his gun. Americans don't take insults. Join the NRA and fight any and all gun control. Find a lawyer with some balls and challenge New York City gun laws as unconstitutional. I'm still laughing at Plaxico Buress going to jail for shooting himself.

Let's face it, we love America. When we watch the Olympics, we cheer for our country and the Black countries when they are playing everybody else. Yeah, America fucks with us because we let it. Chief Justice Taney said, "The Black man has no rights the White man is bound to respect." We finally figured out that you don't earn respect, you take it. Somebody tell Obama that nobody gives a fuck about how smart or intelligent you are. You really can't get mad at him, because as Henry Ford pointed out in *The International Jew*, the Jews control both parties (power of the purse). That's why the Democrats are so quiet while the Republicans make him look like a pussy with his "Let's get together" bullshit.

Don't listen to any pussy argument that it's not just a matter of joining the American gun culture, that it is too simple. No, it's not simple. It means being manly, stepping up, and speaking the truth. That is what King, Malcolm, and Elijah did. They stood up and told the truth, something we do not do.

Our brothers did not die to keep this country as one free of human slavery and united to allow anyone to deny our rights as citizens in this republic. Any attempts to do so either with physical coercion or political chicanery should be met with death. Our rights were gained on the field of battle, in American wars in general and in the Civil War in particular.

Marching on Washington protesting is unbecoming of men. That history is dead and has no use in the twenty-first century. Let the faggots march. Give me a gun.

Extremism in the defense of liberty is no vice.

—Barry Goldwater

By any means necessary.

—Malcolm X

Military Decadence: The Great American Gun Culture

Black people participate in the entire matrix of the American culture except the most important one: the American gun culture. As it turns out, our entry into the American gun culture will solve all of our problems in America, the main one being fear. Whites will not win a race war. Just because we go after the Klan, what are they going to say? That we looked at a White woman? Like Emmett Till, that we raped a White woman? I think a few hoes tried that shit a few years ago. It was hot for a second, but it all collapsed quickly.

The White American conquest of us made him bold enough to challenge the English Empire and win! Did we help in this struggle too, in a bold and most significant way? They very conveniently leave the Black soldiers out of their war chronicles.

Black

Black Cronus (Saturn) has two sons, Poseidon (Neptune) and Zeus (Jupiter). Poseidon was the patron god of Atlantis.

Ancient Ethiopia has her queen, Cassiopeia, as a constellation in the heavens. No White woman is honored as such. God has given beauty power over strength; hence, the strongest man will yield to a woman.

For High School/College Placement Requirement

We should be starting a graduate and college placement expectation plus a draconian academic requirement for players—no class cutting and a 75-percent grade point average to participate. Your school is the second highest Regents-taking school after Brooklyn Tech; don't let these players escape academic excellence. Tell them to transfer now if they think being a player means stupidity. What's the point of winning if the kid can't even go to college?

Dropouts

Drop out of school, and like rappers who say "fuck school and college," which is saying fuck learning and knowledge, you get all these idiots in prison never asking for a book! Want the latest pair of fashionable sneakers, but never heard of Malcolm X or George Jackson? You're a political prisoner and are clueless. Some are real criminals and are so mentally fucked up they need to remain there.

An Open Letter to Anders (Norway Killer of Children)

History as propaganda: White racist superiority deems this delusional. Anders, your entire belief system is a lie, brought about by the indoctrination and falsification of world history where Whites were everything and everyone. Even Achilles of *The Iliad* was made White by a sleight of hand by interpreting that his hair was blond just like yours, Anders. Those early Greeks and Trojans were Blacks.

Now the press is reporting you as a far right-wing Christian. Is that true, Anders? Okay, question: where is the oldest church in Christianity? It's in Africa, Anders—the Coptic Church of Ethiopia. Yes, Anders, Jesus is Black there, as he and his mother were in all the churches of Europe. This changed after the Renaissance when a gay blade like you named Michelangelo painted a White Jesus. Until then, there was no such thing. Anders, there was nothing unusual about this because all of the gods and goddesses of the Greeks were Blacks, but Whites never portrayed them as such!

As a school boy you know that Cronus (Saturn) had two sons, Zeus (Jupiter) and Poseidon (Neptune). Saturn, of course, is Black (you can check with the Jews on that!). And we know that Zeus in literature is frequently referred to as the "Ethiop." Poseidon, who Whites call the patron god of the sunken legendary Atlantis, is obviously also Black, and the father of Hercules (Black). Anders, it gets better: you and your, no doubt, Nazi friends are on this "sons of Aryans" kick like Conan in Marvel comic books, and Whites are running with this from

Blavaskly's *The Secret Doctrine*. But wait a minute, the ancient literature of India claims the Buddha was of the warrior class of the Aryans, and so White. Being these celebrated Aryans is probably nonsense, and they were a minor sect belonging to that. Who came to power in a war with the Blacks, who they defeated, and passed their hegemony to another minor traitorous sect whom we call Hindus today? These Hindus wrote themselves into the ancient text to make themselves appear as the ancient rulers of India, but the ancient texts don't have to refer to Varna (color) as the Whites left when they were in power.

Anders, did I say how terribly cute you are? I looked at your Knights of Templar gear—ravishing before you got face powered. You should have gone through Umberto Eco's fine novel *Foucault's Pendulum*, cleverly discussing the occult history of Europe. If you did you would have understood that Christian Europe was for knowledge and wisdom, which they did not have. Jerusalem was the sidebar and the Arab world was in its flower.

Before I forget, since you are on this hate-the-Arab nonsense, as sections of White America are on the hate-the-immigrant bandwagon, the Renaissance in Europe, where you get your White Jesus, came out of Spain and spread east. Anciently, Spain (look at the people's description in Tacitus) you remember was a Carthegian colony. I suspect you heard of Hannibal. Barcelona carries the Hannibal family surname Barca. It was Hannibal's father, though, who made that imprint. Then the Moors were there for about 800 years. Now, Europe was in the Dark Ages and Islam brought them into the light! When the Spaniards finally drove the Moors out, they celebrated with the slaying of the black bull, which they continue to this day. They became a power in Europe and the Islamic learning they acquired came through Europe.

So Anders, what you consider European culture came through two African religions, Christianity and Islam. That all cultures came out of religion is not even a debatable issue. Now, Anders, the White strategy to world history, which in reality was the history of Black people in our slave captivity in America, was to make it the death penalty for reading, and when caught reading they would blind you! They had to keep who we were hidden. It became so intense with them that even today, in the twenty-first century, it is painful for them to say Egypt is in Africa. Anders, the ascendancy of Whites was done with guns, not culture (which came from elsewhere). They mowed down people who had guns, just like you did, Anders.

Hey Anders, did you see the *Thor* movie? I understand that some people were upset because Hemidall, the guardian of the Rainbow Bridge of Asgard legend, was Black! Everyone knows that the Scandinavian gods are all White. For after all, weren't all the Vikings White?

Anders, I hate to break your pink heart, but those early Vikings were Blacks, and we used to raid all up and down the north coast. I understand the term blackmail came from these raids. McRitchie talks about it in his book *Ancient and Modern Briton* (1875).

Torquemoda, I mean Anders, the Nazis used to liken themselves to the Ku Klux Klan in America. I see your actions as similar to the Republican Party in America. The American president, Obama, is acting a combination of Dr. Spock and a political Jackie Robinson. Like Dr. Spock, he indulges the Republicans as you would a spoil child, hoping bad behavior would improve through enabling. He's like Jackie Robinson because he thinks taking abuse in the long run will benefit his people, but Robinson's actions scarred his soul and led to a premature death. The Republicans, like Anders, have openly racist agendas and see no compromise necessary in their behavior, even under the guise of fiscal responsibility.

Now with the homosexual, butch Nazi movement we're into the god-man philosophy, but it lacked the spiritual underpinning to make it work, so we went to Tibet to get it. The Nazi homos were trying to imitate the homo-warrior cult we had going in Sparta—and it didn't work.* The Jews, notorious faggots, in all their papers will print pictures of gay weddings, gay parades, and gays holding hands and kissing. The Christian right had better wake the fuck up and ask themselves how many media outlets the Jews control. How is it that the words *Blacks* and *Whites* are easy to say, but not *Jew*? Upset when talking about Israel or some holiday, why are foreclosures taken care of in Israel by our tax money, but not for our Americans? How are all those Jew elephants sitting all over their living rooms in White America telling their daughters they can be stars in the adult film industry? Tell the Klan that Betty Lou and Sadie Mae are on the Spice Channel.

We Have Enemies

We have enemies that we have been at war with since the fall of Egypt and Cathage around 10,000 years ago.

We are the founders of all nations and languages on the planet (see *Anacalysis* by Higgins).

We once held sway over the entire globe. Our imprints are found over the entire Earth. All culture stems from us.

We are the Alpha and Omega of all things human.

The doctrine of the god-man wisdom religion comes from us (see *Stolen Legacy* by James).

You cannot be an American without a gun!

Our children are using guns and killing each other. How are we to stop this? Talking to them, showing videos, or preaching history and politics? No. Our families need to immerse themselves in American gun culture; form groups, become draconian toward our youth, and demand and tell them what they are to do. Warn those selling drugs in the communities they are headed for a swim with the fishes. Go into the schools and tell them we expect nothing but the highest scholarship effort from clowns. Hand out directions to the circus for those who wish to clown and not take the war against us seriously. We need scientists, mathematicians, agriculturalists, geneticists, and architects.

It is the duty of every Black man, woman, and child to develop themselves to the fullest to help in the redemption of the African people worldwide in general, and the redemption and unification of Africa in particular. College grads should get military training, be studious, and enter into the armed forces' academies. Go into Africa as a fifth columnist and remind the African what has happened to us from the Whites and Arabs. The unification of Africa will make the race strong globally. All commerce must be taken from the Whites into the hands of the Black Diaspora, so we can raise ourselves. We are one people.

We are going pro-patriotic. We are going to strengthen the empire, not weaken it. How do we do this? We denounce the homosexual movement as being a harbinger of the moral decadence of empire, along with pornography. We support the war efforts of the nation, not so much as we agree with it, but we must support our children who make up a percentage of the troops.

We are going to usurp the Illuminati doctrine of a one-world government! The world needs a one-world government, but not one in the hands of a White minority whose sole concern is the consolidation and control of the world resources, most of which are in the lands of Africa, Asia, South America, and northeast Africa.

Our logistical concern is getting guns to our people in South Africa. Our college grads need to go into the military to get training and then take it into Africa and work as fifth columnists to remind Africa what Europe has done there to our people (and the hated Arabs also). Remind them that the powerful people on the planet are all from United Nations—that the Whites want no trade between the Diaspora and Africa, something that all people do with their global brothers across the globe. Every Black man, woman, and child has a duty to lend in some way to the uplifting of the race: the Black race, the only race!

The Importance of Africa

For Black people to become a strong and feared people once again Africa must be united into one great nation. This will mean running the Whites out of the motherland, particularly in South Africa, with their Jewish allies and the Arabs toward the north. They came with force and must be removed with the same, i.e. war.

The African American must go to every Black nation and remind the people what the Europeans have done to Africa. And curse them out for not knowing the history of the Atlantic and slave trade call tribalism, a historical block to the unification of the continent. The Whites during American slavery literally beat it out of us, mixing the different tribes up so we would be less effective in communicating with each other to revolt against their barbarism. We must reclaim our ancient power and greatness. We are more than a century away if we do not use the gun culture of America.

We Need a Weapon

Meditation on the Ruins of Empire by Count Volney is the book where Volney said Blacks had the first civilization and named the

127

planets and the stars. The crackers edited that out of the text. When Volney, a Frenchman, learned English he made them put it back. The reason they didn't hide the book entirely is because it is a profound philosophical work on the aforementioned.

The second book is by Diop, called *Civilization or Barbarism*. This is an incredible research treatise, and the title gives it away. Diop is also the author of the classic *The Cultural Unity of Black Africa*, which obviously those motherfuckers in Rwanda have not read.

If we were on our game (a force within the political corridors of American power) what happened in Rwanda would never have taken place, for the petty power struggle there would have been replaced with us talking shit about the unification of Africa and running the fucking Arabs out of Africa. How disgraced are we that they hold sway in Egypt, the land of light, the monument to the unparallel glory of our ancestors?

Hey, the reason why we love those kung fu movies is that the central theme is always vengeance—Olu Sesan in Yoruba. In America, our vengeance is limited to asserting ourselves as a political force, which is possible since we are now claiming our American citizenship. However, when we arm ourselves there are two entities that we can exact a merciless vengeance against openly. This is the Klan and the Mafia. As to the Klan, we need not and should not take a posture of self–defense, but to use a popular American term, use "preventive warfare." We will find them and attack and destroy them wherever we can find them for the historical wrong they have done us. Do you think anyone in the country will wonder why we are pursuing such a course of action?

The Mafia humiliated us—it took the numbers game, housed it, put up the Cotton Club, let us sing and dance and not come into an establishment in Harlem. They fucked with us in Chicago also and many of the major American cities. After World War II, Lucky Luciano brought heroin into the Black families—which is their claim to fame. Oh, they are killers, but I think we can remedy that.

The bottom line is this—all that is or has been happening to us is because we are weak, which only means we have no guns. Pick up the gun. Kill or be killed. These scums think that we will be weak forever.

Moved from NYC

I just moved to Florida from New York (retired) and I am loving it. However, I am amused, but not surprised, at the love affair a "working class" state like Florida has with Republicans, who are generally against working class interests. Even the election of Rubio as senator is hilarious. There are pharmacies on every corner and they ridicule healthcare with the Obamacare description. They refuse federal dollars that can bring jobs to the state under the guise of "fiscal responsibility." Hey, the government has been bankrupt since the 1950s! Basically, let's not forget those are White people doing this, caught in a Civil War time warp, still flaunting the Confederate flag, the symbol of the attempt to destroy America and prolong slavery. The classic illustration of fighting against your own self interest for the interest of the rich (plantation aristocracy) is the so-called White, working-class Tea Party sponsored by the billionaire Koch brothers. The wealthy in this country have these Whites licking their boots.

150th Anniversary

Now that the 150th anniversary of the Civil War is here we can reflect on certain facts: it was the Black soldiers that carried the struggle to the Union's victory against traitors who wished to destroy the Union and prolong slavery that were winning the war. When the Black soldiers entered this conflict the situation was reversed. Today the descendants of these traitors and racists can be found in the Tea Party and among Glenn Beck, Hannity, GOP, and Fox News enthusiasts. The Whites, who made up the bulk of the Confederate Army, still historically act and vote against their own interests. White people do this—not Blacks—putting politicians in office who are against national health care and Social Security. Underlying all of this is the ignorant propaganda of White racial superiority, which the doctrine of segregation fostered, and which also created the myth of America as a White man's country. In a working class nation you have millions of White people who continually side with the rich, just as their ancestors did in the Civil War, fighting for the rich slave holders and plantation barons.

Speak As Men

We do not act and speak as men in America. What Black politician has denounced the government for the creation of the AIDS virus, linking it to the syphilis experiment in Tuskegee, and going further back to smallpox blankets given to the Indians? Then we have the World Health Organization spreading the virus in Africa under the guise of vaccinations. What Black politicians denounce the fact that governments control the global drug trade and that the so-called drug war is no more than a scam for the incarceration of the poor? How about the racist murder of a thousand Black soldiers in Mississippi in 1944 for their refusal to kowtow to military racism? How is it that Tim Wise is the only man in America using the language of racial politics? All political language in this country on our part should be racial, because that is the key to politics in America. Everything in this country is still segregated.

One Black man, Farrakhan, speaks the truth to America, and then only occasionally. Who else denounces the Jews?

The State of South Carolina

The state of South Carolina flies the Confederate flag on its capitol building. This is saying "fuck you" to America and Black people. *Make this a point of contention and racial and political conflict—but get your guns first.* Remember, we are taking the position of *pro patria*—only a state flag and the stars and stripes can have the distinction of adorning a capitol building. We give no honor to the symbol of traitors.

Any claim Whites have to honoring their ancestors means you are honoring rebels and traitors who sought to destroy this country and prolong slavery. That piece of shit flag dishonors the Union soldiers in general who fought for a United States of America, and our Black soldiers who turned the tide in that epic struggle.

Claim America

Once we arm ourselves, we can claim America! Right now the conservatives and Tea Party idiots claim this right as their own as the real Americans. We must denounce this and claim our first right as the people whose force of arms saved the union! This distinction belongs to the Black soldiers whose effort beat back the forces hell-bent on destroying the United States and spreading the most barbaric form of slavery ever to exist on Earth. These are the same elements who display the Confederate flag as a badge of honor for trying to destroy the Union. This is the history they are proud of, and whom we should denounce as contemporary traitors because their politic also reflects grade school racism and Republican JHS politics.

America is an empire whose global hegemony is pervasive. The Republican's domestic political agenda espouses a philosophy that government is too big! There are millions of White people who actually embrace this dogma along with openly racist, anti-working class propaganda, particularly in the Republican-dominated states.

Obama and Lincoln

Obama, like Lincoln, is enamored with politics and the art of compromise; like Lincoln, all his decisions are in the middle, and all that he wishes to concede to the other side is never enough.

Lincoln would have tolerated slavery if the South had been satisfied to not expand its territoriality (look at healthcare), but it wasn't. The same thing happened when the Civil War broke out. As in all of America's wars, the Whites wanted to keep the Blacks out of it, but as always, we played a decisive role, none more important than in the American Civil War when we saved the Union and ended slavery, which was the economic power of the South, and defeated White superiority on the field of honor and combat.

Lincoln, like Obama, refused to use the moral force of his office backed by the Abolitionist movement; and in Obama's case, the constituency that put him in office and issues of the aged, i.e., Social Security and national health care for all Americans.

Obama, like Lincoln, seeks to appease a White America by not strongly enforcing any policy that might be construed as favoring Black people. By doing so he gives strength to the notion and myth of a White superiority, which along with slavery led eventually to the American Civil War, which to this very day is the cause of America not reaching the destiny predicted for her.

Sidebar: Picture this—you have two sides, truth and ignorance. One side is to preserve the Union and abolish slavery, which has the country divided into two camps. The South, fighting to destroy the United

States (the Union) and expand slavery, was faced with the due consequence of Blacks joining this war on the side of truth. In 1863, ignorance was winning the war. Lincoln then issued propaganda, the Emancipation Proclamation, to scare the South, cleverly saying that the slaves in the states at war with the Union were free! Of course, he had no power over these states, but so what? To this, the Black soldiers joined the war. The forces of evil and ignorance were now faced with the descendants of Hannibal, fighting to free their brethren from slavery.

The Greatest Conspiracy on Earth

When we hear the word conspiracy we generally think of the secret societies—the Rosicrucians, the Masons, the Illuminati, etc., and how they control nations and preside over all relevant political assassinations—all of which is true. However, the greatest conspiracy extant on the planet is the plan to keep the history of the Black race as hidden and obscure as possible through any and all means. I could say Egypt is the most blatant, because bullshit White scholars can't even reconcile with Egypt being in Africa, let alone comprehend the profound metaphysics that flourish there. You cannot find an imprint on any nation on the planet where we have not left a mark. We founded nations all over the earth. Presently the Mexicans are the only people who have no problem saying we were there first, but maybe that's just because our statuary is all over the place in Latin America. But this is true of many places on this planet. All of this must be sought out with spiritual, scholarly, gun-bearing precision. Do you see this map below! When was the Ethiopian Ocean (Sea) changed to the Atlantic Ocean?

No Culture

The Whites have no culture save that of war, which by no means is insignificant.

The White Jews are at the height of their powers, even to the point of controlling the American armed forces. They control the money, so they have these Whites (gays) by the balls. The American people have never had control of the money since the inception of the Republic, when Lincoln tried to circumvent this with his issuance of greenbacks. He was assassinated. John F. Kennedy subtly tried, and he was assassinated also.

America is right now going through a period of social and moral decadence being pushed by the faggots with their same sex marriage bullshit and rampant pornography, with the Jews as the centerpiece of this garbage. Yeah, the pornography industry in Hollywood is run by Jews, having bubble-headed White girls proudly claiming "I work in the adult film industry" as a badge of honor. It was a Jew, Ralph Ginsberg, and his magazine *EROS* that won a court dispute that allowed pornography to flourish (was the ruling judge a Jew?). Pornography degrades women and no doubt is responsible for the increase in rapes and murders of women in this country. Other points of decline are women boxers and weightlifters.

First Wife

One day I was arguing with my first wife, and her retort on this occasion was, "You know a lot, but you are not doing anything with it." Women always know how to fuck with you. Her saying that (she's a Leo) really bothered me. I then told myself that I would write a book, but on what? This was in 1980. The next task was to decide what to write about. I thought, *There are millions of books written on Black people. Why don't I write something on White people?* This is how it started, but I kept adding different nuances to it, particularly the section on what war is. At that time when I finished, no one wanted to touch it, not even Third World Press. I couldn't understand why no one would be interested in a book that, among other interesting pieces, said that the Ancient Greeks were Blacks, which opened up to me from my incessant reading of *The Iliad.*

Having a love for ancient history, I started reading Greek and Roman histories to see what they had to say about White people. I had no idea what I was doing until I discovered that Whites were called Scythians by the ancients. Then all I had to do was trace this word in various texts; the results are in this book. I also found out that it's difficult to write about White people without including something on Black people, because White historians over the last few centuries have been claiming to be various people who were actually Blacks.

Since I was too divided among my many interests to publish myself, it has given me ample time to reflect on the solution toward the redemption of the Black race and our ultimate use of power in the twenty-first century.

Waging War

Given the nature of institutional racism, the accomplishments of the race are amazing. Imagine what will happen with us operating without the psychological stigma of fear and death and the bullshit notion and the internalization that America is a White man's country. The Tea Party, Fox News, the GOP, and Chief Justice Taney (1859) say "The Black man has no rights that Whites are bound to respect." White men could not save the Union; Black men did. America is what she is based on—the valor of the Black soldier in the Civil War. I say we finish this war and at the same time strengthen the empire.

Actual Policy of Murder

Although random, it's actual policy. The aim is to create an atmosphere of fear and intimidation to stifle us psychologically, and it works. So we have this, coupled with post traumatic slave syndrome, and we've become a basket case of numerous idiotic behavioral nuances including, but certainly not limited to, the clown personality. What the fuck is so funny? These White scums have come into ours homes and killed our grandmothers; come into the slave quarters and had sex with the wife and the daughter before the fathers with a gun in their mouths.

Before you start crying, consider this: in Sparta (Greece) we did the same thing to our White slaves, the Helots. We would go out and randomly murder them to keep them in check. In Sparta we had a homosexual warrior cult. Boys at the age of twelve would be taken from their parents and put into barracks, and these homo relationships would be encouraged, for they knew if their fighters were also lovers, then fighting side by side would make them formidable. They also thought that affairs between other men and boys were good for the political and social development of young Spartan fighters. Of course it was good, for the political and social development of young Spartan fighters was legendary. Apparently when this social nuance became practiced at Athens, these man-boy relationships, they passed a law forbidding it on penalty of death, and this was why Socrates was executed by being made to drink hemlock. We know all about faggots from our own personal and historical experiences. You can always measure the nature of a society by the role of women, who are considered the foundation of civilization. Don't forget the faggot and dyke shows that the Jews have on the television.

My thinking is this: the proclivity of a nation toward homosexuality is an omen, a harbinger for the decline of that nation, and history says this is so. The problem is that many of our families have homosexuals in them. Okay, that's not a problem with them, except when they try to project themselves into heterosexual social mores of the status quo, i.e., marriage. This cannot happen, if for no other reason than the aforementioned. We have an even more selfish reason. We need the American empire to be strong, and us strong in it, so as to influence the unification of Africa, which is tied spiritually to our strength as a people. We want to be strong in a strong America. This we can do politically, but not without picking up the gun. The gun initially used is a psychological prop to ward off the fear psychosis which prevents us from moving as strong men in American society.

Check this out: in America they have a policy of the random murder of Black people through the nation's police forces and racist hate groups. The history of Sodom and Gomorrah must be about us also.

The other piece to this is that homosexuality is anti-state. By this I mean the relationship does not produce children, which is the glory of the state and a function of the marriage state, which is why homos seek to adopt children. Can you be a family without children? Not in any traditional sense, and the family is a mechanism of the state. Faggots do very well in America, pushing their political agenda. They should be suppressed on the grounds of historical evidence and the need to prolong the duration of the Empire.

Disunity

Disunity has Africa divided. Disunity causes a White dyke to head the city council in New York City. This is disgraceful as we head into the twenty-first century in a city where we are the majority.* Our politicians are so stupid they can't even figure out the political consequences of gentrification. As your constituency changes, so will your political life.

One of our brothers on the Council had the nerve to say that the late Black nationalist, Sonny Carson, was a separatist. America is a separatist and apartheid nation. The schools, the cities, the churches— every community save a few are separatist enclaves. No one can represent us who doesn't understand this. Yes, politics is the art of compromise, but only if you understand that "politics is war without bloodshed and war is politics with bloodshed," as Chairman Mao put it. This is a country that has had more colonized people within an empire than any other. We have millions of men in the prisons of America. If we fail to act collectively, we doom future generations. Racism and oppression transcend class differences.

Confederate Honors—to What?

I see the descendants of the nineteenth-century blind Southerners are alive and well in Florida. I'm referring to those worshippers who fought to promote, prolong, and expand human slavery and destroy the United States. They fought for the wealthy (plantation owners) and put their reps in office against their own interests, as they did in the nineteenth century! I recently moved to Florida to see Governor Scott elected and another GOP idiot named Marco Rubio, both of whom are against working class interests in a working class state! But Whites across this country either can't read or watch too much Fox TV. Whatever problems Blacks have, we never vote against our own interests! It always a lesser of two evils with us.

The other piece is someone needs to remind these Southern idiots that the Black soldiers won the Civil War—*hello*. We ended human slavery and saved the Union, not these Tea Party pawns and their Koch brothers billionaire backers or the Confederate flag waving, dress-up fools whose ancestors ignorantly fought proudly for human slavery and the destruction of this great country. Southern apologist demagogues and the stupid like to romanticize the slave South as this noble, genteel, mint-julep-drinking Scarlett and Rhett Butler vision (*Gone with the Wind*).

Despite all of our triumphs as a people in American society, despite murder from all avenues/biochemical wars, and the consistency of a universal institutional racism, we have barely scratched the surface of what is to come with our entry in the American gun culture. We can operate in America without the slightest hint of fear of any kind, and all we have to do is kill some people! How easy is that! Imagine *Semper Fi*—remembering David Dinkins.

Black Face, White Mask: David Dinkins and the Politics of Acquiescence

Our need to have a Black face grace city hall has been a bitter disappointment. What we really wanted was a man, but we wound up with a simple-minded club politician afraid to speak the truth on any matter of substance. Dinkins was constantly trying to please a constituency that had nothing to do with voting him into office. His disgrace was trying to break the boycott of the Korean store in Brooklyn. Dinkins has (had) all the African American and Hispanic people behind him, and he ran scared. He was a bootlicking pawn of the White press. Don't forget, the Asian community voted against Dinkins. He only got 34 percent of their vote.

This is the situation: Governmental forces are going all out to incarcerate as many of our male/female youths as they can get their hands on. This is being done under the guise of combating drugs. However, the truth is that the governments is, and always has been, involved in the distribution of drugs in this country. The aim is to destroy the infrastructure and social fabric of the African American community. The issue is political, not moral or criminal.

Then there is a school system teaching White supremacy. A laboratory created the AIDS virus, coupled with a vicious White press preaching hatred and racism.

Presently there are six powers operating in New York City, and there used to be five. These are the police, the Mafia, real estate, banking, the media, and now the African American/Latino voting bloc. There must be either a hidden or open agenda to break the power of the police and the Mafia. Their war on us is open and without fear. It is possible to compromise with the real estate and banking interests because you don't want to alienate the money, but neither must you genuflect before them. The media must be denounced and ignored.

All the media is going to do is to inflame White fears—so what? Is there a way to please White people? Of course there isn't. They are raised in an environment of racial hatred. The Dinkins administration was not going to change that. No Black man in his right mind should cower to White media sickness. The so-called need for more police is a constant sham emanating from these sick dogs. Did Dinkins laugh and ridicule them? No. He caved in like a welfare peanut butter sandwich, making believe crime is not the effect of the social distribution of wealth, but a matter of increasing outside White New York City police power. Is this what we voted for? A man who let that racist city council attempt to humiliate Laura Blackburne, who was slated to head the New York City Housing Authority? The Whites did not respect Dinkins, no matter what he did. They don't care about the 200 million (people/$$$?) he is bringing to the city through the Demagogic Convention. They didn't care about King, Malcolm, Ida B. Wells, Charles Drew, Garvey, Strawberry, Booker T. Carver, Angela Davis,

Roberson, Dubois, or any person of worth. In fact, the more outstanding you are, the greater the hatred. All the above were vilified by the press. Better to treat the media like scum.

The worst commentary on all of the above is that Dinkins lost the respect of the very people who voted him into office. He has yet to speak on the Maddox[*] situation or call then-Mayor Koch down. One could argue that since Dinkins was the subject of an all out attack by the Whites, why should we further denounce him? After all, look at his appointments of Blacks and Latinos to various posts. This is shallow dressing. If Dinkins acted like a man that would attack, we would have been singing his praises and the Whites here would have trod more softly around him. Has he looked at the films of Nelson Mandela handling the press with total disdain and contempt—right?

Check this out: An analysis was done on Dinkins's first one hundred days in office. This was done by the Institute of Puerto Rican Policy Inc. The report was called "Cracks in the Mosaic" and it clearly demonstrates the butt-kissing antics of Dinkins.

During the first one hundred days Dinkins met with 34 percent Whites, 16 percent Blacks, 5 percent Puerto Ricans/Latinos, and 46 percent non-specific. What this really shows is that we have to come up with ways to make sure that the people that we put in office are accountable to us. We did not put Dinkins in office to show us how many yarmulkes he has. Dave the Slave got over a quarter of a million votes from the Black people in Brooklyn, and not only did he ignore this political hotbed, he had the audacity to come to Brooklyn to try to undermine a boycott because the White people told him it was hurting his administration—with who?

As a people we are weak because of our lack of organization. We need strong people to stand before us and show the children how to face and weather the storm. Perhaps Dinkins represents the weakness I see in myself, that is, *the fear*, the bane of Black men.

The XIII Amendment

Many people falsely believe that the Emancipation Proclamation freed the slaves in the United States. In fact the proclamation was considered by the military astute as the greatest propaganda effort of the Civil War. *The gist of the proclamation is that it frees all the slaves in the states that were at war with the Union.* Lincoln had no power over these states, so the proclamation was rhetorical propaganda at its finest. In fact, the slaves in the states that Lincoln had the power to free he did not free!

Presently the United Sates has the largest prison population in the world. With the fall of the former Soviet Union and apartheid South Africa, Americans had no competition in this field. That the richest and most powerful nation (empire) on Earth has the largest prison population must give cause for reflection.

Basically, prisons have one historic purpose wherever you find them: *the social control of the poor.* Although the state also uses it for the incarceration of ideological and political opponents, its primary purpose is for the incarceration of the poor. "Moreover, the sole invariable characteristic of the state is the economic exploitation of one class by another" (Nock, *Our Enemy, the State,* 1935). This truth is so obscured in American society that the average person would be hard pressed to define the class to which he belonged. The political thinking is that one is a Democrat or Republican, which is, simply speaking, the left and right of the ruling circle. Oswald Spengler pointed out in *The Decline of the West* how historically democracy is always ruled by the families of the rich, going as far back as Ancient Greece. Such insight has no impact on the political electorate in America. The reason for this is that class is obscured by the doctrine of race. Thus, you are White or Black or somewhere in between.

This brings us to the XIII Amendment which, like the Emancipation Proclamation before it, purports to officially free the slaves, but cleverly does not. It says: *"Neither slavery nor involuntary servitude, except as a punishment for the crime whereof the party shall have been duly convicted, shall exist within the United States or any place subject to their jurisdiction."*

I submit that the prison population, which has over one million Black men incarcerated, is a manifestation of the constitutional legalization of the reinstitution of slavery in the United States. Black men are convicted and jailed for crimes that White men do not ever go to court for. The criminalization of Black people in American society is documented in Charshee McIntyre's *Criminalization of a Race.*

Legislative Caucus

Kind Sir,

Black people have more political representation than at any point in our history in the United States. Yet the economic gap between Whites and Blacks is not decreasing, but actually widening!

Follow my argument: There are two methods, or means, and only two, whereby man's needs and desires can be satisfied. One is the production and exchange of wealth; *this is the economic means*. The other is the uncompensated appropriation of wealth produced by others; *this is the political means*. The former was explained very well by Marx, and the latter for our purposes is the history of our enslavement in the United Sates.

The problem with Black politicians is their failure to explore the political means as do their White counterparts (i.e., controlling economics for the benefit of their group).

Numbers dictate we should control the political machinery of New York City. This correspondence relates to how we can do this and the law that is needed to bring it to fruition. The sole intent is to use the political means to control and dominate the civil service apparatus and as a result the subsequent wealth therein for our group. There is nothing unusual in this aim. Other ethnic groups have done the same as they have grown to power in this city. This is historic. Every means, legal and illegal, will be put in place to keep us from doing so.

We need a law in place that requires all citizens to vote. Such a law would give a Black/Hispanic coalition the keys to the city, i.e., the board of education, the police, the fire department, the board of elections, contracts, the judges, etc. Elected office is about scheming for these things, and this is normal! If Black elected officials aren't doing this, what are they doing? The political means is to acquire wealth with the least amount of effort. Are you not tired of slavery, jails, and unemployment for our group? The jails used to be full of Irish, and then they became the police! We can do the same with the proper exercise of the political means.

The irony is that our enemies will have to come out against the law, calling it undemocratic or saying you have a right not to vote! Citizenship should require the exercise of certain duties, one of which should be voting *by law*.

Listen, if I told you that my cousin with a family of four just came to town and needs a job, could you get him one tomorrow? Could you get him a decent place to live? Therein lays the problem. The daycare center, the nursing home, the youth center—this is what you call politics? These are symbols of our ineptness. Please respond as to the feasibility of my observation.

Until Victory,
Dennis James Watson

A Farewell to Arms?

War is the father of all things.

—Heraclitus

There has been a rash of shootings, fratricidal, in which a number of youths have lost their lives. An assembly of voices, individuals as well as in unison, is calling on the youths to turn in their arms and desist from this random violence. The Black community, led by the activist clergy, are preaching an insidious idea of non-violence that was murdered in Memphis over twenty years ago. No one is asking the youths to turn their arms against our enemies. I suspect this is because too many people are either brainwashed or simple-minded, believing force and violence to be evil under any circumstances.

Why such thinking still remains among us is a mystery, considering the publication over thirty years ago of Franz Fanon's classic *The Wretched of the Earth*. Fanon pointed out very clearly why the oppressed engage in fratricidal mayhem. This phenomenon exists wherever there is oppression, and there exists no means to punish the oppressor (at least in the mind). Violence then becomes internalized, and we have historically seen the results, although many would have us believe that this is new among us. If our war veterans and leaders weren't so sissified they would try to direct this energy outward.

Organized force, that is, military organization, is the underlying principle for the formation of the state and of state power itself. It was force and violence that enslaved the race. It was force and violence that liberated us from bonded slavery (the valor of the Black soldier during the American Civil War). Despite everything you have read about, if we did not foolishly turn in those guns after that conflict, we would be a free people today. Take the guns from the kids—you must be mad. Huey Newton used to say that "an unarmed people are subject to slavery at any given time." Is that true or false? The youth of today is the first generation since those brothers who fought in the Civil War who are not afraid of guns. What about the killings, you say? More of our children are being murdered in the public schools. The education of our youth in those schools is murderous, barbaric, and savage.

The other day my daughter told me that a teacher in LaGuardia High School of the Performing Arts boldly told her class that the ancient Egyptians were not Blacks. That's not what Herodotus said and that's not what Plutarch said (Plutarch wrote an essay on Osiris saying he was a Black god, and every English translation of that essay that I have read has edited that fact out. The reason I know this is because other learned men have written about that fact in their books). Diodorus said the Egyptians were Blacks, and so did Juvenal in his *Satires*, calling them "mud faces." Count Volney did as well in *Mediation on the Ruins of Empires* (in this book Volney said the Black race founded civilization. The Americans edited that out. When Volney, a Frenchman, learned English and discovered what they did, he made them put it back in). Then there is also Geoffrey Higgins's *Anacalypsis* and Gerald Massey's *The Book of Beginnings* and *Egypt, Light of the World*. The ancient Greeks were also Blacks! However, the point is, if you don't know who you are, or don't think you are anybody, it is easier to kill your brother, who is yourself. So for me "scholastic murder" if far worse than these fratricidal killings.

Beloved, the duty of men is to protect. The inability to do this is the underlying psychological cause of our fratricidal behavior. We can't protect our children, our women, or ourselves. So we fake a false bravado, masking our fear of White men—we fear them. At least our children are not afraid to pick up the gun, and they may yet save us. As men we are defeated. We let a White Irish Catholic cop kill a grandmother with a shotgun (he also got promoted). You know her name, you Kool-Aid-hearted motherfuckers. We have shown an historic reluctance, fear, and inability to organize force to protect our own, and have the nerve to want respect. We don't deserve it. Then you sissies try to hide behind *The Black Man's Guide to Understanding the Black Woman* and try to blame our sisters for our shameless conduct. To enslave a race the *men* must be defeated, not the women. Fabre D'Olivet stated in his book that "it has been seen how war is always inevitable between the two races, because the races all strive for the dominion and usurpation of the earth. Developed much useful knowledge in the White race, and put it in condition to struggle advantageously against the Black race." What is the Mafia—organized force? If we organized force, would the Italians be stronger than us? The police?

Of course we have our pundits who swear by money and who will say that the problem is economic development, forgetting that military organization precedes economic development. This is why it is said that "he who controls the iron (the manufacture of weapons) controls the gold." If you don't believe this, ask the Jews. Historically, wherever the Jews were strong economically, force removed them. Now they have Israel, a military state, and you can't take anything from them. Meanwhile, the West will look for another Black man to give the Nobel (the inventor of dynamite) Peace Prize to. Are we suckers or what?

Robert Williams, who wrote *Negroes with Guns*, had to leave the country and live in China for almost twenty years behind that book. Do you recall seeing it at your local bookstore? White vigilante terror and state terror (the police) has made us craven cowards and fools.

A certain professor Jefferies, who once chaired the Black Studies Department at City College in New York City, made much of a book called *The Iceman's Inheritance*. This book, written by a White Canadian, seeks to explain through environment why Whites are so murderous, destructive, and greedy. Jefferies, using the book as ammunition, postulates the Ice Culture versus the Sun Culture. He refers to the Whites as the warrior/barbarians. Naturally, the Sun Culture is better than the Ice Culture. However, he should also say, as

Josephus said in *The Jewish War*, "It was unchallenged and immutable law among beast and men alike, that all must submit to the stronger, and that power belonged to those supreme in arms."

Who has ruled this world longer, us or the Whites? Serious research would reveal that the Black race ruled this world far longer than any other people. How did we do it? With peace? I doubt it. We kept the Whites from civilization for so long, and they still hate it. Acknowledged or not, there still is something called karma, the doctrine of cause and effect. I submit that just like we don't know of our rulership on the planet, we also don't know the depth of what we actually did to the Whites. But, based on our history in America, we must have dogged them. We definitely used to take their women from them—"The sons of god who mated with the daughters of men who were fair."

If you read the first page of *The Odyssey* by Homer, you will see that the Black race dominated both the Eastern and Western hemisphere. Incidentally, *The Iliad* and *The Odyssey* are about Black people. We need to teach the superiority of our history and culture, but this should not be separated from our present situation and the fact that we are dominated by those who have organized force and violence. Dr. Welsing reminds us that chess is a war game of the White king against the Black king—and White moves first.

This is the doctrine: One armed man can control ten; ten, a hundred; a hundred, one thousand; one thousand, ten thousand; you get the picture. Armed men rule the world and have always done so. In the classic poem "Prometheus Bound," Black Prometheus is taken by the henchmen of Zeus, who by name are called Force and Violence, to Scythia, the land of the White race, and is nailed to a rock. What this shows is that even the gods use force and violence.

King failed. America has no moral consciousness. The Russian writer who once lived in Vermont has called America a "moral wasteland." If marching in Bensonhurst or Teaneck gets you off, you are misguided; for it certainly has not stopped them from killing us, has it? You can call it creative tension if you want, but we are being humiliated as men. The men who are humiliating us are armed men. Is marching the proper response for naked murder? Marching and crying are the same things. Yielding is the same thing. The guilty will go unpunished.

The kids are out of control because we have no organized force to contain and teach them. Why don't you tell the cops to turn in their guns? More cops die by suicide than in the line of duty, so what is the point of them having guns?

This polemic is not a call to overthrow the United States. We can't do that, but we can protect ourselves and make those who abuse us pay dearly.

Tony Brown has come up with a brilliant idea about how 150 Black organizations, if they had given up their annual conventions in 1992 and used the money to purchase major hotels in various cities, could start some real economic development. As clever as Mr. Brown's idea is, it will not come to fruition because of two things. The first is the Othello syndrome—that is, jealousy and a lack of self-worth. We have everything, just like Othello. It is more than likely that Shakespeare knew who we really were and saw the cause of our downfall, as seen in Othello. The second reason is that we don't have organized force that could simply tell these organizations that they must carry out Brown's idea or pay the piper.

Sports and Play in Culture

All mammals play. This is endemic in nature—cats, dogs, dolphins, mice, monkeys, and of course man. The importance of play/sports has always been an essential element in the culture of men since time began. In Frazer's *The Golden Bough*, he cites numerous accounts of kingdoms and the hands of beautiful princesses that were won by feats of strength and speed. Diodorus, the renowned Greek historian, starts all of his chapters in his histories with the winner of the marathon in a particular year.

If one were to look in the dictionary for the definitions of play, the meanings are so numerous and differentiated you would be hard pressed to decide which was the best. Play at first is associated with the activity of children, but this is misleading. The global world of sports is adult play. This kind of play is very serious. The Incas had a ball game where the losers would have their heads cut off!

For men, a sport is the great metaphor because it mirrors the vicissitudes of life. Sport metaphors are legion in all cultures across the earth. Nature, it seems, appears to continually challenge itself through play, which is easily discerned through the sports of men.

The psychological mood of great cities and nations has been found to be linked to the winning and losing of particular sport teams! The psychological importance of sports/play cannot be understated. The principles that underlie sports unconsciously are the same principles that govern success in life, but the correspondence escapes most people. Science itself is based on experimentation and repetition, and so are sports. You have to experiment to get the proper chemistry on the playing field, and you must repeatedly practice your plays until you get them right. Repetition, it should be said, strengthens the will.

What is the greatest endeavor/hardship men can face on Earth? The answer of course is war! Sports teams constantly evoke the jargon of war when preparing for games. Sports writers call team members "warriors." They call the game a "battlefield." "Being carried out on your shield" means giving your all. One of the most famous quotes in war history was made by the Duke of Wellington when he was questioned about the defeat of Napoleon at Waterloo. Wellington said, "The battle was won on the playing fields of Eton," thus evoking the memories of boyhood competition through sports. All nations practice war "games." In life, the play scenario is always at work.

The importance of competition also plays a significant role in character development. Competition further strengthens the character by teaching the lesson of losing. Losing hardens the personality against the struggles in life. It gives the ability to bounce back from failure. It makes one capable of dealing with disappointment. Life has no favorites; one cannot win all battles. In sports the best players and the best team do not always win. In life you can do your best and lose. You can be the best man and still lose the girl. You can be the best student and not get the best grade. Parents cannot teach these lessons, but sports can.

Lastly, the greatest, and clearly the most significant, aspect of sports is overcoming the self. When all is said and done, it is not the other team or individual that you must overcome, but yourself. This is why our sports figures are better known than doctors, inventors, presidents of nations, saints, etc.

I Smell Pussy

You do realize that our kids are running around with guns and killing each other straight out of Fanon's *The Wretched of the Earth*, his *tour de force* on the psychology of oppression close to and similar to Leary's *Post Traumatic Slave Syndrome*? We (adults) are afraid of them! Do you really think that would be as serious problem as it is if we were an armed people? Black people are so psyched out that they actually believe that guns are the domain of White people only. How are we going to get gun-carrying youths under control if we don't have guns ourselves? Explain that to me. Talking to them is a waste of time. We can't even convince them to pull their pants up, which unconsciously is saying, "We have no place in society". Even in a place like Chicago, where Blacks seem to have more political savvy than we have in New York, the youth are still buck wild and out of control. *We need guns to control and protect our self interest as a people.* We are still operating under Chief Taney's 1859 ruling: "The Black man has no rights that Whites are bound to respect " Court rulings, marches, and freedom riders have yielded very little substance.

After the Civil War, they shipped those Black soldiers west and turned those guns against the Indians, leaving the Black freed slaves defenseless against Southern lynching and murder. Armed Whites would go house to house to make sure Blacks had no guns.

Emmett Till's murder still haunts us, as does the church bombing that left three girls dead, Medgar Evers, Martin Luther King Jr., Fred Hampton, Denmark Vasey, and Nat Turner. You know what? I smell pussy!

Jonathan Jackson was seventeen when he went down in a hail of gunfire trying to free some brothers. His brother, George Jackson, was later murdered in prison for his prowess as a writer for his Black tome, *Soledad Brother*. This is not the 1930s nor Russia in 1917. There is no left in this country. The right I call MSBC leftist. Racism dominates the class struggle. In the last presidential election you had an over-the-top intellectual running against Donald Duck and Mary Poppins. The latter got sixty-six million votes—the "I am White" vote.

The Secret Destiny of the Black Race in America

In Manly Hall's book *The Secret Destiny of America*, he claims as far back as ancient Egypt they knew that a land existed in the west that would someday lead the global world government. He further states that this is also indicted in the symbolism of the dollar, with the eye of Providence and the pyramid, both of which come out of Egypt, but no mention was made of that fact. More than a few secret societies, including the infamous Illuminati, claim this same idea. Most people came to America of their own volition; Blacks were dragged here against their own volition. Blacks were dragged here by guns, whips, and the chains of pirates.

> One of the curious things about these progenitors of ours is that though avowedly searching for peace and happiness for political and religious reasons, they began by robbing, poisoning, murdering, almost exterminating the people to whom this vast continent belonged. Later during the gold rush, they did the same thing to the Mexicans as they had done to the Indians. And when the Mormons sprang up they practiced the same cruelties, the same intolerance and persecution upon their own White brothers.

Every person in the world should have freedom from want, freedom from fear, freedom of worship, etc. Only a world government with sufficient military power to police all nations and protect the small as well as the large from aggression can do this. The reason why Whites cannot accomplish such a lofty aim is that they are basically haters of men and see themselves as separate from other men. What group of men practices apartheid except them? Conquerors in all the ages of men mixed with the people they conquered except them. Their scientists have concocted childish theories of color and race and polluted the world community. This is partly our fault because we kept them away from the civilized world for millennia. The end game here is for us to lead America into the dawn of a new age unprecedented in human history, including the galactic war with aliens for the dominion of the earth, which the government has openly been preparing America for with these alien invasion films and weapons testing in Iraq and

Afghanistan. Ironically, the White Americans are best prepared to fight because they are armed to the teeth, and we must do the same thing.

The Gun Culture of America

In order for us to manifest as men (the ability to protect self and kind) we must immerse ourselves in the gun culture of America.

Why? All of the psycho-social nuances that affect us as a people, from education to bullshit criminality, are rooted in fear. The psychology of the gun eliminates this emotional psychosis which cripples us in degrees unimaginable. We live in a nation with well over a hundred million armed White people. That figure does not include White women and children, who are also part of the American gun culture. This enhances their boldness, as our history of lynching and race murders is ample proof, coming to a public forum where the president is speaking openly brandishing weapons. We tend to think of this as sick, but it is not sick! We better get sick with them. The Constitution says we have a "right to bear arms," and we should do so immediately.

We can never be men if we are unable to speak and act as men. Malcolm and King were assassinated for this because they were isolated within a culture of Black pussies. Who is standing up and speaking the truth? Farrakhan and White boy Tim Wise!

Get a copy of *Post Traumatic Slave Syndrome* by Joy Degruy Leary, Ph.D., but forget Chapter 6, which is on healing. The only healing we need lies within the American gun culture. By doing so, we take away the White initiative through their institutions of murdering us. I say institutions because I don't just mean the police, the Klan, and the White Citizen Council, but also the courts, the politicians, corporations, and any and all organizations which seek our debasement. You do remember when Hollywood gave Three 6 Mafia an Academy Award for music for "Pimping Ain't Easy." This was the Jews goofing on us, obscuring the fact that *all* American music comes from us. How about that female federal judge who said the rights of Black people were not violated when a local sheriff refused to let Black people escape Katrina through his town? If we were an armed people could that kind of shit have happened to us?

Listen very carefully: Professor Smalls and Dr. Jefferies (race men) said on WBAI one night that the race has been at war for 10,000 years! We have ruled this planet far longer than that! Of course we could wait the Whites out; they are hell bent on destroying themselves. However, there is the problem of Africa. Her fall and our fall are connected. As she rises, so do we in the Diaspora. Therefore, it is the duty of every Black man, woman, and child to lend in some way to contribute to the uplifting of Africa in particular and the race in general. What has happen to us is that over the centuries we have been used as cannon fodder for various nations in their wars, which is why you find certain South American countries with few Blacks in them. America is no different. We have lost our military ardor in defense of our own interests and we need to rekindle a military spirit in regard to our own self interest and America can help with this.

How? Our children need to become scholarly and get into the military academies, join the armed forces, and have in the back of their minds that they are training for service to Africa and the race. We also must become stronger in America, but not in a morally bankrupt and decadent society. We must become somewhat conservative so we can get into the political corridors of the nation's foreign policy. We want and shall demand the African Desk and openly support her interest, which in the long term will be greater for America than fighting proxy wars for the Jews.

We are going *pro patria*. We are going to strengthen the empire, not weaken it. How do we do this? We denounce the homosexual movement as being a harbinger of moral decadence in historical empires, along with pornography. Since the philosophical ideals of the homosexual lifestyle, the man-boy doctrine, came from those Black Greeks, we are best qualified to speak of its pitfalls.

Life is Spiritual, Not Material

All nations have a spiritual underpinning, but life itself is spiritual, not material. Why has communism failed? They recognize civilization as economic and define man in his relationship to production. However true that is, there is no spiritual underpinning and failure is inevitable.

Man is a spiritual being, even if he doesn't know it. In ancient Egypt, the religious, the philosophical, and the scientific were one.

In Greece, the spiritual underpinnings of the state were the oracles. When they declined so did the state. Plutarch has an essay called "The Decline of the Oracles." The homosexual "butch" Nazi movement was into the God-man philosophy, but lacked the spiritual underpinning to make it work, so they went to Tibet to get it (true story). The Nazi homos were trying to imitate the homo-warrior cult we had going in Sparta (read *The Pink Swastika*) and it worked for a while. The man-bitch at war is cruel and vicious. Most people think the Nazis hated homosexuals. They hated the feminine type, not the macho Village People type.

The Jews, notorious faggots who dominate the media, will start printing pictures of gay weddings, of them kissing, holding hands, of gay parades, and use the electronic Jew* to continue showing gay sitcoms and shows like *The L Word*. Bobby Fisher said the Jews control America, but the White Christian is sitting next to the Jew elephant in his living room saying to his wife, "What do the Blacks want?"

Indaba, my children: What is called Greek history is ours and we cannot shy away from the homosexual doctrine that flourishes there, particularly among the Spartans with their warrior homosexual cult. There is much written about this save the fact that these were Black people. Also, the reputation of the looseness of Spartan women begins to make more sense when you figure the bisexuality of the men those times must have been rampant.* All of this is to say we know about the "faggot" thing and are saying in the long term this is not good for the state. Even in the situation in Sparta, the men had to couple with women so the state would have children! Our beef with same sex marriage is that it does not produce children for the state, so the gays want to adopt children to be a family. Children are the glory of the state and the family is a microcosm of the state. America is not Sparta; gay marriages are in essence anti-state because these unions don't produce children. Somewhere it says "be fruitful and multiply." Of course you find gays in all walks of human life, and some very famous, but so what? They are in our families (my family too). So what? We love them as people. Their sexual lifestyle is their business, but we have no intention of celebrating it within the culture. Our history tells us not to. Malachi York, in one of his last scrolls, claims to have found the genetics of homosexuality! This is deep.

A brother is now in a government prison in Colorado on child molestation charges that his followers say are false. The Rasters hate him, calling him a faggot, but the government locked him up, I think, because of his extensive knowledge of past and present alien involvement on Earth. Oh, you didn't know about aliens? Get off your ass and do some research. Nancy Fullwood has an interesting piece on the spiritual karma of homosexuality in her book *The Song of Sano Taro*. Another important book that I hear was panned by a gay Jew night show host is *The Pink Swastika*. This will clear your mind about the Nazis. The authors are Scott Lively and Kevin Abrams.

What the fuck do we look like, champions of homosexual rights? Our biggest issue is *manliness*, duh! Get a fucking gun(s). That's our problem, acting like faggots, allowing these ethnic Whites to fuck us, afraid of our children because they have guns and we don't. It's the reason we call the cracker the *man*. Our time may be coming because it is getting popular to say "man up." My translation of this is to join the American gun culture before they make an amendment to the Constitution. Most of you don't know this, but Clarence Thomas made a ruling explaining why a Black man should have a gun—check it out!

The absolute worst guy in a cowboy movie is the guy selling guns to the Indians. These were men trying to help the Indians from being exterminated because they had no weapons to defend themselves. Plaxico Burress went to jail for shooting himself in a New York City night club! What! He should have challenged the gun laws that jailed him, because they are different in many states. The Constitution says he can carry a gun. It does not say where he cannot. If it did, they would not have jailed him. Burress was jailed because he was Black and they don't want Blacks and Indians with guns.

Duties of Students (HS/College)

Harken, you gods and goddesses of the ancient world. Have your parents ever told you we have enemies? Have they ever discussed slavery in America and what was done to us? It was so vicious, barbaric, and inhumane, that from guilt the White world is an armed camp, waiting for a war of retribution. We are given Nobel Peace Prizes while entire White families are trained in the use of weapons. Wake the fuck up. What is our response to the Tuskegee experiment with syphilis on our people over a forty-year period? What is our response to the manmade virus, AIDS, and the World Health Organization spreading it throughout Africa in the guise of vaccinations? What is our response to the "change doctrine" as outlined in this book, where everything that was ours they claim as their own?

We need scientists, not rappers (we are a race of poets and dancers; Dubois commented on this in his classic *Black Reconstruction*). We need math majors, physicists, engineers, geneticists (not to create another White man!), architects, historians, and doctors. Listen: it's important for all of you to read Herodotus and Diodorus so you can grasp the legacy of the race, while many of us have developed into basket cases of intellectual cowards ("I can't learn this or that"), petty fucking criminals, homo thugs, women haters, and the women, man haters. We have males who believe being a pimp is a noble endeavor. What we need out of these gangster types are soldiers willing to put people in the ground who are against the self interest of the race, not for drug turf, or a "look," or jealousy, or better looking, etc.

Who is going to create a virus against our enemies effective on people with no melanin?

Some will argue falsely, "How I could be *pro patria* given what America has and continues to do against us?" For the same reason the ancients had a geocentric view of the universe, not the Catholics, who for 200 years hid the fact that the earth revolves around the sun, but the principle that "where you are is the center." In martial arts, the direction that you're facing is north, regardless if it is south, west, or east. Don't forget we have a destiny to fulfill here in the creation of a one-world government. The wisest of the Whites have tried with the League of Nations and the United Nations, but the United Nations is hated by White people—they just don't get it, and then racism has made them unfit to lead and has bored them in a corner. Dealing with the Chinese must be killing them! Can you remember when the US had no relationship with China, the most populous nation of Earth? What kind of foreign policy was that? Look at Cuban policy.

Going back to the students: how many chemistry, biology, and physic majors do we have? How many of them ever get together to discuss the AIDS virus aimed at us? It is trying to depopulate Africa. It's called biochemical warfare and some of our brightest people in the sciences haven't the faintest notion of responding to this. You piece of shit cowardly fuckers, whatever your major—change it. Do something in the sciences and math to help our people. Carver asked the peanuts, "Why did God make you this way?" And the peanut told him how to figure it out! The rest is history!

Immersion into America Gun Culture

This immersion into the American gun culture must be a family outing, just like our White counterparts in America. Our veterans must open gun clubs for our people and teach the safety of weapons. Again, we do not speak and act as men in America. The government policy of arbitrary murder of our people is to instill fear, as is the inability to protect our family from hostile ethnic forces, the Tuskegee syphilis experiment, the genocidal AIDS onslaught, our children with guns, and the murder of 1,000 soldiers in Mississippi in 1944.

Veterans

The Golden Age of Black Nationalism: 1850-1925 states, "In every war since the American Revolution, Black people and their leaders have been beguiled by the idea that fighting the nation's battles would inevitably lead to an improvement in the status of Black Americans."

Humiliating

There are American arms, Russian arms, Chinese arms, Vietnamese arms, Israeli arms, and Cuban arms. By "arms" is meant military prowess. Has anybody heard of African arms? The Africans have guns, but they are tribal, selfish, jealous, and aimless, lacking in racial consciousness. China had similar growing pains, but was helped by the invasion of China by the Japanese, which forced unity among the warlords, nationalists, and communists.

Zulus

Hey Zulus, have you ever heard of a place called Ireland? English settlers went there in the twelfth century. The English came from a cold, rainy, windy, foggy place of an island with no natural resources to speak of. They got on boats and went all over the world, killing natives and settling in places where people had more than they did. The Irish are still fighting them, but they won't leave. Don't forget our children, the various nation states have been warring against us for 10,000 years. Untold millions have died. The Europeans and Arabs have devastated us during this period.

We are unarmed and subject to any and all humiliations. Disgracing the names of our forefathers, we are shamed in front of our women constantly. Is it any wonder that our women hold us in contempt, secretly and openly (*Colored Girls Who Contemplated Suicide When the Rainbow Wasn't Enuf*)? Black men treat their women badly in response to being afraid to organize violence against the death forces in defense of the race, or some political objective, or just plain revenge!

Wars are to be undertaken in order that it may be possible to live in peace without molestation.

—Cicero, De Officiis

All violence should be aimed at acquiring local power, and all should be done without *braggadocio*. Our race does not lack talkers, so violence will have its defenders and detractors. The local power concept is based on the ability to control the police in a given community. Any group that is able to control the police within its boundaries will demonstrate its capacity for organized violence, and therefore political leadership. Is this so difficult to understand? We shall never control the destiny of our race unless we first demonstrate our ability to control the very streets and communities that we live in. This can be done by organized violence and only by violence. The Black man is not voting his way to respectability—fighting is what gives men respectability, not cleverness in rhetoric, useful though this might be. Organized violence by Black people will signify a qualitative jump in consciousness, and we will be reckoned a serious political force. It is simply a matter of killing.

Malcolm said that we were afraid to bleed! Do we have any men willing to kill and die for the race? The ancient Egyptians held that the truth is in the living. Meanwhile, we will continue to cry for a "theoretical framework" while they murder us daily.

Princes ought, therefore to make the art of war their sole study and occupation for it peculiarly the science of those who govern . . . By neglect of this art it is that states are lost and by cultivating it they are required.
—Machiavelli, *The Prince*

There are circumstances in war when many cannot attack the few, and others when the weak can master the strong.
—Sun Tzu, *The Art of War*

You fools—the "fool" is the first tarot card. A symbol of undifferentiated consciousness, it pictures a man heedlessly getting ready to walk off a cliff, smiling all the way. He appears a fool, but the smile indicates that he knows there is no death! Of necessity, the wise always appear foolish to the unlearned. Don't you know that people love fighters more than any other kind of man? Why do you think the heavyweight champion is the most popular man in the world? Do you remember the reception the Jewish soldiers received when they rescued the hostages in Uganda at Entebbe Airport? Even Jew-haters applauded this act because it was brave, daring, and successful. People admire men who fight for what they believe in, as opposed to talking about it! It has already been pointed out that a fighting organization is the only true identity card of a nation struggling for its liberation. (Remember, speech is silver but silence is golden, for a warrior is a fighter, not a rhetorician.[*])

On the local level, the police, the Mafia, and Jews are the enemies in the eternal power struggle. The first two use force and coercion so they can only be opposed through arms—is this clear? The third uses deceit and legal chicanery. This should be a *silent* war.

157

War is the principal motivational force for the development of science at every level from the abstractly conceptual to the narrowly technological.

—Report from Iron Mountain

The rule of class warfare in America since 1865 is *silence.*

In Sun Tzu's *The Art of War*, "doctrine" is the fifth most important factor in waging war. Again, the idea that we must organize around a political philosophy is bullshit. *We must organize around the need to use violence and participate in a war that is already being waged upon us by the state and the different ethnic groups who struggle for power in America.* What philosophy do these other groups espouse other than self-interest? Do we need more than this?

The results of organized violence will lead to effective political leadership, in that political aims can be backed by force, implied but never open. At the same time, we should deny the existence of any violent organization whose aims are political! In fact, we should denounce all acts of violence, appeal to reason, and appear rational in view, and meanwhile wage selected warfare—isn't this what they do to us?

In Hakis's book *Enemies* he says, "We can't out violence the White man." War is not a question of the amount of violence but of how, when, and where. First, we must make ourselves strong before we can fulfill any lofty ideals. (Most of us do not even work out, we eat too much meat, we are sexually overindulgent—mental energy and sexual energy are the same energy—and it is either up or down. Where is yours?) Inasmuch as we are not in the position to overthrow the armed forces of the United States, I would suggest playing local cloak and dagger to serve immediate economic-political ends and to get practice.

Where are our killers, men-slayers, and race lovers—do we only kill when ordered to by White men or moved by the passions, like children? Even the Jews in New York have organized themselves for violence. Is it any wonder these people think we are children? "Political power grows out of the barrel of a gun," as Chairman Mao said, not out of ideology.

As long as there is a division of labor there will be classes in society.
— Protocols of the Wise Elders of Zion

The Russians are nationalists just like everybody else. Let me rephrase this — all nations, large and small, are nationalist. Nationalism is the key idea that characterizes the political epoch in which we live. The world is a gladiatorial arena of struggling nationalisms. Remember the talks about international brotherhood? But what about US? It is good to profess these things, like the Chinese and the Russians, giving lip service only. The American presidency is talking about human rights — say one thing, but do the other. This is how the game is played. In America we could get away with murder if we played the game this way. Some classics in rhetoric are "there is no such thing as the Mafia," and "America is a free and democratic society," and "the situation is difficult though not impossible," and "I'll call you," etc.

The Italians are murderers of the lowest sort, yet these dogs are romanticized in the movies for two reasons: people relate to violence, and the Mafia believes in public relations. Mafia activities include assassination, extortion, pimping, kidnapping, murder, loan sharking, theft, pornography, and gambling, but more than this, they are Italian nationalists. They do what they do for the elevation of their group and the economic gratuity that goes with it.

We must clean house, build unity among the herd and rekindle trust, make a pact with Yama (the god of death), read the Bagavagita, and reflect on Fanon's immortal first sentence in *The Wretched of the Earth* ("National liberation, national renaissance, the restoration of nationhood to the people, commonwealth; whatever may be the heading used or the formulas introduced decolonization is always a violent phenomenon").

War is the highest form of struggle for resolving contradictions, when they have developed to a certain stage, between classes, nations, states, or political groups, and it has existed ever since the emergence of private property and of classes.
— Mao, *Selected Works, Vol. II*

The US president wears a business suit and he is commander in chief of the armed forces. We had better wake up. We will never control the schools until we control the streets. We must begin to plan our ascension based on two things: the use of force and the cultivation of the art of concentration. This can be done by studying *The Spiritual Sciences*, meditation, yoga, Tai Chi, Kabbala, and other ancient arts of the Black race, especially all those things which are called occult (hidden).* Our ancient power of concentration made us the most dreaded race on Earth and it is the key to our redemption. In ancient times we were considered a race of magicians (See *Egyptian Magic* by Budge).

The trial of a Jew named Shcharansky in the Soviet Union attracted world press, along with the comments of Andrew Young concerning political prisoners in the US. One of the charges that the Soviets held against Shcharansky was passing secret information to Western journalists on Soviet experiments in parapsychology. This is a Western term for the science of consciousness (exalted). The East has many systems dealing with this science—yoga, magic, astrology, I Ching, Kabbala, Tai Chi, etc.

The sages and wise men of ancient times comprehended that men spend more time dead than alive, so a wise man would occupy his time in the study of death, the great mystery of existence. In ancient Egypt, the last initiation rite is said to have been the revelation of the secret of death. This was done by magically removing the consciousness, or doer, from the physical body and then bringing it back, thus a man was twice born.

Let it be said that it is not cowardice, but lack of opportunity and arms that prevents our ascension.
— Capricorn, *Business as a Terrorist Front*

The word *magic* frightens a lot of people. Good. Magic is dependent on imagination. Imagination is dependent on the ability to concentrate. Magic, then, is the art of concentration. Concentration is based on the breath. Meditation and concentration are the same. Everything which men have created in the world began as an idea. It must first have been seen in the mind. The mind thinks in symbols or

160

pictures. If this picture is strong enough, it will manifest on the physical plane.

The ancients left two great texts concerning the doctrine of death. The first is famous and anciently was called *The Book of the Master of the Secret House* but is now called *The Egyptian Book of the Dead*. The second book is equally famous and more comprehensible by the dead (the ancients considered a man dead if he was ignorant of things spiritual). This text is called *The Tibetan Book of the Dead*.

Recently, I was informed by an astrologer that when Kwame Nkrumah was president of Ghana, the Rosicrucians sent members of their cult his picture, saying that Nkrumah was a troublemaker and was causing problems in Africa! The members were asked to concentrate on him on certain days at certain hours in order to affect what he was about. This is a clear example of spiritual warfare, and speaks to the power of concentration.

The Rosicrucians are an organization whose spiritual doctrines and practices have been handed down by the Black race, the Egyptians in particular.[*] They, like the so-called White brotherhood, the Theosophists, and other spiritual quacks and vampires, all claim a White origin of occult science and spiritual development. Ha! These groups have many dupes who imagine that somehow they will be led to enlightenment and self-realization by a group engaged in hate concentration, and diabolical practices exemplified by the Nazis of Germany.[**]

Check this out—the government has found the Klan extremely useful in its program of domestic terror against the first of its soldier-citizens (the Blacks).

It should be pointed out that although we are historically, and by eyewitness accounts, the finest soldiers and fighters within the nation and the world at large, the Whites have constantly dared us to show our prowess within the nation, for all their behavior toward us is provocative of war. Indeed, they are already waging a campaign of extermination. The conclusion of this drama will end happily once we resolve to participate.

If the dread technological might and power of America could not defeat "small"[**] brothers, the Decamisamos of Southeast Asia,[***] can they defeat us here in America?

Senator Jackson, a realistic fascist, knows very well that the danger to America is internal. Neither Russia nor China is going to attack this country with missiles. Why should they risk the destruction of their entire nation?

The nation has a bloody legacy of the physical, emotional, psychological, and spiritual mutilation of Black people and has done its utmost to ravage our collective psyche (soul).

We can mention the Ninja, the stranglers of Bombay (worshippers of Kali), the assassins of the Middle East, and the Tong society. None of these can compare to the CIA-Mafia-Nazi triumvirate that has organized murder on a scale hitherto unknown to man—an international network of death dealing.

When the Panthers happened, all they got and continued to get was criticism. This was because they were fighting and dying, and scared Negroes all over the country, admitting to it or not, did not and do not want to put their lives on the line. This is the result of 400 years of naked brutal terrorism, lynching, the Ku Klux Klan, police murder, the prison system, etc. In short, violence is used to intimidate us and make us fearful and cowardly, and it's working!

Meanwhile, Italians teach their sons how to use a Stiletto Magnum .357 and push dope in the ghetto! The Irish push their children on the police force and the jails are full of Black and Hispanic people. The Jews are the judges and run the school systems, amongst other things, and still there are people walking and losing themselves in international politics! Our ability to organize local violence to serve our political aims will definitely put us in a significant international position. At this point in time we are spineless creatures, given to rhetoric-protesting to the police when they murder one of us.

An Unanswered Letter to a Learned Professor (A Marxist)

Dear Sir:

In looking over the reading material for Political Science 602 and 453, I noticed the absence of texts on revolutionary warfare—the absence of texts dealing with the application of political science in warfare! Politics is war without bloodshed and war is politics with bloodshed.

What a metaphor on the class struggle! But the practical purpose of using warfare texts is bibliotherapeutic, that is, books that inspire action. Books of this kind not only contain doctrines but themes of heroism, sacrifice, courage, and all those qualities necessary for a people struggling for liberation to have a strong identification with. Literature, like music, can be very subtle but devastating. The Marxist theory of the state defines the *army* as the chief component of state power!

In *The Wretched of the Earth* Fanon outlined the therapeutic value of violence and its redeeming psychological benefits for the colonized!

In fact, in the North, the word is that this political inability to espouse organized violence is the cause of a host of problems. What claim to nationhood can we legitimately make without the chief component, or even a small component, to enact our *will*? We need to understand that a fighting organization is the chief identity card of a nation fighting for liberation.

In America, the chief psychological ruse is fear: from the Ku Klux Klan, police in the dawn hours, lynching, jail for the flower of our youth, and assassination of all the men among us who have risen to the occasion. A military spirit must be cultivated to offset this programmed fear psychosis. Consider New York City—the Irish are the police, the Italians have the Mafia, the WASPs have the Army, the Navy, the Marines, the CIA, etc.— and each is an institution of organized violence. Being unarmed, we are forced to talk about the situation. When Mao said that "political power grows out of the barrel of a gun," he was not trying to be abstract. Malcolm X's "ballots and bullets" speech was an obvious call for organized political violence. The Nazis nipped this in the bud. Bobby Kennedy was killed in LA, and soon afterward Martin Luther King Jr. was in Memphis. Nixon was coming to power—this string of assassinations bears a similarity to what was going on in Germany before Hitler's rise to power, when there were 397 political murders.[4]

Interestingly, the question of revolutionary violence created an obvious schism within the Black Panther Party. Curiously enough, the party was organized around the right to bear arms!

The seriousness or importance of an organization can be judged by the enemy's reaction to it. In the case of the Panthers the reactions included assassinations, daily arrests, conspiracy trials, and exiles—in short, open warfare. When they were not being attacked by the enemy, rival Black organizations condemned and/or attacked them! The Panthers, although not the first Black communists, certainly were the first to thoroughly articulate in erudite Marxist language the colonization of Black people in North America in particular, and its relationship to US imperialism in general. More important, their example points out that no organization that seeks the liberation of Black people can operate as an above-ground communist Black-White united type. Conversely, the necessity of any group operating as an underground organization dialectically implies, and does indeed mean, the use of violence.[*]

Again, although war is used as an instrument of national and social policy, the fact that societies are organized for any degree of readiness for war supersedes its political and economic structure. War itself is the basic social system within which other secondary modes of social organization conflict or conspire. It is the system that has governed most human societies of record, as it is today.[5] The men who have best articulated this need to fight have been Franz Fanon, Malcolm X, and George Jackson. Jackson's book, *Soledad Brother*, did this so well that the fascists had him assassinated, but his book is not on the list of required readings for this course. I did not see *The Suppression of the Atlantic Slave Trade* (Dubois). Young scholars should be constantly reminded that Western capitalism as we know it today has its foundation in the slavery of the Black race and that "the evil system of colonialism and imperialism arose and throve with the enslavement of Negroes and the trade in Negroes, and it will surely come to an end with the complete emancipation of the Black people."[6]

Epistemology—"All ideas and all the various tendencies, without exceptions, have their root in the condition of the material forces of production."[7] Mao said, "All knowledge originates in man's perception of the external world through his sensory organs. If one denies perception, direct experience, and personal participation in the practice of changing existing condition, one is not a materialist."[8] Are these statements true? In all the history of human thought, in all the forms; without exception, which this thought has ever taken, people have always divided the world into the visible and the invisible, and they have always understood that the visible (external) world, accessible to their direct observation and study, represents something very small, perhaps even something non-existent in comparison to the invisible world.

Such an assertion, that is, the division of the world into the visible and the invisible, has existed always and everywhere. It may appear strange at first, but all existing general schemes of the world, from the most primitive to the most subtle and elaborate, divide the world into the visible and the invisible and never free themselves from this division. This division of the world into the visible and the invisible is the foundation of man's thinking about the world, no matter how he names or defines this division. The fact of such a division becomes evident if we try to enumerate the various systems of thinking in the world. First of all, let us divide all the systems of thinking about the world into three categories: 1) religious systems, 2) philosophical systems, and 3) scientific systems.

All religious systems, without exception, from those theologically elaborated down to the smallest details as in Christianity, Buddhism, and Judaism, to the completely degenerated religions of savages, appearing as primitive to the modern knowledge, invariably divide the world into the visible and invisible. In Christianity there is God, angels, devils, demons, souls of living and dead people, and heaven or hell. In paganism, the gods personifying forces of nature—thunder, sun, fire, spirits of mountains, woods, lakes, water spirits, house spirits— comprise the invisible world.

In philosophy there is the world of events and the world of causes, the world of phenomena and the world of numina. In Indian philosophy, especially in certain schools of it, the visible or phenomenal world, that is *maya* or illusion, which means a wrong conception of the invisible, does not exist at all.

In science, the invisible world is the world of small quantities and, strangely, it is also the world of large quantities. The visibility of the world is determined by this scale. The invisible world is, on the one hand, the world of micro-organismic cells, the microscopic, and the ultra-microscopic world. Still further, it is the world of molecules, atoms, electrons, and vibrations, and on the other hand the world of invisible stars, other solar systems, and unknown universes. The microscopic expands the limits of our vision in one direction, the telescopic in the other. But even with increased visibility, very little exists in comparison to what remains invisible. Physics and chemistry have demonstrated the probability of investigating phenomena in such small quantities or in such distant worlds as will never be visible to us. This strengthens the fundamental idea of the existence of an enormous, invisible world around a small, visible world.

Mathematics goes even further. As was pointed out before, it calculates such relations of magnitudes and such relations between these relations as has nothing similar in the visible world surrounding us, and we are forced to admit that the invisible world differs from the visible, not only in size but in other properties that we can neither define nor understand, and that only show us that laws inferred by us for the visible world cannot apply to the invisible world.

Invisible worlds, the religious, the philosophical, and the scientific, are more closely related than they would first appear. And these invisible worlds of different categories have commonalities: first, incomprehensibility to us, that is, incomprehensibility from the ordinary point of view through ordinary means of cognition and perception; and second, they cause the occurrences of phenomena in our visible world.

In the invisible world of the religious systems, invisible forces govern people and visible phenomena. In the scientific, invisible world, the causes of visible phenomena always come from the invisible world's quantities and vibrations.

In philosophical systems, the phenomena are only our conception of the numina, that is, an illusion, the real cause of which remains hidden and inaccessible to us.[9]

In the future, the so-called ancient religions and myths will be found to be systems of classification of invisible phenomena. Catholics have accused the communists of stealing their doctrines, but this is not unusual because it has already been said that "Modern science is ancient thought distorted, and no more."[10] The question arises as to how the ancients (Blacks) were able to classify phenomena only recently discovered by science. What about the pyramids and the Sphinx in Egypt? The pyramids, more than any other wonder of the world, tell us that we are quite wrong to consider that our ancestors were hairy-tailed quadrupeds. Our ancestors were very rich and eminent people, and they left us a powerful, bountiful legacy, which we have completely forgotten, especially since the time when we began to consider ourselves the descendants of monkeys.

The Sphinx is indisputably one of the most remarkable, if not the most remarkable, works of art in the world. Nothing in the world is comparable to it. The Sphinx appears unmistakably to be a relic of another, very ancient culture, which was possessed of a knowledge far greater than ours.[11]

"The type of the great Sphinx, the age of which is unknown, is African, not Aryan or Caucasian. The Egyptians themselves never got rid of the thick nose, the full lip, the flat foot, and weak calf of the nigritian type, and these were not additions to any form of the Caucasian race . . ."[12]

Quite recently a tribe in Mali, the Dogon, captured the curiosity of the scientific world because of their incredible knowledge of astronomy. This knowledge has been concealed in their religious mysteries and ceremonies! But this is also true of the Bambara, the Bozo, and the Minianka (and countless others, I imagine).[13]

Consider the ancient geocentric view of the universe. "If as science tells, there is no fixed center anywhere in the universe to which everything else can be related, then any point may be taken for in a center as well as any other. For in this case a center is a useful concept, becomes only a reference point, not a universal objective reality."[14]

This explains and shows the superiority of the ancient geocentric view of the universe — conceptually where you are is the center! In astronomy, the Earth, in astrology, man. "In a circle there can be no real beginnings and endings, no question of absolute progression from one point to another, as there is in a straight line. In the circle, if one goes far enough in either direction he ends up where he began. Indeed, there is not even any question of really ending. The terminus of one sequence is the starting point of another.

"Man likes to think in starts and finishes, of fixed centers and fixed boundaries. . . It pleases him perhaps only because having but one set of vocal chords, he can sing only one song at a time, to think of progress as a movement in one direction only — a straight line that admits no return."[15]

The Russians are still claiming that "the Marxist dialectical materialist theory of knowledge is based on the recognition of the objective world, its objects and phenomena as the sole source of human knowledge."[16] But only publicly. The Russians are said to lead the world in psychic research (spiritual inquiry?).

If we can judge by the recent disclosures that the CIA has been experimenting with LSD, as well as other mind-expanding drugs, since the fifties, we can be assured that the US is well aware that there are other ways of *knowing*. The public has been thrown off by the word *hallucinogen*. This is like saying terrorists. Acid, LSD, purple haze, sunshine, mescaline, peyote, pot, and, to a lesser extent, chemically-awakened centers in the body lead to exalted states of consciousness. The traditional methods of experiencing these states are the practice of yoga and/or magic, alchemy, Tai Chi, religious zeal, etc. LSD has helped people achieve that which usually takes many years of practice and devotion in the aforementioned arts to acquire, namely, greater awareness or consciousness.

The US government's political position on drugs is "everything goes"—keep everybody high and out of it! Reefer, coke, heroin, angel dust, pills, uppers and downers, and methadone are plentiful, but there is no LSD on the street! The drug culture in America is without acid, and it has been this way for decades. To say that the government stopped it for the health of people can only incite laughter. When acid guru Timothy Leary was with the Panthers they were ridiculed by practically everyone except the government! "In our culture naturally-occurring hypnotic-like experiences tend to be regarded with some misgiving, if not as outright pathology. Consequently they are little talked about, but this does not mean that they occur with less frequency or profundity than in cultures where they are encouraged or institutionalized. In many cultures such experiences are seen as a vital source of creative inspiration and gratification."[17]

Consider Adolf Hitler and the Nazi party. Hitler was not only knowledgeable of yoga.[18] He also took a peyote trip trying to scale the walls of transcendental consciousness.[19] Contrary to love and flowers, the Nazis were into serious satanic worship and rituals. The world leaders kept this from the public. It was Churchill himself who was insistent that the occultism of the Nazi party should not under any circumstances be revealed to the public.[20] It's a matter of common knowledge that Hitler copied very carefully America's racial tactics. For instance, Harold Callender says in *The New York Times* of August 4, 1940 that when he saw the Nazis in their beginnings in Munich in 1931, Rudolph Hess defended his stand by pointing to the racial discrimination in the United States and saying "we are very much like the Ku Klux Klan."[21]

Paying back the compliment, the American people on the whole (Whites) were pro-Nazi prior to, and to a greater extent even after, the bombing of Pearl Harbor. The book *A Man Called Intrepid* states this very clearly. Nazi racism appealed to American Whites, and still does for obvious reasons.

With the fall of the Third Reich, General Richard Gehlen (head of Nazi SS intelligence) was brought to the US to reorganize the OSS, which is now the infamous CIA, a brotherhood of occultists, political assassins, racist murderers, and White nationalists whose economic and political philosophy is capitalism. Gehlen was given $200 million to bring in other Nazis and racists to help him in his job of reorganization based on the experience of barbarism in Nazi Germany, which was a testing ground for the new order.[22] Families from Eastern Europe, Russia, and Germany, screened by Gehlen, immigrated into cities all over the US, particularly in the Southwest. Many of these people still dream of a war against Russia or Asia, and an examination of their backgrounds would reveal why wars against Asians, Blacks, Chicanos, and Indians, all non-white people, are taking place today.[23] These Nazis are extremely influential in today's world. This can be seen by the worldwide emergence of right-wing death squads, who murder without pretense anyone who threatens the status quo. This is the German experience.

During World War II, the Nazis were working with Tibetan Lamas, harnessing evil spiritual forces—too much, right? Ravenscroft's book says: "Three years after the first contact had been made with the adepts of Agarthi and Shamballah a Tibetan community was established in Germany with branches in Berlin, Munich and Nuremberg. But only the adepts of Agarthi the servants of Lucifer were to support the Nazi cause. The initiates of Shamballah who are concerned with the advent of materialism and the furtherance of the machine age, flatly refused to cooperate. Serving Ahriman, they have already made contact with the west and were working in affiliation with certain lodges in England and America."[24] History talks about German fascism, but never is anything mentioned of this unholy marriage—German science and technology with Eastern mysticism and occultism! This marriage for world conquest was stopped only by their own fanaticism—the siege of Russia!

As a man watches the sun rise and the light of the moon, he seldom thinks that the sun is not rising—the earth is spinning and the moon reflects the light of the sun. Things appear one way but are actually another. Men, too, say, "my body." *My* is a possessive pronoun. Can men appear to be one thing but actually be another? When a man says "This is me," he is generally speaking to his way of being.

"But if the . . . question is raised what thought and consciousness really are and where they come from, it becomes apparent that they are products of the human brain and that man is the product of nature."[25]

Consciousness? "Consciousness is another mystery, the greatest and most profound of all mysteries. The word consciousness is unique . . . Its all important value and meaning are not, however, appreciated. This will be seen in the uses that the word is made to serve. To give some common examples of its misuse: It is heard in such expressions as 'my consciousness' and 'one's consciousness' and in such as animal consciousness, human consciousness, and psychic, cosmic, and other KINDS of consciousness. And it is described as normal consciousness, and greater and deeper, and higher and lower, inner and outer, consciousness: and full and partial consciousness. Mention is also made of the beginning and of a change of consciousness. One hears people say that they have experienced or caused a growth or an extension or an expansion, of consciousness. A very common misuse of the word is in such phrases as: to lose consciousness, to hold consciousness: to regain to use, to develop consciousness. And one hears further, of various states, and planes and degrees and conditions of consciousness. Consciousness is too great to be thus qualified, limited, or . . .

". . . Consciousness is the ultimate reality, the final reality. Consciousness is that by the presence of which things are conscious. Mystery of all mysteries it is beyond comprehension. Without it nothing can be conscious, no one could think; no being, no entity, no force, no unit, could perform any function. Yet consciousness itself performs no function. It does not act in any way; it is a presence, everywhere. And it is because of its presence that all things are conscious in whatever degree they are conscious.

"Consciousness is not a cause. It cannot be moved or used or in any way affected by anything. Consciousness is not the result of anything, nor does it depend on anything. It does not decrease or diminish, expand, extend, contract, or change or vary in any way. Although there are countless degrees 'in' being conscious there are no degrees of consciousness: no planes, no state, no grades, divisions, or variation of any sort; it is the same everywhere and in all things . . . Consciousness has no properties, no qualities, no attributes it does not possess; it cannot be possessed. Consciousness never began; it cannot cease to be, consciousness IS."[26]

Concerning the brain itself, Peter Tompkins's and Christopher Bird's *The Secret Life of Plants* will force most men to reconsider all theories concerning the brain and its true function. The text shows that plants think, feel, read minds, are emotional, and a countless host of things one would never imagine. Plants don't have brains! Now, if we agree that man is on a higher scale of the evolutionary plane than plants, and that the ability to read minds is certainly a very high level of functioning, to what do we attribute this brainless activity?[27] If men could read minds, people would be talking about the brain! "Matter is the opposite of consciousness. It is the 'darkness' in which the light (of consciousness) shines, yet it knows not the light."[28]

Materialism is certainly in its own right an old doctrine. The Russian Academy of Sciences, in a study of Buddhist logic, confirms this. On materialism they said, "The Indian materialist denied the existence of any spiritual substances, as all materialists indeed are doing. Therefore no soul, no God. The spirit is only a product of certain material stuff, just as wine spirit is the product of fermentation. They therefore first of all, admitted of no other source of our knowledge than sense perception. Knowledge for them consists of, so to speak, physiological reflexes. They, next to that, denied every established order in the universe other than a haphazard order. They admitted of no priori, binding eternal moral law . . . It is a noticeable fact that materialism was fostered and studied in India, especially in schools of political thought. Political men, having thus freed the conscious from every moral tie, preached a business-like Machiavellism in politics."[29]

"Failure to define life as the *formless*, has led to the confusion and difficulty raised by the idea of a world without beginning and without end. It is the formless, life, it is the self which has no beginning and no end. The world, form, has a beginning and an end. The difficulty has been compounded by the 'scientific' hypothesis that life is the effect of material organization. This is a good example of *maya* (illusion). If we make correspondence to drama, life can be viewed as the one theme to which all manifestations relate as dialogue, action, etc. That there is only one principle, one subject, one theme, one verse, and that all forms relate to this one, is the essential meaning of the absolute.

". . . Underlying all forms is one energy/matter, which in its undifferentiated mode does not exhibit any differences in its vibratory rate, accent, direction, etc., i.e., one homogeneous substance. Life in its quiescent state is thus referred to as No-Thing, void (empty of forms, things). The differentiation of its energy/matter into patterns (organized lines of forces) constitute what we call forms, things. Form is the differentiation of any homogeneous substance, or undifferentiated vibration, or undifferentiated vectors, rates of motion, etc. This underlying energy/matter which assumes the many forms we apprehend as through emotions, etc. Consider the fact that 'science' has discovered that the elements of chemistry are not in essence, separate and different substances but different rates of vibration (weights) of the same substance, hence the possibility of "transmutation." This law applies to all forms in the world."[30] Certainly this is $E=MC^2$—the law of relativity!

May I say that, contrary to popular opinion, it is not dialectical materialism that makes communism attractive, however sweet this song might be. Communism is superior from a *moral* point of view. It was known and elucidated upon 2,000 years ago that the first factor in war is *moral* influence; second, the weather; third, terrain; fourth, command; and fifth, doctrine.[31] This order has not changed despite the obvious differences in armaments of today and those of 2,000 years ago.

The Vietnam War was opposed from a moral, not a political, point of view. All over the world! This affected America and her armed forces, and served to undermine the fighting capacity of the colonizers.

The doctrine of war clearly reveals why Capricorn sage Martin Luther King Jr. had to be assassinated by our sworn enemies—moral influence, the first factor in war. King's prestige and influence had the entire world in our corner, which as history has shown can be crucial to the victorious. When King was murdered, the race rebelled all over the country. Certainly this is unprecedented in our history here in the land of the free and home of the brave—moral influence.

Communism invariably has the moral advantage. This is one of the reasons why men of varying religious backgrounds can embrace its doctrines. The outstanding example in the West is the famous Camillo Torres of Colombia. "Camillo Torres was no orthodox politician. Nor was he a particularly competent one. Had he not taken to the hills and been killed fighting with the guerillas, he would have been remembered as a sociologist and a rebellious priest. But his heroic death ranks him with Che Guevara in the pantheon of the Latin American left."[32]

Hoffer has commented, "The religious character of the Bolshevik and Nazi revolutions is generally recognized. The hammer and sickle and the swastika are in a class with the cross. The ceremonial of their parades is as the ceremonial of a religious procession. They have articles of faith, saints, martyrs and holy sepulchers."[33]

To the communist, I quote Garvey: "We have sympathy for the Workers Party. But we belong to the Negro party, first, last and all the time. We will support every party that supports us, and we appreciate the attention the Workers Party has given us in sending this friendly communication. But the communists have a long time ahead of them before they can do anything for themselves in this country. When they get there we will be for them. But meantime we are for ourselves."[34]

"The Occident is, indeed, at the dawn of an age of a truly new science. The old science of today, based upon a study of phenomena rather than numina, will, like the now absolute materialism of nineteenth century physicists, give place to a science, or a way of knowing now called occult not because it is really hidden or inaccessible but because it is transcendent."[35]

We should all remember, "Science of today, the superstition of tomorrow. Science of tomorrow, the superstition of today."[36]

1

2

3

* See *The Pink Swastika*
* What is the nature of the slave mentality that allowed us not to promote one of our own as speaker?
* Disbarred for defending the rights of Black people.
* Television
* Atlanta has become Black Greece!
* Ali—the exception proves the rule!
* Egypt, home of occut scure (??)
* Ironically the Rosicrucians in America were started by a black man.
** Read *The Spear of Destiny* by Ravenscroft. The Whites aren't slouches. They didn't acquire what they have by being idle!
** The Vietnamese are obviously very big. The countries in Southeast Asia can verify this.
*** Shirtless ones.
4 Trevor Ravenscroft, *The Spear of Destiny* (New York, 1973), p. 262.
* No underground organization—hence, no violence!
5 Leonard C. Lewin, *Report from Iron Mountain on the Possibility and Desirability of Peace New York*, 1967, p. 29.
6 Mao Tse Tung, *Statement by Comrade Mao Tse Tung, Chairman of the Communist Party of China, in Support of the Afro-American Struggle Against Violent Repression*, April 16, 1968 (Peking, 1968), p. 4.
7 V.I. Lenin, *The Three Sources and Three Component Parts of Marxism* (Moscow), p. 28.
8 Stuart R. Schram, *The Political Thought of Mao Tse Tung* (New York, 1965), p. 126.
9 P.D. Ouspensky, *A New Model of the Universe* (New York, 1971), pp. 61-63.
10 Joseph F. Goodavage, *How to Write Your Own Horoscope* (New York), p. 21.
11 H.P. Blavatsky, *The Secret Doctrine* (Pasadena), p. 579.
12 Ouspensky, p. 319.
13 Ibid., p. 320.
14 Gerald Massey, *A Book of the Beginnings* (Seacaucus), I, pp. 18-19.
12. Robert K.G. Temple, *The Sirius Mystery* (New York, 1976).
13. Swami Kriyananda, *Your Sun Sign as a Spiritual Guide* (New York), p. 39.
15 Ibid., pp. 40-41.
16 V.A. Fanasyev, *Marxist Philosophy* (Moscow, 1968), p. 156.
17 Charles T. Tart, *Altered States of Consciousness* (New York, 1968), p. 395.

[18] Ravenscroft, p. 26.

[19] Ibid., p. 80.

[20] Ibid., p. Xiii.

[21] J.A. Rogers, *Sex and Race* (New York, 1967), I, pp. 1-2.

[22] E.H. Cookridge, *Gehlen, Spy of the Century*.

[23] *The Realist* (August 12, 1972), No. 93, p. 39.

[24] Ravenscroft, p. 255.

[25] V.I. Lenin, p. 21.

[26] Harold Waldwin Percival, *Thinking and Destiny* (New York, 1971), pp. 25-26.

[27] Peter Tompkins & Christopher Bird, *The Secret Life of Plants* (New York)

[28] R.A. Straughn, *The Realization of Neter Nu* (Brooklyn, 1975), P. 320

[29] Th. Stcherbatsky, *Buddhist Logic* (New York, 1962) I, pp. 15-16.

[30] Straughn, p. 32.

[31] Sun Tzu, *The Art of War* (New York, 1963), p. 63.

[32] Richard Gott, *Guerrilla Movements in Latin America* (Garden City, 1972), p. 269.

[33] Eric Hoffer, *The True Believer* (New York), p, 27.

[34] Tony Martin, *Race First: The Ideological and Organization Struggles of Marcus Garvey and the Negro Improvement Association*, Westport, 1976, p. 221.

[34.] Alan Leo, *Saturn* (New York, 1973), p. 11.

[35.] W.Y. Evans-Wentz, *Tibetan Yoga* (New York, 1975), p. XXVI.

[35] George Padmore, *Pan-Africanism or Communism* (Garden City, 1971), p. 303.

[36] Charles Fort, *The Book of the Damned* (New York, 1972), p. 193.

So when we beheld him thus, we became unconscious of our existence, our fear was vehement and our terror was violent, and through the violence of our fear and dread and terror we became as dead men.

—Arabian Nights

Self Defense

Those of you into sports know that a championship team always has a good defense—defense being the ability to prevent the enemy from implementing his plan of aggression on home territory. Observation has shown that the best defenses are aggressive, punishing, and flexible. You simply cannot allow the enemy to impose his will. Whites score many points against us because our defense stinks. We have consistently been unable to mount any semblance of defense in protection of the race and our interests.

Now, urban guerilla warfare has not been successful anywhere. In fact, the only group to use city violence in a prolonged, effective manner is the Mafia. We can benefit from their reactionary example.

The great lesson, of course, is silence. The purpose of the violence should never be declared under any circumstances.

Peligroso

Ask yourself which of the two countries, the US or Russia, would be more likely to reach first into its nuclear arsenal and why.

The answer to this question tells you which of the two is the most dangerous.

The answer is, of course, America. The reasons are: America is a younger nation, hence it lacks wisdom; America has already used nuclear weapons in conflict; and the multi-national corporations and their political apparatus (the US government) have no idea what the true interest of the American people is, and are concerned only with the profit margin. How can a nation with a facade of democracy maintain an empire? How many democracies have maintained empires in world history? America's use of nuclear force will be to maintain position and place, something no nation is guaranteed "in perpetuity," to use an American treaty phrase. The development of new power relationships in the world is confusing to Americans, whose policy is containment and not cooperation. In American sports this is called the zone defense.

For example, the Russians and the Chinese expect the developing nation to begin to assert more control over its economy, particularly the natural resources; America does all in her power to suppress this kind of activity. Consequently, America is dealing with this from the standpoints of hidden and open belligerence, and by so doing has become the chief stumbling block to Third World development. The technology of America belongs as much to the world as the 60 percent of the world's resources that are used here.

The West has a history of attacking Russia, unsuccessfully I might add. Russia rightfully should be scared to death that the US will attack her, even though unprovoked.

Ancient Egypt under Sesotris seems to have been the only nation ever to conquer Scythia (Russia)! Cyrus tried and was crucified by the White warrior queen; Darius went presumably to avenge this earlier outrage and barely escaped! Napoleon had his turn, and it is well known what happened to him; and finally there was Hitler and the Nazis, the most dreaded White men ever—dreaded because of their open use of "evil" spiritual forces to conquer the earth (as if there is not enough evil here already!).

The US now threatens Scythia. America is provoking the wrong country. She cannot overcome the Russians in conflict. History and time are against her.

The Decline of an Empire

Question: Is the United States declining as a world empire?

Answer: Yes, and the major reasons are the rise of nationalism in Africa, Asia, and South America; a consistent inability to see the political writing on the wall; failure to heed sound intelligence advice; and the decline of a military spirit in White youth, who see no reason for defending the interests of Gulf and Western and other corporations. Of foremost importance is the lack of domestic support for foreign military adventures, the failure to reevaluate foreign policy to meet the needs of a changing world, a refusal to acknowledge that what goes up must come down, the secret Hitlerian wish to have a thousand-year Reich, the increased exploitation of the domestic population, the idiotic refusal to recognize that the world at large is colored, and the refusal to adjust its domestic racial policy—this is the reason why the UN gets so much bad press in America. Carter and the trilateral commission tried to deal with this through Andy Young and then tried another little Black parrot articulating US foreign policy interest—nevertheless, the nation wishes to maintain its identity as a White racist country and is hoping it can take this policy into the twenty-first century.

Militarily, the US is at a point of diminishing return—she has so much power she can't use it. The use of force is an understatement since the true power is nuclear. In truth, force for America has little meaning. For us, however, it is everything.

With all that has been said of guerilla strategy its ultimate weapon is time, which no man can defeat save the self-realized.

This strategy, in which military intervention is no longer needed because client states can get all the military equipment needed to suppress their own populations, has reached its epitome in South America, where practically every regime is engaged in terrorizing and killing its own people. In Central America the dominoes are falling.

Israel represents US military interest in the Middle East and makes no disclaimers on this point. The US, though, is being forced to reconsider this policy based on the new Arab oil power. Keeping the balance of power in the Middle East does not require Israel. Islam alone is more than enough for the communists because the commies haven't figured out a way to present "Islamic Communism" (Communism with Allah!).

The Jews benefit greatly from the Black-White conflict, in that the Blacks are the scapegoats of political America. The history of these Jews in Europe makes some things indubitably clear. They have caught less heat in America than anywhere in Europe. This has allowed them to accumulate great wealth and wield great influence. They are unrealistically confident that they can always swing American foreign policy on the side of Israel, even though American policy makers have been reconsidering their positions. This seems to have begun during the

Nixon administration and is, no doubt, one of the reasons Nixon got the ax.

It was the Jews (B'nai Brith) who pushed the Bakke case. The Jew is the image maker in America (in the media—Hollywood). This kind of deviousness on the part of the Jew can also be seen in Israel's blood-brother relationship with South Africa. Jews are heavy into diamonds, aren't they? Gold too, huh?

As long as the Whites control South Africa the Jews there can do their thing. They recognize that if this were to change they wouldn't have much fun there. Most people aren't aware that the Jews favor the fascist USA (Union of South Africa).

The Klan Personality: Nowhere Man

> *He's a real nowhere man, living in his nowhere land, making all his nowhere plans for nobody.*
>
> —The Beatles

Innately, men want to become more than they are—this is called ambition! America as a nation gives the illusion that it's easy to satisfy this aim. Obviously, this has made the Whites insane to the point that many numbers of them have slain their families and themselves over the loss of jobs!

The frustration and rage of the Whites is tripled when they contemplate that there are Blacks living on parity with, and even better than, they—*all this is based on the political, economic, social, etc. assumptions that America is a country of the White man. This was never true but was promoted through the use of murder and terror as it still is to this very day.*

The lie of a White American has made the White men savages, for they seek to uphold what is not. The doctrine of White supremacy in America needs no advocates, since it is reflected in all the institutions of the nation.

The Divine Sparks

Those of you who insist that the organization of matter is "life" are in for a rude awakening. We, the divine sparks who have incarnated into the mortal sex body for the purpose of awakening mankind to the divine descent, also swore in heaven to wage "tearful war" upon all those who wish to uphold such a decadent philosophy, as all beings on this earth do die. To say that existence is designed for the accumulation of material wealth, as do the capitalists, the Jews, and the Communists, whose entire doctrine is based on economics and man's relation at the point of production, is rather ludicrous. We do not deny that there is some truth to these doctrines, but all of them deny the primacy of the Divine. The Blacks who are Marxist are in reality denying the history of their own people, the Black race having been characterized by historians of all ages as a people wholly given to religious pursuits and fervor of all sorts. According to the Marxists, the Blacks of Egypt, whose knowledge and divine wisdom is apparent to all who have ever studied ancient Egypt, were in reality a foolish people because of their religious doctrines! For is not religion the opium of the people? In addition, these men fail to realize that every major theological doctrine practiced on Earth was founded by the Black race. There are numerous books written on this subject.

Neo-Slavery

According to the world press (Western) and history books, Africa seems to be a new land. In fact, Africa and her people have always been at the very center and heart of world affairs since ancient Egypt. The slave trade (the foundation of Western wealth) and the Berlin Conference (1885), when Africa was geographically carved up by the European powers, laid the groundwork for World War I and World War II, when the colonial powers were fighting each other over markets and peoples!

Let it be also said that the two great wars increased the consciousness of the Black race and revolutionary Africa, and Black power America says this is so! The next great war shall end the cycle and put us back in power, so it is this that we should be preparing for as sure as the sun shall rise tomorrow. Our race shall never, never be independent in America without a fierce struggle. America is the most heavily armed nation on Earth, despite what the press says! America, too, has a long militaristic history of intervention in foreign nations. Yet the average White man in this country is in possession of arms! What is he afraid of? The Blacks! In every nation where Black and White "co-exist," the dichotomy is the same—a heavily armed White population wont to "hunt" an unarmed Black population hunting for work!

Whites always think that Blacks are coming to get them. This underlies all the racism and fear that has always engulfed the nation, and so we come to US African policy.

US African policy is the same policy it has for the Blacks in America—neo-economic slavery.

Blacks in America will have come of age when we begin using political, as opposed to emotional, violence. This will be a qualitative leap in our struggle for liberation. We must remove the chains on our minds. Each man holds the key to himself.

The American Civil War

America, the land of the free and home of the brave, was held together by the valor of the Black soldier. Many of these Blacks were free men prior to their entry into the war the South was winning! Lincoln did not want to field the Black soldier—he wanted the distinction of saving the Union to be held by White men, which they proved incapable of doing. *This is our country by right of valor.*

Don't forget the Draft Riot of New York City when the Irish had no wish to "free the Niggers." The White people in this country did not want the Civil War to be fought over slavery! The White northerners did not want to be accused of having fought to free the Black race. The Civil War was fought to "preserve the Union," or class-wise, it was the Northern industrialist and railroad interests against the agriculturalist South, the struggle between the new and the old, democracy versus oligarchy. Slavery had nothing to do with it!

Now, the Black soldiers who were fighting with the Union were fighting against slavery, and they knew it. The Irish knew it too. The Civil War could only be anti-slavery. To defeat this power slavery had

181

to end, had to be abolished (the abolitionists!). The Black soldiers destroyed slavery and preserved the Union.

"White Trash" is the name given to the huge White population in the South that was destitute and poverty-stricken. Many writers have commented that these Whites lived worse lives than the slaves. In the South the slaves did all of the work. Consequently, these Whites could not sell their labor and hadn't the slightest means of earning a living. Guess who made up the bulk of the Southern Confederacy's soldiers?

Here was an ignorant White population ready to right until death to preserve and extend a system that was responsible for their own impoverishment and destitution! Nevertheless, these illiterate dogs were beaten back by Black soldiers.

In modern times, these Southern Whites are the members of the Ku Klux Klan, the Nazi party, and other reactionary hate groups. The Whites seem readily able to organize themselves around the principles of hate, envy, jealousy, and murder.

Still, a man hears what he wants to hear and disregards the rest.

—"The Boxer" by Simon and Garfunkel

The Lost War

Everybody knows that Blacks were brought to America, North, South, and Central, during the infamous slave trade years. But what seems to escape most who discuss this topic is that we would never have been here had we been victorious in arms. We lost a war. That is why we are here. The firepower of the White men is what got us here — not their cleverness, intelligence, or their pale color, but their guns. To this day it is their guns that have kept us subjugated, terrorized, and cowardly. This lack of comprehension of the doctrine and philosophy of war is the sole reason these Whites have been able to keep us in check. We have had only eight men who have tried to explain this to us—Malcolm X, Robert William, Huey Newton, Gabriel Prosser, Denmark Vesey, Nat Turner, Walker, and a White man named John Brown. Everybody else has been busy trying to inoculate and brainwash the Blacks with a decrepit theory called nonviolence, which simply translates as non-action in the midst of deadly violence. People who refuse to organize themselves for violence deserve death because they have not made any move to protect themselves. I always thought self-preservation was the first of nature's laws, not nonviolence! To preach a philosophy of nonviolence in America is self-deceiving. America is the most violent nation on Earth. It is the only nation where White men periodically freak out and commit mass murders. This kind of phenomenon is peculiar to the White American, who is raised on gun culture. No race enjoys killing and practicing terror tactics more than these passionless killers. If the victims are Black it is even more enjoyable, because all we are going to do is march, picket, or protest but never bring death to these psychopathic dogs. We can never acquit ourselves as men as long as we allow men to continue the institutionalization of the murder of our race in this country.

I Pity the Poor Immigrant"—*Bob Dylan*

What is an American? Historically speaking, he is a White immigrant, despised in his native land for being either poor, a convict, an indentured servant, a prostitute, a slaver, or a good-for-nothing louse who couldn't make it in his own country and came to a land where degenerate Whites held Blacks in abject slavery. Yes, America, where the despised is the Black, not the Jew, the drunken Irish, the Italian throat-cutter, but the Black. Here is a land where we can lose our identity of shame and be an American! The scum of Europe were called to the American shore so that America would be a White country. Why is the presidential residence called the White House?

In social science circles it is common knowledge that the Blacks and other minorities suffer from a negative self-image and self-hate stemming from the barrage of racism that these groups are subject to in this land of hate and murder. But, as a college counselor, I began to observe and question various Whites, concentrating on the educated. I discovered that these people seem to hate themselves also. In fact, they hate themselves even more than the minorities, for these people really try to lose themselves in Americanism. The Irish are the worst, followed by the Jews and the Italian throat-cutters. Imagine growing up with the sole desire to be a professional murderer! The WASPs have set up the social dynamics which govern this godless country.

Black-on-Black Violence

It's no secret that most of the ethnic groups engage in fratricide. This violence sometimes masks the violence that is practiced by the state. Italians do kill Italians, Puerto Ricans kill Puerto Ricans, and Blacks kill Blacks in an orgy of unconscious self-hatred.

In psychology there is the term "indirect aggression." This is a response situation where anger and aggression are taken out in an area other than where they should be. Sometimes this is good, sometimes it is bad, i.e., being mad at your wife and becoming angry with everybody at work.

In the Black communities throughout America, the violence that should be directed at the state and our ethnic enemies is being used against us because the men are afraid and unwilling to organize force against our enemies, but will kill a "nigger" in a minute! We do not "feel" ourselves as men. Because of the crap we have to take from White men, our anger is turned inward and toward our own people to cover our cowardice and shame.

This is why when a man comes home after taking crap all day on the job, where he is emasculated because he must earn a living, he will sometimes nearly kill his wife, who seeks to further humiliate him. Yes, men beat women for a variety of reasons, the chief of which is a loss of sense of dignity. When your woman tells you to "go fuck yourself," or other such expressions that men do not use unless they're getting ready to fight, the reaction at times can only be violent. Now this is not to say that society doesn't treat women unfairly or that men shouldn't begin to view women differently because they should, but the effect of White society on the Black man and the Black woman is the same yet different at the same time. The Black woman knows this very well, and you can see this in the way Black male children are raised. The women are generally overprotective of them. In fact, the women have been protecting us since we have been here! "Be a good boy, Johnny," "Don't run in the streets," "Be careful around policemen or White men generally."

The emasculating treatment of young males is due to the unconscious and conscious recognition that America seeks the death of the Black man and our women want us to live. The result of this is a nation of pampered, cowardly men, spoiled, conceited, and self-hating.

The women must now tell their sons that we are at war and that they must fight until death to free us from slavery in America—for if the men do not fight, who will? They must tell their sons of the immortality of the soul, the divine descent, and the life everlasting.

This brings us to an interesting point, namely, sex and violence—either of the arts can lead to death! In astrology, sex and death are in the same "house" (the eighth).

Now a man chasing ass all day isn't likely to be interested in warfare against other men, but is more likely to be concerned with the war of the sexes. The resulting dissipation drains the individual of both mental and physical strength—any boxer can tell you this!

Chaka, the great Zulu war chief, hated married men. Marriage makes man soft and domesticated as well as enamored of sex. Chaka, in his wars with the British, kept the men separated from the women. The wars of the Zulus with the British are legendary. These Zulu warriors had no modern arms, but their courage and fearlessness were no less than spectacular.

The day we organize ourselves for violence in this country will alter the entire world situation. *The Whites in America can remain strong only so long as they keep us subjugated. If we break free the whole social order as it now exists will change, and not just here—everywhere.*

What Price Freedom?

We know that the words freedom and liberty have been misused and we know that freedom itself, as well as liberty, has also been misused. We know that the Greeks and the Romans talked much about their freedom and liberty, as have the Americans. All three were slave states. As we study history, we can see that when men talk about the ideals of freedom and liberty they are referring solely to themselves.

As to the price of freedom, it has remained stable since the dawn of history and has not deviated one iota from its original asking price—

death. Slavery is universal because not many are willing to pay that price. In America, we know very well that any bold move of self-assertiveness or confrontation with the White power structure is going to end in death. We know this and they know this. Our problem is admitting it to ourselves and facing the fear that this implies—fear is the killer. Once we face this fear and overcome, *we can then open up hostilities against our enemies after we clean up our own neighborhood* (people who live in glass houses. . .).

The Slave Relationship

Is there anything worse than facing an enemy who is abusing you openly and having no way to strike back at him? Is this not the classic slave-master relationship? Is this not the situation we find ourselves in today? The psychological rage this causes among Black men is manifested in the pseudo-macho-loverboy style being the hip trip. These behavioral patterns masquerade the fact that when it comes to self and group protection we are sorely lacking, to say the least. There is no stomach for organizational violence in defense of the race. In every major war Black men have defended White America. Is this not disgraceful? We need an army, but small groups will do just fine to kick the ball off.

The Klan

They're the scum of the land
The Ku Klux Klan (they have three mottos—hate, hate, and hate)
No one has told them that the world is colored
That all men are brothers
These men burn the cross
Deny what was lost
Want to be apart, never smart
Terror and hanging and God bless America
In the West they have cousins
Devils on wheels
Called Hell's Angels by the policia
In Germany it was the Nazi clan
And their satanic band

186

And California had Manson and his female fans the Zebra Killers
The Faggot thriller
Too many people are practicing hate
Generally because their lives are fake
Never had no cake or a true mate
No vision of God
No comprehension of Mars
No love for the soul but for murder and for gold
How much more can we take
Men cannot live beside poison snakes
Now the Klan in New York, Ohio, Detroit too
On the police, in the street, the prison guard,
The Georgia farm, the construction gang, in Zooland
Can't dance no disco steps, do the boogie, get no snookie
Love to hate, kill, maim, and burn
Eat glass, forsake shame
Murder has become virtue and virtue—vice
Hitler their hero, terror their delight
There's only one thing we can do
I know and so do you!
I know and so do you!
I know and so do you!

No great art ever yet rose on Earth, but among a nation of soldiers . . . there is no great art possible to a nation but that, which is based on battle . . . that all great nations learned their truth of word, and strength of thought, in war; that they were nourished in war, and wasted by peace; taught by war, and deceived by peace; trained by war, and betrayed by peace—in a word they were born in war and expired in peace.

—Ruskin

This "peace" is killing us! Everywhere in the Black community you hear "peace, brother" and "peace, sister." "Peace" has become the most popular greeting, particularly among nationalist folk. But there is no peace on Earth. Everywhere men are fighting. Peace, therefore, is a desire or wish greeting.

Now, the ancients have stated that true peace is within, and the modern sages concur with this. Therefore, seek your peace within and wage war on your enemies without—this will give you real peace.

In fact, despite all the pain, torture, and death which are to come, nothing would make the Black man happier than facing down the White man in America—NOTHING!

We need to do this more than to breathe the sacred breath, for we shall never be whole until we confront these men and force them to yield.

Will is the law, not weapons or terror—*will*.

Military Spirit

The major cause of all of the problems facing Black people in America is the lack of a military spirit, which translates into an inability to organize force, or better said, the reluctance to do this based on 300 years of murder, torture, jailings, and every device of brutality which could be thought of. These activities have turned the men of the race into sniveling cowards in America. Foreign wars are different. In short, the Black man is the psychological victim of programmed terror (the KKK).

We are dominated because we have no force to counter the force of the enemy. We are in America because we lost a war, not to better men, but to men who were better armed.

This is why in sports the Whites always emphasize teamwork—for only in a tightly organized team can they ever hope to overcome the individual prowess of the Black athlete (race).

Growing up in Canarsie, in the projects, some of the fellows would get into fights with the Italian locals. Naturally these Italians would get their asses kicked (there are more fighting champions who are Black than there are among any other group of people). These were always fair fights—no one saw a need to gang up on one White boy in a fair fight! Inevitably what would happen is that the Italian, who had been beaten fairly, would bring back all his family and the entire neighborhood to attack one or two people and raise hell in the community, because they would also be armed.

The Italians are organized for force. This is their claim to fame. The Mafia is an organization of murderers romanticized in novels and movies.

Firstly, force and terror have always been used as a wedge and advantage over all those who have no knowledge of their usage. Because of this lack of use of arms we have been forced historically into using moral persuasion to calm the wrath of our enemies, always appealing to the higher and nobler sentiments befitting a great and noble race, yet humiliated daily by the branches of the Scythians.

Didn't Black people start the numbers? Didn't force take it? If Blacks were organized for force would we have problems with the Italians? We owe the Italians something that only force can remedy! Haven't the Italians brought in all the dope with the government to practice chemical warfare against us, make millions, and destroy the social fabric of Black communities throughout America?

Heroin usage is different from, let's say, pot or cocaine, in that pot and cocaine use do not have to affect the nuclear family, whereas heroin usage does. The nature of the addiction leads the addict to constantly steal, and who is he stealing from? You and me. In addition, the overall effect of junkies is demoralizing, sickening, and shameless. Of course, if the community could rely on the death penalty for such behavior this kind of activity would not exist.

It should be also noted that not having an organization of violence has caused us to turn out young people who are not self-disciplined. It is this kind of slack that results in youths sixteen and under being absorbed by the drug trade, leaving school, and in all manners messing up. Force is the only thing that can remedy this situation. In New York City in the fifties the young toughs were always confined to their own neighborhoods because of the street gangs that then existed, and if someone roamed the streets because and they were caught in the wrong place their teeth would be kicked out. The concept of the neighborhood gang must take on a modern, that is, political perspective.

When you were asked to join these gangs you could not refuse for several reasons, the two foremost being that the toughest, meanest, and craziest guys were members of the gang and, worse than this, they all

189

lived in the neighborhood so you could not avoid them unless your family moved, or if you were an athlete or a faggot.

> *Either death is a state of nothingness and utter unconsciousness, or as men say, there is a change and migration of the soul from this world to another . . . Now if death be of such a nature I say that to die is a gain; for eternity is only a single night.*
>
> —Socrates

Deathlessness: The Warrior Doctrine

Fear is always the bottom line—the fear of success, the fear of punishment, the fear of God, the fear of death whom all men meet, fear, and the fear of fear.

Right now the Black race in America, its men specifically, is all overwrought with fear. If we were not we would have organized secret violence against our enemies years (centuries) ago. More than death, I think we fear killing. For certainly many men have abused and humiliated our race openly. Yet we have been unable to counter with serious responses, other than the violence of spontaneity that dots our history. With a few notable exceptions, we have grown afraid to plot the death of men, villains who deserve immediate execution—men who dare murder our children in the street, import dope specifically for us, shame our women, and deny us our dignity. We must organize militarily. We are in the Americas because we lost a war.

Since we are doing a great deal of dying anyway, it can't be death that we're afraid of. It's killing!

Somehow, for many years we have been wasting our time trying to organize politically, forgetting that Mao said, "political power grows out of the barrel of a gun."

Military organization precedes political organization. Just as life is not the result of the material organization of matter but rather the force that organizes the matter, the military is the force or spirit for the organization of the state. Indeed, many men have said that the origin of the state was at first the apparatus of conquest in order to better organize the spoils!

The family is the state in miniature. Is there not war in the family, rivalry, hatred, jealousy, vengeance, etc.? There's war between men and women, cats and dogs, Vietnamese and Cambodians, men and the environment, government and people. There is also the sacred war that man wages against himself in search of divinity and his true nature! Man, know thyself. Life seems to be a doctrine of strife, so no one fares better if he struggles because resistance creates friction and friction causes fire and fire is the spirit, and this is what men unknowingly are really after, and can be found in the camaraderie of arms.

The bond between the state and people is one of force, not the so-called social contract. The state offers its citizenry protection, but the ones who control the force use this same force to protect themselves against domestic opposition to this monopoly on power. This is true regardless of the political stripes of any regime. For this reason all people who aspire to replace those who rule must have recourse to force, not elections. Allende was "elected" in Chile, but force overthrew him precisely because he had no force to back him up—just ideals. Allende was dreaming.

Consider this: Four Black men have received the Nobel Prize for "Peace"—Lithuli, Ralph Bunche, Martin Luther King Jr., and Bishop Desmond Tutu. Talk about psychological warfare! The Whites, who are using every violent tactic conceivable, are urging Blacks to be peaceful and many Blacks actually believe that peace is the only way: "How can we fight against the armed might of the White man?" Men fight wars, weapons are the tools, and tools can always be gotten.

A United Africa

We have previously discussed how America, China, and Russia are all vast nations made up of numerous peoples (nationalities) united. The lands of these nations are divided into provinces or states that are autonomous but directed by a central government. So far Europe has been unable to unite, though she is trying to do so through the Common Market.

Question: How have America, Russia, and China been able to unite many nationalities under one nation?

Answer: Warfare!

Africa will unite when her people feel themselves strong enough to undertake what necessity demands, history calls for, Garvey predicted, and what Nkrumah died for.

Recently, the Nigerian head of state was in Morovia at an OAU meeting denouncing Tanzanian interference into Ugandan politics and calling it a "dangerous precedent"!

The very fact that the OAU is unable to put together an all-African military force means that one of the great African peoples must take up arms in defense of Africa and should project itself as the defender of Africa. Certainly this was not the reason given by Tanzania when it helped overthrow Idi Amin—but the point is that military force used to overthrow a neighboring state should have as its aim be the uniting of Black Africa.

No African nation seems to feel itself strong enough to defend the interest of the Black Race and say so openly. This is why the Cubans came halfway around the world to save the Angolan Revolution at a crucial hour—had the Nigerians gone in they would have won glory all over Africa.

What about when the French sent troops into the Congo? Somebody must take the lead!

The Cause of Ego

Although the White man has very little spiritual vision or talent, he has nevertheless conducted himself like a god, which he is and doesn't know it (all men are the Sons of God). Now, pray tell, what could have given him this kind of ego?

It is conquest that gives a man supreme confidence in himself. And although the word conquest is used in relation to all struggles, its very meaning evokes the war drama.

Granted, the god Time and the other cyclic forces decreed the ascension of the Scythians during the age of the Kali-Yuga (the Age of Spiritual Darkness), but *the psychological springboard was the conquest of the Black race.* After this the Scythians willed themselves invincible.

192

Aren't we the greatest fighters in the world, the fastest runners, the strongest, the best singers and musicians, the most spiritual, the only people ever given the appellation "wise" on Earth (the wisdom of the Egyptians)? Aren't we the creators of every major theological doctrine on the planet, East and West? If you conquered such a people what kind of ego would you have? *Their power is our subjugation.*

Race Conflict Is a Power Struggle

The power of the Whites in the world is relative to their control over us.

A man who is not physically stronger than you are is not supposed to rule you, but a technological innovation has given him a unique advantage. That technological innovation is the gun.

Africa, excluding South Africa, to this day is the least armed of all the continents on Earth. There's an armed embargo on Black Africa. Huey Newton, the Aquarian agent and bold spirit, reminded Blacks that Mao said, "Political power grows out of the barrel of a gun." Our problem is trying to believe this truth, bitter and harsh as it is. We know the acceptance of this truth means death and dying; it's easier to be a basketball player, a singer, a street hustler, a blue or white collar worker, a pussy hound, a coke freak, or a clown, anything but the man you must be if we are to free our race from the American horror show.

J.A. Rogers said the key to world peace was racial sympathy and this is true to some degree, but the so-called racial conflict is simply the surface expression of the struggle for power.

Sex and Violence

The subject matter was mentioned before but the importance of it (that is, sex and violence) needs to be elaborated a bit more fully.

Some Black men relate stories that involve the hot pursuit of a female who is finally cornered. This woman is then propositioned to "fuck or fight."

Marriage is sometimes like this as well, sometimes a combination of both. The point is that the sexual energy seems also to be the energy concerned with violence.

This makes sense astrologically because in the eighth house we have the sign Scorpio (sex) and the planet Mars (violence, war). In astrology, the eighth house is called the house of sex and death, contrawise regeneration and immortality—that is, sublimated sex can regenerate you, and knowledge of death can lead to immortality.

From this relationship you can also see why we hide ourselves in sex day and night. What are we chasing women around for while White men are killing our children in the streets? How can voting be more important than organizing men to protect the community from bloodthirsty policemen and ignorant Black youth? The men are chasing ass, trying to make believe that we do not have the duty to slay as many of our enemies as is possible. "Ain't Supposed to Die a Natural Death"—what do you think Van Peebles meant by this?

You know very well that we have no business letting men run around in White sheets, sowing terror and death. A spineless group of Black lawyers in North Carolina has petitioned the government to put an end to the activities of the Klan! If the court thought the Klan inimical to its own interests, the Klan would have been crushed long ago. Is there no honor left? Have Black men sworn off courage for Anglo-Saxon jurisprudence?

There is only one law—*will*.

In 1980, Vernon Jordan was shot in the back in Klan country. Jordan represents, as King did, the appeasement principle. Yet this does not stop the Whites from throwing lead. It inspires them to greater crimes and infamy. These men must be put to death! But if Black men are more intent on fucking than fighting the Klan and the reactionary forces of the state, we will remain a subjugated and humiliated people.

For peace with justice and honor is the fairest and most profitable of possession, but with disgrace and shameful cowardice it is the most infamous and harmful of all.

—Polybius

APPENDIX

Music–Dance–Theatre

American history can be traced through the particular music of each era—blues ragtime (1890s), dixieland (1920s), modern swing-jazz (1930s and '40s), rock 'n' roll (1950s and '60s), and disco (1970s and '80s).

What is unsaid about this music is that its source is the Black people in America. In each of the above eras, and those in between, the Whites have always capitalized on our creativity through rank imitation.

Al Jolson, the Jew, was the Jazz Singer. You have only to listen to him once to realize that he is mimicking the Blacks. Benny Goodman, the Jew, was the King of Swing; Elvis Presley, the Southern Jew, was the King of Rock 'n' Roll!

All of the popular music being played in the world today, for the most part, derived from the music of Black people (the soloist with the background singers—call/response). The world is quite literally dancing to our music—yet the Jews and Italians make more money off it than we do.

It seems that Blacks are also the creators of all the dances being danced, that is, the Twist, the Jerk, the Watusi, the Dog, disco, mambo, cha cha, conga, tango, samba, the Charleston, the Jersey Bounce, Roller Disco, you name it.

Does this mean that Blacks are the mart of the cultural life in America? The answer is obvious if music and dance reflect the cultural life of the nation, nay, the world.

Young–McHenry

The US government is, and has always been, engaged in genocidal practices against Black people in this country.

Sam Yette's book *The Choice* documents this activity very clearly.

So, for Black man to be a representative of the US government in an international capacity is contemptible, not to speak of the false image of the well-being of Blacks in the country that such representation projects.

Wasn't the US government involved in the assassination of Martin Luther King Jr.? Wasn't Young assumed to be a good friend of King? Why was he working with his murderers? Are you listening, Carl?

As it was, the Whites tried to use every subterfuge to make these bootlickers and niggers appear as assholes, and deservedly so, because they have no business representing the US interest (monopoly and capitalism) anyway.

Supposedly these niggers were trying to persuade the government to adopt a more liberal policy toward Africa—who were they kidding?

American Arms

When Theodore Roosevelt charged up San Juan Hill, who was with him? The Brothers.

When the white trash soldiers of the Confederacy were winning the Civil War, who carried the victory for the North and saved the Union? The Brothers.

In World War I, who was given first honors in the victory parade (refer to the film *Men of Bronze*)? The Brothers.

Who fought with Patton, not in the movie, but in reality? The Brothers.

In short, the terror of American arms has been the Black soldier— of course the Black soldier is hated in the armed forces!

The trick is to war for yourself! The Black soldier is first in distinction in conflict and last in civil liberties, whose prerogatives were won through arms.

Since the Black soldiers have had more frontline combat experience vis-à-vis the Vietnam War, how is it that our White fellow citizens claim to be stronger and braver than we? Let war decide the issue.

The Scythians represent the minority interest of mankind. If this is based on color, as such, I fail to see why we should leave the fate of the world is in the hands of people so stupid they think that poisoning the environment is unworthy of serious attention.

The so-called technology of the White race, the pride of the Western world, is in reality as great a threat to man as nuclear war.

It is common to hear an American say, "You've got to die of something." This is always said in justification of some poison feature of American life—like three meals a day!

The sages have said that the four classes of men have ruled the earth in turn; that is, the Priest-Kings (Theocracy-Monarchy), the Soldiers (Dictatorship), the Merchants (Democracy), and the workers (Communism-Socialism).

The rise of America heralded the civilization (I'm using the term loosely) of the merchant. Living in the era of the merchant, it is only natural that wealth would be considered the greatest good, along with thrift, savings, and those things concerned with business. Thus the Protestant ethic reads like a man trying to start a business.

It is also "natural" that a people who have a great love for golden calves attain much prominence in such a superficial setting where money is the criterion for merit.

The Weight of Freedom

African society on the whole is characterized by its order of position and place. In fact, the world was like this prior to the rise of capitalism (based on the slavery of the Black race). In a capitalistic society, men could now choose what they wanted to be, that is, the pursuit of wealth became open. If a man starved it was his own fault—this is and was the capitalist ideal. As with most things, this is a double-edged sword.

The point is that there *is* a certain amount of freedom in America. This freedom is limited, but what in life is not?

That this freedom does exist can be measured by our reaction to the education and prison systems (I mean the weight of this freedom as reflected by our participation in those two institutions).

Say what you will, but the school represents not only knowledge but economic advantage and advancement (applicable to the entire country). How is this known? It is trumpeted throughout society. Even the Mafia knows that "a man with a briefcase" (i.e., a lawyer) can steal much more money than a bank robber!

Now, how is it that our youngsters are dropping out of high school? Remember, the capitalist ideal is that if you don't make it it's your own fault. Now our young people are copping out, afraid to use the freedom to further their advancement, but spending countless numbers of hours in frivolous pursuits. Our young people should be severely rebuked for this slack. Quitting school takes away the discipline of freedom, that is, the discipline that is necessary to educate one's self properly. Psychologically, the "weight" of succeeding is less since now you are a high school dropout. Not much can be expected of you, right?

It is the same thing with prison. The ex-jailbirds keep going back, because each time they are let out, the weight of going straight—that is, making it in society—is slapping them right in the face. Rather than deal with the freedom of action, they cower and engage in some nonsense that they intuitively know will land them right back in jail.

Have we been free to organize forces against our enemies? Of course we have. Have we yet done so?

WILL: The Autobiography of G. Gordon Liddy or How Assimilation (Anglophobia) Leads to National Chauvinism.

Recently on WBAI, I heard a White boy, who had political savvy, say that the Gordon Liddy's book was "on," not from a leftist point of view, but from that of the right, and should be checked out.

Then I saw Liddy on Dick Cavett's show. During this interview, Liddy said that during the sixties the US government was at war domestically. I thought to myself, *Aha, a right wing fanatic.* * *I must read his book.*

The book exceeded my expectations. I had never had any interest in the Watergate situation, viewing it only as a vehicle of powerful enemies of Richard Nixon. With all the laws Nixon had broken previous to Watergate, I was baffled as to why there was such a fuss over Republicans spying on Democrats, to the point of actually forcing Tricky Dick to give up his reign on the mountain. This was the same Nixon who won by a landslide, was anti-Black, right wing on all domestic programs, stopped the Vietnam War, opened relations with China, criticized the US intelligence community, and was critical of US-Israel policy. These latter deeds caused him his own Watergate! As for Liddy, the subject here, his claim to fame is not being a squealer.

Liddy did not rat on his superiors and associates, and his book ranges from him growing up in New Jersey to his adventures as a spy for the Republicans and his further adventures as a convict in the largest prison system in the world. Central to all of this is his strong will, which he uses to extricate himself from troublesome situations. His method of developing this will is the "test of fire," in which he burns his arm in order to harden his resolve. These self-inflicted burns are light stuff compared to the overall hilarity of the book and the psychological profile I got of Liddy pertaining to who he is.

Follow this closely: Liddy is half-Irish, half-Italian (is he a mongrel?), but loves the so-called German-Anglo ideal. There are numerous passages in his text relating to the German this or that (his selection of a wife based on genetic factors and considerations is laughable).

In one particular episode, Liddy is recruiting women (whores) for the Democratic convention and says that as far as women are concerned his style is "Northern European." This is all the result of what is called assimilation (Italy and Ireland are not in Northern Europe!). Nixon is a German-Anglo and Liddy was loyal to him like a dog.

From a military point of view, *all Black men should read this book to get an understanding psychologically of how White men feel and think about guns. Liddy's stance on gun fighting is worth the whole book.*

Intellectually, Liddy seems not to comprehend motive, lawyer notwithstanding! For instance, he presents his hawkish views of the Vietnam conflict but nowhere says why.

Liddy does not comprehend, much less understand, the reason behind the conflict, but the best insight into this is *Pentagonism* by Juan Bosch.

Liddy loves America because he can be White and not Irish or Italian, which are still bad words among the ruling elite.

In true slavish mentality, Liddy is resigned to be loyal and obey the orders of hierarchical superiors, whose aim is the control of all markets and capital and the suppression of wars of liberation, but mostly the perpetual domination of the Whites for the control of the mundane world—an impossible task spiritually, historically, psychologically, and practically.

Liddy claims that a hundred million Americans have firearms, that is, the civilian population is an armed camp of gun-carrying White men. In an illuminating part of the text Liddy shows us his efforts at steeling his emotions for the killing art.

Many are going to say that Liddy is a sick man, but with a hundred million armed men in the country, for me he is the symbol of the whole.

The hunter kills for pleasure, doesn't he? "Happiness is a warm gun."

Though Liddy is able to disguise his self-hatred through loyalty and national chauvinism, these Irish can't fool me. I know Liddy loves America and I know why. I love America too, but I also hate it.

Liddy sees himself as a White American, period. Not as an Irishman or an Italian.

---

* It is true that war takes many forms and disguises—but war, to be true, must be organized. Frustrated random attacks on the state by the oppressed and romantics cannot be considered war.

These Blacks were wont to portray themselves as satyrs frolicking with White and Mulatto women. The women seem to be having great fun!

Dennis James Watson

Hercules in Egypt. The reader will notice the afro. Check out the blackness of the Egyptians and yellow Mulattoes. Black with Red Hair- Only Blacks have assess like this! "Red Hatred Menataus"

Scene from a gymnasium. The two youths are practicing the javelin under the supervision of the *paidotribes* (on the right), who has a peg in his hand, ready to mark their throws. (New York. Metropolitan Museum)

Two boxers practicing to the accompaniment of the flute. Exercise in the gymnasion and the palaistra was often accompanied by music (New York. Metropolitan Museum)

Reconstruction of an ancient gymnasion. The young men are practicing running, jumping and wrestling in the open area in the center, accompanied by the flute. The gymnasia were much-frequented places; in addition to the youths, philosophers, orators, and politicians used to gather there, because this was where they found a ready audience. Music and philosophy lessons were often held in its stoas. (Reconstruction: K. Iliakis)

LEARNING RESOURCES

READING AND WRITING, THEN, AND SONG AND INSTRUMENTAL MUSIC, were the first things the youth learnt. It is perhaps worthwhile emphasizing the special significance the Greeks attached to music; musical instruments and song were used to accompany the dance, which connects man with the gods, according to Plato, and distinguishes him from the animals. The other animals have no sense of order and disorder in movement, which we call rhythm and harmony. This means, he continues, that the man who is achoreutos (not trained in the dance) is uneducated, while the educated man is one who knows how to sing and dance. However, as a result of the fact that hardly any element of the music created throughout the whole of Greek civilisation has survived, we frequently forget the important role of music—and dance—in the education of the Greeks. For the rhythm and harmony that we admire so much nowhere find such clear, lively and sensitive expression as in the sphere of music and dance.

In the light of this fundamental assumption, we can better understand the importance of gymnastics and athletic training in the education of the young in Athens. The body was exercised, originally naked under the sun or the shadow of the leaves, in contests such as wrestling, boxing, the javelin, discus, running and jumping, under the supervision of the paidotribes (physical trainer) and to the rhythm of flute music. The presence of the flute player in scenes, of the palaistra, depicted on large numbers of Attic vases, is revealing: it attests irrefutably the essential content of physical education . . . . Music and song, dance and exercise are aimed at a complete education that will imbue the young man with rhythm—that is to say, will make him able to achieve the harmonious functioning, both of the body and of the soul. Within a strong and agile body, with harmonious proportions and rhythmic movements, there will be cultivated a psychological attitude at once vigorous and balanced, vibrant and exhuberant, but also quiet and calm; in other words, a balance of the tendencies and drives that lead a man to action or inaction. An education and training of this sort could produce the state and the citizens hymned by Perikles: the state and citizens who "love beauty without excess, and love wisdom without being weak." And if rhythm constitutes the harmonious reconciliation of the opposing tendencies in the world and in man, then we can understand the whole point of the eulogy in the *Funeral Speech*. It is nothing less than a picture of this harmony in the social, economic, political and cultural spheres as achieved by the Athenian democracy under Perikles, which had succeeded precisely in reconciling these opposing forces that threatened, through their lack of rhythm, the balance of the citizen and the state.

This is the education described by Perikles as a free way of living and opposed by him to the laborious exercise of the Spartans, and it is this that allows him to describe Athens as the School of Greece. It is difficult for us today to appreciate the beauty and charm of this education, after so many centuries of a divided existence that has led us to feel scorn and shame for our body, and to separate the exercise of it from musical rhythm from song and from poetry.

Dionysus or Bacchus. A symbol of the higher self evolving in all the lower members and down to the soul.

205

Zeus and Python. Zeus was a Black god, as you can see for yourself, and his blackness was often mentioned in the writings of the "Greeks."

Miscegenation follows conquest and is an age-old "scheme." From Plutarch: "A Greek woman who bore a black infant, and was accused of adultery, discovered that she was fourth in descent from an *Aithiops*."

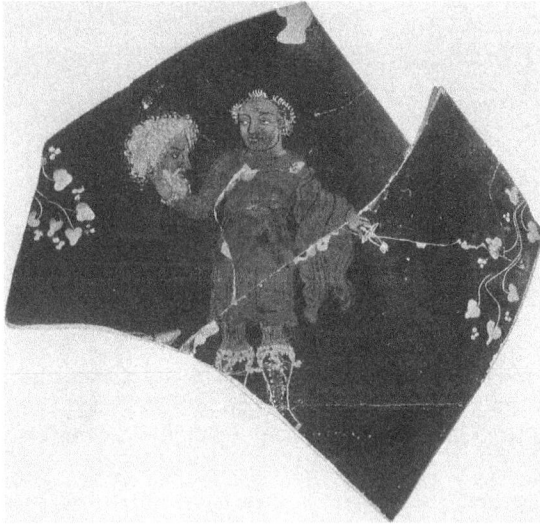

Greek Actor. Do these faces look familiar? I saw ten guys on 42nd Street who look like this.

Achilles and Ajax. Check out those thin ankles. These two were the meanest fighters in the Greek forces during the siege of Troy. The details of the cloth material that the warriors are wearing looks exactly like the cloth you get from West Africa.

An orgiastic Dionysian *komos* with satyrs and maenads. Following the artistic convention, the women's bodies are painted white. However, note that the satyrs are not painted according to the conventions of the second half of the sixth century onwards; that is, they do not have tails or bestial faces.

". . . though in the strength and number of its armed forces, it was very definitely inferior to the Scythians, who are beyond comparison bigger than any other European people. In fact, if the Scythians were united, there is not even in Asia a race that could stand up to them by itself, though of course in governing themselves wisely and in making intelligent use of their resources, they are below the average level." — Thucydides, *The Peloponnesian War*

The Hunter. "I saw a white man who walked a black dog." —Dylan. "I see a black man who walked a white dog." —D.W. History is cyclic, not Michael, Angelo.

Satyrs. These black Greeks often portrayed themselves as satyrs having serious fun with white and yellow women. "By beast and man together (satyr) is signified man as to spiritual and natural affection." —Swedenborg

Arjuna. This is the Wayang representation of Arjuna, the central character in the Indian epic *The Bhagavad Gita*, sometimes called the Song Divine or the Song of God. As you can see, he is B-L-A-C-K.

A Persian courtier, from the frieze on the stairway to the palace at Persepolis. As the reader can see, he is shown with an Afro. (British Museum)

211

A panel from the "Black Obelisk" of Shalmeneser III. Jehu, king of Israel, prostrates himself before the Assyrian king, while behind him stand Assyrian guards. (British Museum)

Polychromatic leather Wayang figures

BIBLIOGRAPHY

NOTE: This bibliography is provided so that readers can consult the sources for much of the information as well as some of the ideas in this book. Since research into publication sources and the availability of many editions (especially of older and revered works such as the *Bhagavad Gita*) are now easily obtained by a search on the Internet, complete publishing information has not been provided here.

Anonymous, *Lives of the Later Caesars*.

Apuleius. *The Golden Ass*.

Aristotle. *Politics*. Loeb.

Arng, Lee-Ying. *Lee's Modified Tai-Chi For Health*.

Arrian. *The Campaigns of Alexander.*.

Bailey, Alice. *The Labours of Hercules*.

Bandon, Franz. *Frabato the Magician*.

Bandon, Franz. *Initiation Into Hermetics*.

Bandon, Franz. *Magic Evocation*.

Beeton, Samuel Orchart. *Beeton's Classical Dictionary*.

Bernard, Theos. *Hatha Yoga*.

Bhagavad Gita.

Blavatsky, H.P. *The Secret Doctrine*.

Bragdon, Claude. *Yoga and You*.

Brinton, Daniel Garrison. *Races and Peoples*.

Budge, A.E. *Life and Exploits of Alexander the Great*.

Chang, Garner C. C. *The Hundred Thousand Songs of Milarepa: The Life-Story and Teaching of the Greatest Poet-Saint Ever to Appear in the History of Buddhism*.

Chang, Stephen C. *The Tao of Sexology*.

Churchward, James. *Cosmic Forces of Mu*.

Clark, Edward. *Daleth*.

Conford, Francis M. *Thucydides Mythistoricus*.

Cookridge, E.H. *Ghelen, Spy of the Century*.

Cooper, Milton William. *Behold a Pale Horse*.

D'Olivet, Fabre. *Hermeneutic Inter pretation of the Origin of the Social State of Man and the Destiny of the Adamic Race*.

———. *The Golden Verses of Pythagoras.*

———. *The Hebraic Tongue Restored.*

Debrunner, H. *Witchcraft in Ghana.*

Delouise. "Blacks are More Psychic than Whites." *H.E.P Magazine.*

Diodorus. *The Historical Library of Diodorus the Sicilian.*

Douglass, Frederick. *A Narrative of the Life of Frederick Douglass, an American Slave.*

Dubois, W.E.B. *The Suppression of the African Slave Trade.*

———. *The World and Africa.*

———. *Black Reconstruction in America.*

———. *The Souls of Black Folk.*

Dupuis, Charles-François. *The Origin of All Religious Worship.*

Ehret, Arnold. *Mucusless Diet Healing System.*

Einstein, Albert. *Ideas and Opinions.*

Elkins, Stanley. *Elkins on Slavery.*

Encyclopedia Britannica. 1958.

Evans-Wentz, Walter. *Tibetan Yoga and Secret Doctrines.*

Everybody's Plutarch. Dodd/Mead.

Fanasyev, V.A. *Marxist Philosophy.*

Fort, Charles. *The Book of the Damned.*

Fullwood, Nancy. *The Song of Sano Tarot.*

Gallery of Antiquities. London: British Museum.

Gaskell's Dictionary of All Scriptures and Myths

Gayley, Charles Mills. *The Classic Myths in English Literature and in Art.*

Gibbons, Edward. *The Decline and Fall of the Roman Empire.*

Goodavage, Joseph F. *How to Write Your Own Horoscope.*

Gott, Richard. *Guerrilla Movements in Latin America.*

Haley, Alex. *Autobiography of Malcolm X.*

Heliodorus. *The Ethiopics.*

Herodotus. *The History of Herodotus.*

Hesse, Hermann. *Siddhartha.*

Higgins, Godfrey. *Anacalypsis.*

———. *The Celtic Druids.*

Hislop, Alexander. *The Two Babylons.*

Hoffer, Eric Row. *The True Believer.*

Homer. *The Odyssey* (different translations are referenced in the text).

———. *The Iliad* (different translations are references in the text).

Hotema, Hilton. *Ancient Tarot Symbolism Revealed.*

I Ching (Wilhelm Edition).

Jackson, George. *Soledad Brother.*

James, George M. *Stolen Legacy.*

Jochannan, Dr. Ben. *African Origins of the Major Western Religions.*

Josephus. *The Jewish War.*

King, Martin Luther. *Letter From a Birmingham Jail.*

Kirkyand Feng. *Tai Chi . . . A Way of Centering and the I Ching.*

Kornman, Robin and Lama Chonam, translators. *The Epic of Gesar of Ling; Gesar's Magical Birth, Early Years, and Coronation as King.*

Kriyananda, Swami. *Your Sun Sign as a Spiritual Guide.*

Lenin, V.I. *The Three Sources and Three Component Parts of Marxism.*

Leo, Alan. *Saturn.*

Lewin, Leonard. *Report from Iron Mountain on the Possibility and Desirability of Peace.*

Livingstone, Charles and David. *Narrative of an Expedition to the Zambesi and Its Tributaries.*

Livy. *The Early History of Rome.*

———. *The History of Rome.*

Lubicz, R.A. Schwaller. *The Temple in Man.*

Machiavelli, Niccolo. *The Prince.*

Manuel d'Histoire. Paris.

Martin, Tony. *Race First: The Ideological and Organizational Struggles of Marcus Garvey and the Negro Improvement Association.*

Massey, Gerald. *A Book of Beginnings.*

———. *Egypt, Light of the World.*

McGovern, William. *The Early Empires of Central Asia.*

McRitchie, David. *Ancient and Modern Britain.*

Mutwa, Fusamazulu. *Indaba My Children.*

Ouspensky, P.D. *A New Model of the Universe.*

Ovid. *Metamorphoses.*

Oxford Bible Atlas.

Padmore, George. *Pan-Africanism or Communism.*

Parker, George Wells. *Children of the Sun.*

Percival, Harold Waldwin. *Thinking and Destiny.*

Petrie, Flinders Wm. *A History of Egypt.*

Pinkerton, John. *A Dissertation on the Origin, Progress of the Scythians or Goths.*

Pliny. *National History.*

Plutarch. *Age of Alexander.*

———. *Fall of the Roman Republic.*

———. *Lives.*

———. *Selected Works and Essays..*

———. *The Rise and Fall of Athens.*

Protocols of the Elders of Zion, The.

Pryse, James M. *The Magical Message According to Ioannes-Commonly Called the Gospel According t o St. John.*

Ptolemy. *Tetrabiblos.*

Ravenscroft, Trevor. *Spear of Destiny.*

Rawlinson, George. *Egypt and Babylon From Sacred & Mundane Sources.*

Regardie, Israel. *The Art of True Healing.*

Rice, Tamara Talbot. *The Scythians.*

Rigaud, Milo. *Secrets of Voodoo.*

Rogers, J.A. *100 Amazing Facts About the Negro.*

———. *Africa's Gift to America.*

———. *Sex and Race Vol. I, II, III.*

———. *World's Great Men of Color.*

Russell. *A View of Ancient and Modern Egypt.*

Saggs, H.W.F. *The Greatness That Was Babylon.*

Sallust. *Jugurthine War/Conspiracy of Cataline.*

Sanders, N. K. *The Epic of Gilgamesh..*

Schram, Stuart R. *The Political Thought of Mao Tse Tung.*

Schuman, Frederick L.. *International Politics.*

Sergi, Giuseppe. *The Mediterranean Race.*

Stadter, Phillips. *Plutarch Historical Methods.*

Stcherbatsky, *The Buddhist .Logic.*

Stinger, Penny & Douglas, N. K. *Sexual Secrets.*

Straughn, R.A. *The Realization of Neter Nu.*

Tacitus. *The Agricola and the Germania.*

Tart, Charles T. *Altered States of Consciousness.*

Temple, Robert K.G. *The Sirius Mystery.*

The New York Times. Cl. January 15, 1980.

The Realist. Number 93.

Tompkins, Peter & Bird, Christopher. *The Secret Life of Plants*.

Trotsky, Leon. *My Life*.

Tzu, Sun. *Art of War*.

Veith, Ilsa (translator). *The Yellow Emperor's Classic on Internal Medicine*.

Vivekananda Foundation. *Living at the Source: Yoga Teachings of Vivekananda*.

Volney, Count. *Meditation on t he Ruins of Empire*.

Wathen, George. *Art, Antiquities, and Chronology of Ancient Egypt*.

Weigall, Arthur. *Akhnaton*.

Williams, Chancellor. *The Destruction of Black Civilization*.

Williams, Eric. *Capitalism and Slavery*.

Windsor, Rudolph R. *From Babylon t o Timbuktu..*

World Masterpieces #1. W. W. Norton.

Yogananda, Paramahansa. *The Autobiography of a Yogi*.

Zimmen, Alice. *Home Life of the Ancient Greeks*.

CONCLUSION

Consequences

Doubt: What will be the consequences of Blacks organizing themselves for violence?

Force: The emergence of a New Black man, the one The World has been waiting for. Repression, race war, then civil war.

Doubt: But if the Black is only using force for his own protection how can this lead to civil and/or race war?

Force: Easily, what you must never forget is that the power of the Whites in America is psychologically rooted in the subjugation of the Black Man. Once this is broken it will change the social order, not only here, but world-wide, for if open warfare breaks out, and we should do our best to see that it does, we can then preach a doctrine of global warfare to all our people in every country, those where we should hold power and do not.

Question: Are you mad? What about the Napalm nuclear weapons? The Neutron bomb?

Force: Friend, did this mighty arsenal scare the Vietnamese? Basically, your question speaks only to the fear of death, and as long as men are afraid to die they will never free their race, you dig? The whole history of the relationship between us and the Scythian in America has been a relationship of force. For instance, the KKK has been allowed to operate because it uses force, fear and terror. These are the same tactics used by the police forces, so the Klan serves a positive state function from their point of view and makes their work easier.

Doubt: Wasn't Manso trying to start a race war?

Force: Yes, but a race or civil war is not going to help the interests of the Whites either in long or short terms. Such conflict will only be beneficial to the Blacks. We are already repressed. What more could they possibly do to us? And they do to us only what we allow them to do. This is what we have to understand.

Doubt: If you're so smart how do you propose to get Black people to untie--ha, this is impossible!

Force: Not really, we will unite the same way and for the same reasons other people do (I am well aware of how it is said Blacks can't stick together).

Doubt: You haven't answered the question!

Force: The best way to unite people is through warfare, for anything short of this is not going to get results. External confrontation is sure to bring about cohesion. As the Black vets about the camaraderie among the Black soldiers, dread fighters abroad.

Doubt: You will admit that war is a somewhat extreme solution to the problems facing Blacks in America?

Force: Actually no, historically speaking this lack of the comprehension of arms and the meaning of war to nationhood have really put Blacks on the cross. If, in Garvey's time they had pondered this question seriously they could have done it then. If you have no army, no enforcers, no fighters, then you have no nation, for who is going to protect this nation? This is why the Blameless can be murdered with utter contempt.

Question: What about nonviolence?

Force: Ask King? Seriously, what nonviolence does is simply demonstrate moral superiority and the mass of men, although affected by morality, cannot use it when confronting the state or other reactionaries unless morality has some guns on its side. You are also negating the fact that violence is necessary from a psychological point of view if only to prove that we are more than capable of defending the right and dignity of our race. It should also be clear that since the murder of Blacks has been institutionalized, we really have no choice as to how we respond, do we? The truth is that men who are humiliated and stripped of their dignity react only one way--war, war got us here and war shall free us.

Doubt: But wasn't it said that these Whites represent the destructive power of God and Blacks the creative, so how can they defeat them?

Force: The same way the destructive forces can harness the creative forces to do their bidding the opposite is also true. This has been previously demonstrated. Blacks have ruled far longer than they, and as history cyclic the ruling scepter is again being passed to the Blameless, but only if we are willing to seize it, to do, to will, to dare, and to know. Binary star system.

Doubt: Where and when do you think this organizational violence will take place?

Force: Hopefully in the South first.

Doubt: Why the South?

Force: Because the South is the spiritual home of the Black race in America. Probably the Whites, too, since the country has its beginnings in the South. If the Blacks in the South start dealing righteously with the Klan and repressive forces of the states, the action will become widespread. There are at least fifty to seventy-five million[1] Blacks in this country, so despite the many contingency plans of the Pentagon to contain the Blameless, it will be impossible.

Doubt: As a henchman,[2] it is only natural for you to attribute everything political to violence and force!

Force: You make me laugh, you imply that people can have their liberty and freedom without fighting for it. Of course you cannot cite any example in history, ancient or modern, where such a thing has happened. Ideas such as yours are rooted in American propaganda, which professes that voting is the only true means of legitimate representation. Is this why America supports every military dictatorship on earth?

Doubt: But America has a civilian government!

Force: Yes, but the President doubles as the supreme commander of the United States Armed Forces. It should be noted that the so-called democracies where civilians have constitutional control over armed

---

[1] I have been hearing that there are twenty-five million of us for about twenty years. I just doubt it.

[2] Force and Violence are the henchmen of Zeus in "Prometheus Bound"

forces, these nations are imperialist, whereas the average military dictatorship has no expansionist policy and is solely concerned with internal repression to maintain its hold on power. In both cases the people have no choice except to arm themselves and struggle for power.

Doubt: I cannot help thinking that yours is the philosophy of anarchy.

Force: You coward, you would say that! Please recall that in ancient times murder was not a civil offense. An "eye for an eye" justice existed and if you killed someone you had to leave your country because family and friends of the injured party would definitely come after you. In fact, on reflection, it seems that Egypt was the only country where murder was a crime! In later times the beginning of a trial by jury can be seen in the story of Orestes, pursued by the furies for killing his mother, who has killed his father. Orestes is given a trial, that is, the old law of an "eye for an eye" justice is being replaced by civil institution called a court. Orestes is freed, which is significant for under the old law he would have been automatically killed.

Doubt: This is all very interesting, but what are you trying to say?

Force: I'm saying that it is now necessary to go back to the old law because the court are incapable of dispensing justice. COurt are also doing all that is in their power to incarcerate as many Blacks as possible. If anarchy does exist you should look to the court, where the best example of it can be seen. Look also in the white hoses and the Nation Association of Manufactures-- this is anarchy which is sanction by law.

Doubt: You are sick, using every subterfuge to justify violence which any sane man knows is evil.

Force: You are perfectly correct in what you say, for the colonized man is a sick man until he has purified himself in the blood of his enemy. Fanon documents this therapy in a scientific manner!

Doubt: You are twisting my word around! Who is Fanon?

Force: Fanon was a psychiatrist whose book <u>The Wretched of the Earth</u> documents the struggle of the Algerian people against the French. He argues in the book that violence was the therapy which changed the Algerians from servile bootlickers into positive men. Arguing in this way he provides "before" and "after" examples.

Doubt: Isn't this rather extravagant, "way out?" Besides, I heard that this Fanon was married to a white woman and wrote this way because white society rejected him! Ha!

Force: White society rejects all black people so that argument holds no water. History will also bear testimony to the analysis of Fanon. Men who struggle undergo change. It makes them bolder and more self-assertive. Why won't you acknowledge that the Whites dominate through force, fear and terror?

Doubt: You have blundered here! Society is held together, not as you claim, but by law!

Force: My ignorant friend, the very fact that a nation has laws implies that there is some power which can enforce these laws, so when you say "law" you automatically mean that somewhere is armed group of men who enforce the law. Otherwise, the "law" has no meaning. You still have yet to acknowledge the historic use of terror to subjugate the Black race and how our inability to meet this external force has caused us to turn on ourselves.

Doubt: You're trying to get me to second your passion!

Violence: I have been following this dialogue with interest and would like to give my opinion. If I may?

Doubt: Where is Force?

Violence: Vengeance needed him and you know how much he likes her.

Doubt: Evidently you wish to espouse the same philosophy!

Violence: Certainly, first of all let me say to you who are squeamish of heart that Force and I do work for Xeus, who is the King of the Gods, demonstrating that even the high gods have use and regard for our services.

Doubt: This is blasphemy and outrageous!

Violence: You are pretending that you have never heard of the wars in heaven! The Whites even on earth, air, water and fire.

Doubt: Alright, so they dirtied up the environment a little but, Mankind has to take some risk in the name of progress. What do you mean by fire? What have Whites done to fire?

Violence: You are an ignoramus! This cavalier attitude about the environment convicts you. The human body is a breathing machine, air being the most important element connected with the functioning of the body! You can can go without food and water for days but five minutes without air will take you across the Elysian fields. The earth is the medium through which men get their food and three quarters of the earth's surface is water. An attack on these elements is an attack on the creative forces of the universe, is it not? By fire, I mean the spiritual element in Man. This is the age where God is dead, right?

Doubt: Okay, your arguments are compelling but the Blacks in America have little use for you or Force except every now and then, on a hot night or if the lights go out. Other than that, you are wasting you time. You even admitted that they do not understand what your uses are. They have forgotten their history. Whose fault is that?

Violence: Listen, I...

In walks Terror, Fear and Self-Hatred

Violence: Are you the three on your endless search for the cowardly?

Fear: That's not necessary, there is enough Black men for everybody!

Terror, Self-Hatred and Doubt all burst out laughing

Violence: Your wit is sharp today, old friend.

Fear: Thank you. Tell me, why are you trying to wake up the Blameless?

Violence: Their time is coming and they're going to need me.

Fear: I am older than you and i say Doubt is right. I am speaking from personal experience, for is it not I who has placed fear in their hearts? Besides, you know very well that once I enter their hearts they will never have any use for you and will find all kind of excuses not to take you up.

Violence: Yes, but admit that you only affect them at home.

Fear: This is true. For some strange reason I have no power over them outside America and their valor in warfare proves this, but this is America. In the guise of a KKK or a policeman, I make them shake in their shoes.

Terror: Don't I deserve some credit for their cowardly behavior? Haven't I lynched, burned, stoned, stabbed, kicked, castrated and used every method to make them weak kneed? Haven't these methods worked? They are not fighting back, are they? We can even kill their children. Can we get them more frightened than this?

Self-Hatred: Terror and fear have told their stories, but the wise will concede that without Self-Hatred, terror and Fear would have no effect. A man who has self-knowledge has no fear and cannot be terrorized. I prevent this knowledge by having men engaged in all endeavors that lead away from essential self

Fear: Let's face it, the tree of us work well together! Our combination has the Blameless totally confused.

Violence: You seem to forget that all of us can be used by anyone!. Despite all your bragging you all know that the destiny of this race called the Blameless is influenced by the position of the sun and its relationship (aspect) to its central sun. The earth's sun has traveled its furthest distance from its central sun, but is now on its way back. Correspondingly, as the sun moves back toward its center, the power and might of the Blameless will increase.

Self-Hatred: Mysticism and Prophecy do not suit your nature.

Doubt: You fellows are very clever.

Violence: Our use requires sagacity.

Doubt: You and your friend can never convince me that Blacks can only achieve dignity in America if the organize themselves for violence. I will never accept that.

Violence: It's not unusual for you to feel this way. In fact, most Blacks don't believe it. They are also afraid at the same time

We Have No Friends
SPECIFICALLY THE BRZEZINSKI MEMO AUTHORIZED UNDER PRESIDENT Carter in 1978 combined with the official position on race and the powerful Trilateral Commission are sufficient to cause strong hearts to flatter.

"In 1978 President Jimmy Carter ordered this Nation Security Advisor, Zbigniew Brzezinski, to study the following subjects:

- Long term tendencies in Africa for the purpose of determining if they are consistent with U.S interest and goal.
- The danger of African leader interacting with the African American community.
- Appropriate steps to prevent a coalition of African leader and the American American Community from exerting pressure on U.S policy toward Africa and the Middle East.

Brzezinski's conclusions were:

- Select African natural resources are a strategic value of the U.S.
- African American and Arabs have a common ancestry. Knowledge of this fact will cause black Americans to be more sympathetic to the Arab cause. Such an identification is therefore against U.S. policy

In light of the danger posed by the African Americans involvement in Africa and the Middle East, the following is recommended:

- Discouraged the African American from associating with Africans and Arabs.

- Influence the AFL-CIO from promoting the union movement in Africa.
- Prevent the emergence of a monolithic American leader, especially one with an African/Arab consciousness
- Establish programs to keep the Black community divided through the dissension and hostility toward directed progressive Black organizations.
- Promote class and elite divisions in the African American community.

Promote Black political empowerment as a means to control the black community through their political leaders."

The one thing the above memo shows us is the importance of linking up with Africa, racially, politically, and economically. None of this can be done if we remain in FEAr and remain PUSSY by allowing armed men to continue to murder and jail the flower of our youth a process that has been around our necks for centuries. The answer to all of this is GUN AND SECRECY

The Lost Books of Africa Rediscovered/ pages 155-157
Dr. Khalid Abdullah Tariq Al-Mansour

Review Requested:
If you loved this book, would you please provide a review at Amazon.com?

Ingram Content Group UK Ltd.
Milton Keynes UK
UKHW011814080523
421421UK00001B/32

9 781631 355370